Fathers' Rights

The Best Interest of Your Child Includes You

Second Edition

Fathers' Rights

The Best Interest of Your Child Includes You

Second Edition

James J. Gross
Attorney at Law

SPHINX® PUBLISHING
AN IMPRINT OF SOURCEBOOKS, INC.®
NAPERVILLE, ILLINOIS
www.SphinxLegal.com

Published by: **Sphinx® Publishing, An Imprint of Sourcebooks, Inc.®**

Naperville Office
P. O. Box 4410
Naperville, Illinois 60567-4410
630-961-3900
Fax: 630-961-2168
www.sourcebooks.com
www.SphinxLegal.com

This publication is designed to provide accurate and authoritative information in regard to the subject matter covered. It is sold with the understanding that the publisher is not engaged in rendering legal, accounting, or other professional service. If legal advice or other expert assistance is required, the services of a competent professional person should be sought.

*From a Declaration of Principles Jointly Adopted by a Committee of
the American Bar Association and a Committee of Publishers and Associations*

This product is not a substitute for legal advice.

Disclaimer required by Texas statutes.

Library of Congress Cataloging-in-Publication Data
Gross, James J.
  Fathers' rights : the best interest of your child includes you / by James
J. Gross. -- 2nd ed.
      p. cm.
  Includes index.
  1. Parent and child (Law)--United States--Popular works. 2.
Fathers--Legal status, laws, etc.--United States--Popular works. I. Title.

KF540.Z9G76 2006
346.7301'7--dc22

                                                                2006024608

Printed and bound in the United States of America.
CRDP — 10 9 8 7 6 5

DEDICATION

To my sons, Jake and Nicholas. They are—and let's be honest about this—the best boys a father ever had.

CONTENTS

Mediation
Parenting Plans
Sample Parenting Plan
Collaborative Law
Negotiation through Attorneys
Arbitration

The Three Phases of a Lawsuit
Threshold Legal Requirements
Beginning the Lawsuit
Notice
Sample Summons from Montana
Service of Process
Pleadings
Sample Caption and Title for Pleading
Sample Verification
Sample Certificate of Service
Complaint
Answer
Sample Answer
Pretrial Proceedings
How Long Does it Take?
How Much Does it Cost?
Sample Trial Budget
Sample Trial Timeline

Investigation
Interrogatories
Sample Interrogatories
Requests for Documents
Sample Request for Documents
Requests for Admissions
Sample Request for Admissions
Stipulation
Depositions
Subpoenas
Expert Witness Statement
Limitations on Discovery
Making the Other Side Respond
Pretrial Preparation

INTRODUCTION

I like my job. I am a fathers' rights attorney. People think it must be depressing to hear one sad story after another, but it is not. My work involves guiding fathers successfully through the legal system. I give them confidence and courage when they have to face their fears, uncertainties, and doubts about the outcome of their cases and their future roles with their children. I defend them against false accusations. I untangle their finances, protect their backs, and send them on their way with their troubles mainly behind them. Best of all, I get to help the children enjoy the participation of both a mother and a father in their lives—and that is exhilarating.

In my practice, I see a lot of things that fathers do right—and a lot of things they do wrong—when fighting for their children. A dispute over children can arise in several contexts, such as legal proceedings involving divorce, paternity, termination of parental rights, or child support. Disputes over children may be adversarial and hard fought. The situation is tense and the stakes are the highest they can be, because children are involved.

I wrote this book as a practical how-to legal guide for fathers. It helps you understand your rights and how to assert them. It is an explanation, in plain and simple language, of the laws affecting fathers' rights. It takes you step-by-step through the actions you need to take to protect your children and yourself. It provides you with the information and tools you need as a father to enforce your rights. This book can help you take control of your case.

This book gives you information about the law that will make you more knowledgeable as you go through the legal process. You may be reading this book because you have received a letter from an attorney who represents the mother of your children. Maybe your wife has announced she is leaving and taking the kids. Perhaps you have been served with some legal papers. If you are going through a divorce, paternity action, or other dispute over children, this book helps make your struggle less difficult. The information you are about to read is a clear guide to your rights as a father and your children's rights to have you participate in their lives to the maximum extent possible.

This book takes a constructive approach to specific cases, as well as fathers, mothers, lawyers, and the courts involved in fathers' rights cases. It is for fathers who want to help themselves and who want to be constructive in resolving their cases. It can help you grow in your life and make your dispute over your children a growing experience. You may even become better friends with the mother of your children at the end of the legal process than you were at the beginning. After all, the two of you will still be partners—in the business of raising your children—for some time to come.

There are some mothers who alienate children against fathers, withhold visitation, deny access to school and medical records, or make false allegations of abuse. They want you to be frozen out of the picture altogether with no voice in the parenting of your children, or to be a Disneyland dad who just gets the kids on the weekends. This book tells you how to deal with those circumstances calmly and rationally.

This book *does not* beat the drum for the fathers' rights movement. It *does not* complain about the poor treatment of men by women or the legal system. It *is not* about gender bashing. This book is about being a good father to your children and protecting their best interests. This book is about looking out for your children, who deserve two good parents.

This is not a legal treatise and it cannot substitute for three years of law school, the bar exam, and expertise that comes from years of trying cases. However, it does explain the law and the legal system in plain English.

You may very well decide to hire an attorney to help you negotiate the legal system. New laws are being passed by the legislatures, new cases are being decided by the courts, and the law is constantly changing. The laws of each state are different. Also, every case is different. A lawyer cannot give you legal advice without knowing the specific facts of your particular case.

Chapter 1 talks about fatherhood. Chapters 2 and 3 suggest some interventions to resolve disputes over children and what to do in case of an emergency. Chapter 4 explains the legal system with respect to fathers' rights. Chapters 5, 6, and 7 are about the children—namely custody, visitation, and child support. Chapter 8 discusses special federal and uniform laws that may affect your case. Chapters 10, 11, 12, and 13 explain the litigation process. Chapter 9 discusses alternatives to trial. Chapter 14 discusses aspects of posttrial life. Sample documents you might see in litigation are found throughout this book.

There are several appendices to the book. These include laws and summaries of the most important federal, uniform, and state laws affecting fathers' rights, and resources you might need in your case.

Cases are used throughout this book to illustrate certain points about fathers and mothers engaged in struggles over children. The cases are true, and they are a matter of public record; however, the names have been changed to protect the privacy of the parties involved.

There is simply no substitute for the love, involvement, and commitment of a responsible father.
—The Fatherhood Initiative
Department of Heath & Human Services

–1–

FATHERHOOD

My father taught me how to bait a hook, punch a punching bag, swim, dive off the high board, ride a bike, and shoot straight. I am delighted to be passing these skills on to my sons. One thing you learn as a father is that it is not about you anymore. Sometimes it seems that your job is to carry the playpen, drive the car, and pay for everything. However, being a father also means playing the role of a hero to your children, teaching them, and setting an example for them. It is both an exciting and frightening role.

A woman can be the best mother in the world, but there is no way she can be both a mother and a father. A man can certainly claim the role of father if he is the biological parent of a child. A man can also play the role of a father if he has a legal or emotional connection to a child. However, the law and courts sometimes view these three types of connections—biological, legal, and emotional—differently. If you become involved with the courts through a dispute over children, you will need to understand your rights and responsibilities, because the court has the power to restrict or terminate your rights as a father.

Custody litigation has high stakes. It takes place in the context of divorce, paternity determination, or termination of parental rights. Frequently, there are allegations of adultery, domestic violence, cruelty, desertion, substance abuse, or other fault. Both fathers and mothers want to spend the maximum time available with their children. No one wants to be relegated to the position of visitor with his or her own children. The judge tries to look into a cloudy crystal ball and determine the best outcome for the children. This creates tense emotions and sometimes *win at all cost* strategies on the part of the parents and their lawyers.

Judges can decide matters such as custody, visitation, and child support. While fathers have a constitutional right to raise their children as they see fit, that right is not without limits. The court has the power to intervene to protect children under the legal doctrine of *parens patriae*, which literally means *father of a country* and more figuratively means *the government as a father* (kind of like a super-father).

The following is an example of what not to do. Tom's case shows the mistakes you can make. He did not get the rights he wanted or expected, and the court took away his time with his children.

TOM'S CASE

Tom's children did not want to visit with him. They were afraid of him. He had to drag them kicking and screaming from the car each time. Tom blamed his ex-wife for this, and took her to court for contempt of the visitation order.

"You mean to tell me that a judge knows more about raising my kids than I do?" Tom asked his lawyer in the parking lot at the courthouse. "How can that be? I'm their father. The judge is not their father. Nobody is going to tell me how to raise my own kids."

Tom's lawyer attempted to rehabilitate him. He arranged for Tom to go to counseling. He set up a limited visitation schedule and got the judge to interview the children. He arranged for a parenting coordinator to help resolve visitation disputes between Tom and his ex-wife.

Unfortunately, Tom was inflexible. He knew that he was right and everyone else was wrong. He was convinced that he had to take a stand on matters such as physically disciplining the children and forcing visitation.

At the hearing, Tom asserted his rights to parent his children as he saw fit, free from any interference by the court, and asked the judge to enforce his visitation rights. The judge found that the children were afraid of Tom, and that forced visitation might have a harmful effect on them.

As a result, she ordered no visitation until the next status hearing in three months, when she would review the case again. Tom's case continues with high conflict and no resolution in sight.

You may not agree with the law, or understand the reasons for some laws, but you will not win your case by telling the judge what the law ought to be. You may be angry, as Tom was, with your ex-spouse, the lawyers, the judge, the legal system, and the circumstances of your case, but anger is not a useful tool in court. It is better to understand and accept the law, and then use it to your advantage.

FATHERS' RIGHTS

Fatherhood, by law, gives you certain rights and responsibilities with respect to your children. You do not need a court order to obtain your rights as a father. You already have them. They are guaranteed by the United States Constitution and the laws of your state. As a father and as a parent, you have the right to:

- be an influence in your children's lives;
- be involved, interact, and spend time with your children;
- love and nurture your children without harassment from the other parent;
- decide where your children will live;
- participate in the parenting of your children;
- see your children's school and medical records;
- attend and participate in your children's extracurricular activities;
- have custody, care, and control of your children;
- select your children's school and determine whether it will be home, public, or private;
- determine your children's religious faith and practices;
- determine your children's doctor, dentist, and medical treatment;
- follow your own beliefs and parenting style during your time with the children without interference from the other parent;
- guide and discipline your children; and,
- decide what is best for your children.

The law provides that fathers also have certain duties, obligations, and responsibilities. You have the responsibility to:

- support your children;
- provide your children with food, shelter, and clothing;
- see that your children obtain appropriate medical treatment;
- provide access to your children's schooling; and,
- protect your children from harm and neglect.

CHILDREN'S RIGHTS

Children also have rights. Children have the right to:

- be fed, clothed, sheltered, and educated;
- be loved, protected, and nurtured;

- ◆ be free from the conflict of the parents;
- ◆ not be used as a spy, messenger, or bargaining chip;
- ◆ be a child without having to make adult decisions;
- ◆ inherit from their parents;
- ◆ have the benefits of relationships with the extended family of both parents;
- ◆ have two parents—both a mother and a father;
- ◆ spend as much time as possible with each parent unless a parent is unfit;
- ◆ develop a meaningful relationship with each parent; and,
- ◆ enjoy and love each parent without disapproval of the other parent.

PATERNITY

Fatherhood may be legally established by court order through a paternity case. In a paternity case, the court determines who the father of a child is and decides custody, visitation, child support, and related matters.

You do not necessarily need a court proceeding to establish that you are the father. If you are married and a child is born during the marriage, there is a legal presumption (in most states) that you are the father. In some states, that presumption is irrefutable. In those states, this can result in certain paradoxes. For example, if you are the biological father, but the mother is married to someone else, you will not be the legal father with rights to custody or visitation. On the other hand, if your wife has a child by another man during your marriage, you are presumed to be the legal father. You could then be required to pay child support for a child that is not biologically yours.

If you are trying to assert your rights to custody and visitation with your child and the mother disputes that you are the father, you can ask the court to decide. Paternity cases also arise when a mother is trying to obtain child support from a man who claims he is not the father.

Paternity Disputes

You can avoid a paternity dispute by voluntarily admitting paternity and signing an *affidavit of paternity* declaring that you are the father. The affidavit is signed by you and the mother in front of a notary, and filed with the court. Once the judge signs the affidavit, if required by state law, that will make you the legal father. This is true even if you are not the biological father.

If you do not believe you are the father of the child in a paternity case, you have the right to ask the court for a paternity test. *Genetic testing* has replaced blood tests for determining paternity, because blood tests could rule you out as a father, but could not say with certainty whether or not you were the father of a child. Genetic testing can pinpoint the father with almost 100% accuracy. The testing is done by using a cotton swab to take a saliva sample from the mouth. You can hire a private lab to conduct the test or you can request that the court order a test. The cost is around $500 and sometimes insurance will pay a portion of the cost.

You have the right to ask the court for a determination of whether or not you are the father. You have the right to obtain custody of your child, whether or not you are married to the mother. You can also ask for a hearing to determine if you are fit to have custody. If you are the father of a child and the court grants you custody, then you will have a say in how the child will be raised. The mother of the child must discuss the various parenting issues concerning the minor child with you, such as religion, education, medical treatment, and other decisions. You have the right to be informed of the activities of the minor child, and you have the right to participate in those activities. You also have the right to see medical records and school records.

If you do not wish to have custody or if the court does not grant custody, you still have the right to have visitation with the minor child. Visitation will depend on the facts and circumstances of your case. For example, if you have not had a relationship with the child or you have no experience in raising children, then you may have to start with *supervised* or *graduated visitation.* (see Chapter 6.)

If you are the father of a child, you have the responsibility of supporting that child. If the mother has custody, then you will be required by law to pay her child support. Some states make child support retroactive to the date the mother files a petition in court for child support. Others allow retroactive child support to the date of birth, and require some reimbursement of medical expenses for the birth.

If you are declared the *legal father* of a child, your name will be recorded as the father on the child's birth certificate and your surname will be entered on the birth certificate as the child's surname.

If you are declared the legal father of a child, you are the *guardian* of that child. That means you have the right to consent to medical decisions, marriage, or enlistment in the armed services before the age of majority; invest money belonging to the child; and, take legal action on behalf of the child.

ADOPTION

Another way to become a father is by adoption. You can adopt a child, whether you are single or married, by filing a petition for adoption with the court. You can adopt before or after the child is born. In a stepparent adoption, the natural parent and the stepparent are co-petitioners. Agency or private adoptions do not involve stepparents or relatives.

Usually, the court has detailed rules for preparing an adoption petition and exhibits. Your petition will be rejected if you fail to follow these rules carefully. For example, sometimes certified copies of documents are required and photocopies are not acceptable.

All adoption files are confidential to protect the privacy of the child and the parties involved. The caption of the petition usually does not name the child. Adoption files are sealed at the courthouse.

It is wise to give notice to every person with an interest in or right to participating in an adoption proceeding. Also, give a list of these persons to the court. That way, a relative or other party cannot disrupt the proceeding later by claiming lack of notice. Any such person may object to the proceeding within a short period of time and the court will hold a hearing on the objection.

Adoption hearings are usually closed to the public. Only the petitioner and prospective adoptive child may be present, with their counsel, unless the court desires the presence of some other person. Each petitioner will give brief direct testimony and confirm that the statements in the petition are still current and true. The judge will then decide whether or not the adoption is in the best interest of the child. Both adoptive parents must be fit and proper. If the court finds the adoption is in the best interest of the child, the judge will grant a *judgment of adoption.*

In order to adopt, you usually need the consent of the children to be adopted (if they have reached a certain age) and consent of the birth parents. This does not apply if the birth parents are unavailable or dead, or if their parental rights have already been revoked. Consents are filed with the petition and may be revoked within certain time limits before the adoption.

To prevent the brokering of children and adoptions, only certain payments are allowed. The adopting father can pay for filing fees, attorney fees, agency fees, necessary medical care, and counseling for the birth mother and child.

If you plan to be present during the birth of the child, see the child in the nursery, and take the child home from the hospital, you will need a custody order from the court. It is a good idea to have the adoption petition and other documents in order and filed even before the prospective adoptive child is born. You may also need consents signed by the birth parents after the birth of the child, medical information, releases for each birth parent and the child, and the birth parents' signatures on hospital forms, such as nursery admission authorization and consent to remove the child from the hospital.

TERMINATION OF FATHERS' RIGHTS

While the law favors the relationship between father and child, there are cases where the court will sever all parental rights. This is a drastic action, and once terminated, these rights cannot be restored.

Termination Law and Procedure

You cannot voluntarily terminate your rights and responsibilities as a father—for example, stop paying child support—unless there is another man willing to take your place as a father through an adoption proceeding. However, the court has the power to terminate a father's rights when a father neglects or abuses a child, or when the father consents to termination or cannot be found in an adoption. Bill's case is an example of how a termination of parental rights might occur.

BILL'S CASE

Bill was the only father that Teresa, age 4, had ever known. Although he was not her biological father, and he had not adopted her or signed an affidavit of paternity, Bill never objected to paying child support when he and his wife, Kelly, divorced.

When Kelly remarried, she began a campaign to gain full custody of the girl. She stopped all visitation and filed numerous motions, including a petition for sole custody.

The court ordered a custody evaluation. Bill told the evaluator that Kelly was alienating the child from him.

He insisted that joint physical custody be reinstated immediately.

Much to Bill's disappointment, the evaluator recommended a *graduated visitation schedule*. Bill felt that he was being punished for his good behavior, while Kelly was being rewarded for kidnapping the child. His lawyer told him he could fight it in court with his own private evaluation, but the judge would probably follow the court-appointed evaluator's recommendation.

On the eve of the custody trial, Bill instructed his lawyer to make a settlement proposal. He agreed to let Kelly's new husband adopt Teresa. He believed this was the best solution for all, because it brought an end to the litigation, took the child out of the middle, and resolved the long-running conflict with his ex-wife.

Petitioners

The court will only act to terminate parental rights if someone asks it to do so. Termination petitions can be filed by the custodial parent, a state or county welfare agency, the children's attorney, a grandparent, or any other interested person.

Grounds

You need *grounds* or reasons to petition the court for a termination of parental rights. Grounds for termination include abandonment, abuse, incarceration, mental incapacity, and neglect.

Defenses

The best way to defend against a petition for termination of your rights as a father is to show that it would have a negative effect on the child. Show the judge that there is a bond between you and the child. Pictures of you and the child having fun together can help.

Now is the time to volunteer as an assistant coach for the child's soccer team. Know birth dates, clothing sizes, favorite pajamas, friends, teachers, and doctors so you do not get tripped up on cross-examination by a clever lawyer. If you are accused of improper behavior, you will want to show the judge that you have taken corrective actions, such as therapy or drug rehabilitation.

PATERNITY FRAUD

More and more fathers are challenging paternity fraud in cases across the country. Under common law, a married man is presumed to be the father of a child born during the marriage. Even if you are not the biological father of the child born of the marriage, the courts in a majority of cases will hold you to be the legal father of that child, and will require you to pay child support. This is true even if you present DNA evidence that you are not the father.

What should you do if you are tricked into paying child support by the mother for a child who is not your own? A Michigan man paid $80,000 in child support over fifteen years to his ex-wife, despite DNA evidence that he was not the father. The father sued, and after a long court battle, finally settled with the ex-wife and had his child support canceled.

Some state legislatures are looking at the problem of paternity fraud and enacting laws to give some relief. Colorado passed a new law allowing men to challenge paternity during a divorce, separation, or child support action; Florida is considering a law that would terminate support if a man proves he is not the father; and, Michigan is looking at a bill to require the courts to end support in such a case. Other states have also made similar changes to their paternity laws to allow men to challenge paternity, including Alabama, Maryland, Georgia, and Ohio.

There is a model law—which has been adopted in Delaware, North Dakota, Texas, Utah, Washington, and Wyoming—that permits genetic testing within the first two years of a child's life. If the test shows the father is not the biological parent, then he has the right to disestablish paternity. The idea is that this is better for the child than letting anybody sue anytime.

Of course, courts are trying to look out for the child, and terminating child support is certainly not in the best interests of the child, especially when the real father cannot be found. There is also the trauma to the child of finding out the parent he or she thought was his or her father is not. The courts do not want children to be fatherless. Nevertheless, a California court threw out a child support order when a construction worker proved he was not the father, saying, "[W]hen a mistake occurs in a child support action, the county must correct it, not exploit it."

Some men are bringing suits against the biological father to recoup the cost of raising a child who turns out not to be theirs. In New Jersey, a man recently won the right to sue the biological father for over $100,000. He found out the child was not his some thirty years after the birth.

–2–

CONFLICTS

Even if you are the best father in the world, you may still end up in a conflict over your children. You might have to ask the court for access to your children or to establish custody. A mother might engage in conflict over custody as a way of hanging onto the lost relationship with the father. A mother who feels she has failed in the relationship with her spouse or lover may set out to prove she can be successful in her relationship with her children—the only relationship she has left. She is determined to prove that she is a better parent than you. The opposite is true as well—that is, the father may be the one fueling the conflict.

DISPUTES ABOUT CHILDREN

A dispute over custody can arise in the context of a divorce, paternity suit, domestic violence petition, or other legal action. While some disputes can be resolved gracefully and peacefully, it is an unfortunate fact of life that many cannot. If you are in an adversarial situation involving your children, you cannot afford to let yourself be shocked into inaction. It is important for you to take responsibility, think clearly, and take control of your case.

You might receive a letter in the mail similar to the one on page 15. Most family lawyers use an initial letter similar to this to begin a divorce, custody, or other legal proceeding.

Child custody cases are the worst of all lawsuits. They are expensive and mean-spirited, and they put the children in the middle of the conflict between mom and dad. Children bounce back, but the bounce hurts. There are enormous currents of emotions at play, as well as major legal and financial issues, in disputes over parenting. Custody fights are just as traumatic to the parents as they are to the children involved. This chapter discusses the emotions and thoughts that fuel high-conflict custody disputes. It also presents *interventions*, which are effective methods of bringing clarity, control, and order to the emotional chaos swirling around conflicts over children.

DEALING WITH EMOTIONS

Women are not the only ones who have to deal with emotions. If you are a father caught up in a struggle over your children and you are *not* feeling uncertain, insecure, or depressed right now, then there may be something wrong with you. You should consider seeking professional help immediately. If you are going through a divorce or other lawsuit involving your children, and you *do* feel uncertain, insecure, angry, or depressed, do not fear—these are normal emotions. However, you may want to obtain some counseling to help you cope with your feelings. While this is not a particularly pleasant life lesson, you will survive it—becoming much stronger and wiser in the process.

The rest of this section discusses some of the emotions that you may recognize if you are in a dispute over your children, and provides some ways of dealing with them.

Anxiety. Worry and anxiety are common human emotions. People will find something to worry about even when times are good. When going through a divorce or other legal proceeding concerning your children, you will find many things to worry about—and you will have good reason to worry. However, instead of letting your mind be consumed with worrying about how bad the situation is, concern yourself with what you can do to solve your problems.

6/15/07
Mr. John Doe
123 Easy Street
Anytown, MD 55555

Re: Doe Family Matter

Dear Mr. Doe:

This firm has been retained by your wife to represent her in connection with the present marital difficulty. She is committed to resolving the issues pending between you in an amicable fashion with the least amount of disruption to the family.

Toward this end, she has expressed an interest in negotiating a fair and equitable separation agreement that takes into consideration not only her needs, but your needs and those of the children as well.

Please contact us, or have your attorney contact us, within the next ten days. Thanking you for your time, attention, and courtesy, I remain,

Sincerely yours,

ATTORNEY & ATTORNEY

John Q. Attorney
John Q. Attorney

JQA/dms
cc: My Client

NOTE: *Outline your problems in writing—it will help you focus clearly. Then, destroy the notes so they cannot be used against you by the other side.*

Shame. The failure of a relationship results in hurt, shame, and embarrassment. This is even more so when the breakup is abrupt, unexpected, or traumatic. You may feel embarrassment and humiliation that you are involved in a divorce or custody dispute with the mother of your children. You may be feeling like a failure or a loser in relationships right now. These feelings can happen whether you are the one leaving or the one being left. These are normal feelings, but do not let them drive you into isolation. You will need to tell your friends and family about your situation, because you will need their support. You may also want to consult with a therapist and a lawyer. These people will be sympathetic to your circumstances and will not judge you— they are in the business of dealing with cases like yours.

Depression. Depression is another fairly common experience in custody conflicts. Psychologists say that depression is anger directed inward—toward yourself rather than your spouse. You may find yourself sleeping more, crying, and unable to concentrate or work. You may even have thoughts of suicide. It is important to see a therapist as soon as possible if you are feeling depressed.

Blame. The parties to a lawsuit frequently view it as an assessment of blame. Each party wants to show that they are right and the other side is wrong. Each party wants the judge to say who is good and who is bad. People are willing to pay thousands of dollars for this assessment. You will benefit in the long run if you can hold the desire to blame in check, especially when you are under attack by the other side. Instead, concentrate on the practical, legal, and financial aspects of your situation. That is what the lawyers and judge will be doing.

Anger. Your children's mother may have deserted you, deceived you, insulted you, or betrayed you in some other way. It is only natural for you to feel angry with her. Do not take your anger out on her or your children—take your anger out on a punching bag or racquetball.

NOTE: You need to be cool, calm, and collected to deal effectively with legal and financial issues.

Revenge. Akin to anger is the desire for revenge. However, revenge will not help your legal case. Two old sayings will come in handy if the desire for revenge is getting in your way: *revenge is a dish best served cold* and *the best revenge is living well.*

If you receive a letter like the one on page 15, a *Complaint*, or a *Protective Order*, then you are in an *adversarial situation.* You need to be aware that you are in a fight. The fight may be over assets, alimony, child support, or custody.

While there is plenty of room for cooperation, collaboration, and settlement in the legal system, it is, by nature and tradition, an adversarial process. Traditional lawyering requires representing a client as an advocate. While it may not be appropriate in cases in which families and children are involved, that sometimes means kicking the other guy when he is down.

Your wife or the mother of your children, who may have been your friend, lover, confidant, and ally, is now plotting against you. At this very moment, she may be planning with her lawyer to drain the joint bank accounts, charge up the joint credit cards, accuse you of cruelty and misconduct, and take the children and leave.

She knows your vulnerabilities, your insecurities, your weak spots, and where every skeleton is hidden. Failure to get control of your emotions, think clearly, plan, and take early action can have dire consequences, as Jerry's case illustrates.

JERRY'S CASE

Jerry was a hardworking father of two and a good provider for his family. He loved his children, but his marriage had not been going smoothly for a number of years. He was still trying to make it work, but one night he had another argument with his wife and harsh words were exchanged.

The next evening, he answered a knock at the door and the sheriff's deputies were there. They told him he had five minutes to collect his things and leave the house. He checked into a hotel with an overnight bag, his toothbrush, and the clothes he had on. He did not go to work the next day because he was too depressed. He missed an important meeting and was fired.

Depressed and confused, Jerry was paralyzed into inaction. Although the possible dire consequences were printed in bold letters on the papers he received, he did not really understand the procedures or the stakes involved, and he missed his next court date.

His wife told the judge that Jerry threatened her. She also said that he made over $100,000 a year, but failed to mention that he lost his job. Because she did not work, she said that she and the children needed $5,000 a month in living expenses. Since her testimony was unopposed, the judge entered a permanent protective order requiring Jerry to pay alimony of $5,000 a month. The judge also gave custody of the children to Jerry's wife. Jerry failed to appeal within the next thirty days, and the order became final.

INTERVENTIONS

Jerry needed some help that he did not receive. The following techniques, called *interventions*, can resolve or mitigate conflict, and can help you avoid Jerry's circumstances.

Intervention #1—Establish a Support Structure

In general, men are reluctant to share their problems with others. Instead, they try to figure out a solution in their heads. This is a poor strategy for conflicts over children. There are some things that are beyond your control. You will never figure it out by yourself. You need some support.

Counseling can benefit anyone. It can be very valuable to you during a divorce or other legal conflict involving children. It is a time to confront the problems in your relationship and your life head-on. It may take time, but eventually you will be able to get on with your life. Counselors can be psychiatrists, psychologists, or licensed clinical social workers. They can cost about $150 per session, and sessions are usually once a week. Insurance may help pay a portion of the cost. There are also low-cost clinics. Ministers and other religious and spiritual leaders may also provide good counseling at no cost to you.

Distinguish your emotions from your legal case. Your legal case involves legal and financial issues. You will want to discuss legal and financial matters with a lawyer. When you talk to your lawyer, he or she is mentally sorting the facts according to the legal elements that must be proven at trial. About 90% of the things clients tell a lawyer are very important to the client, but not very important to their case or their lawyer, so if you feel like your lawyer is not listening to you, you are probably right. Discuss emotional issues with a good therapist.

The support of friends and family is invaluable during a custody case, but one word of caution is in order. Your family and friends will offer you advice about your case. They will tell you about someone that got full custody or someone that did not have to pay any child support. Often, such advice is incorrect, so you need to take it with a grain of salt. The facts and circumstances of your marriage, divorce, or children are unique. This is not your neighbor's case or your cousin Joe's case. It is your case, and it is different from anyone else's case.

There are support groups for separating and divorcing parties. You can find support on the Internet, where there are virtual communities of fathers, separated parents, and divorced parents.

Intervention #2—Get Your Head Together

This is a crisis that requires clear thought and action. To protect yourself, your rights, and the shirt on your back, you will need to get your head together and think clearly.

A lot of men make the mistake of thinking their wives or girlfriends were responsible for all the good things in their lives. But you are the one that created your environment—where and how you lived, the money, the lifestyle, and the happiness. You did it once and you can do it again. The trick is to realize that you are responsible for your happiness, your finances, your case, and your life.

Right now, things may be spinning out of control in your life. This makes you crazy because you like to be in control. You will have to accept the fact that certain things are beyond your control, like your wife or girlfriend, her attorney, the legal system, the judge, and maybe even your attorney. However, there are other things that you can and should take control of now, such as your emotions, your finances, your legal case, and your future.

Use this analogy in your legal situation: Two men come out of their houses one morning and find that someone has vandalized their brand-new automobiles. One takes his car to the repair shop and has it repaired. The other worries and frets about it for six months, then takes his car to the repair shop and has it repaired. The only difference between the two men and the outcome is that one has an extra six months of worry and feeling sorry for himself.

Get to work on your case now. Act swiftly and effectively. Do not let worry and feeling sorry for yourself immobilize you for long periods of time. Your emotions are independent and separate from your legal case. Put your emotions in one basket and discuss them with a counselor or other support structure. Put your financial and legal matters in another basket and review them with your attorney.

Intervention #3—Acknowledge Each Others' Feelings

Something has broken the bonds between you and the mother of your children. She may be making you feel like the split or the problems the children are having with the separation is all your fault. You may be laying a guilt trip on her. There is always plenty of blame to go around in a custody fight.

You may be headed toward a costly legal battle that is more about proving—once and for all—who is right than it is about determining access and child support. The legal system will feed this kind of thinking. It is set up as an adversarial system with one winner and one loser. Parties can hire aggressive lawyers to make the other parent look as bad as possible in hopes the judge will ultimately agree. Lawyers use anger, contempt, derision, and theatrics as weapons in their arsenal to win a case.

How do you avoid this? Acknowledging what the other parent is feeling is one step that can go a long way toward resolving conflict.

MIKE'S CASE

Mike was divorcing Marcia after a sixteen year marriage. They had three children together, ages 7, 9, and 10, who were living with Marcia. The youngest, Grant, was caught shoplifting. He was also having troubles in school. Marcia called Mike to inform him. When Mike responded, Marcia thought Mike was saying that Grant was having problems because she was a bad mother. Mike did not think that, and did not intend to convey that message.

The parties went to mediation. Mike asked for 50% time-sharing with children. Marcia resisted and wanted no overnights during the school week. She said she wants the children to have routine and stability, and to wake up in the same bed each morning.

In a private conversation in the hall, Marcia's lawyer told Mike's lawyer that Marcia believed this is just another indication that Mike thinks she is a bad mother. Mike wanted the children 50% of the time so he could save them from Marcia's bad mothering.

Mike's lawyer stopped the mediation and pulled Mike aside. He explained the situation and asked Mike to acknowledge Marcia's feelings, then apologize sincerely in front of everyone. Mike was reluctant at first, because he felt he was apologizing for something he did not do. But he agreed to do it upon on the advice of his lawyer, who believed it would help his case.

When the mediation resumed, Mike said, "Marcia, I acknowledge that you think I blame you for Grant's recent problems. You think I believe that you are a bad mother. I want you to know that I do not believe that. I believe Grant's problems are a result of our getting a divorce. And I apologize if anything I have done or said led you to believe that I think you are a bad mother. I believe you are a good mother, and I hope that we can work together to raise our children."

As the mediation continued, Marcia agreed to allow the children to spend some more time with Mike.

Intervention #4—Respect Your Opponent

If the bonds of human interaction have been broken, the way to restore them is through respect. Respect is shown by small gestures, words, and courtesies, such as saying *hello* to acknowledge that the other person is present. No matter what anger or ill feelings you may have toward your ex-girlfriend or wife, you are still partners in the business of raising your children. The following suggestions will smooth the way to resolving your disputes and restoring social bonds between you and the mother of your children.

- Pick your battles and fight for the things that matter. You do not have to respond to every provocation.
- Stop talking and trying to persuade the other side that you are right and she is wrong. This is a time to ask questions, listen to the answers, and gather intelligence.
- If you can remove minor irritations between you and the children's mother at no great cost to you, then do so.

WHAT TO SAY TO THE KIDS

The courts frown on exposing the children to the conflict between the parents, but you have to explain the situation to them. To the extent you can coordinate this with the mother, plan together what you are going to say before you say it. Depending on their ages and the circumstances of the legal proceeding, your explanation may change. In general, you should try to convey the message that sometimes adults cannot live together, but that has no effect on the children's relationship with either parent. You will always be their dad and their mom will always be their mom.

Custody proceedings are very emotional, and parents sometimes use children to seek revenge. Try to keep the children out of this. If they must be involved, prepare them properly without poisoning their minds about their mother. Obtain professional advice if possible, but do not try to use your child's therapist to gain an advantage in a custody battle. Tell the children that the divorce is not their fault and they will still have both parents.

Make a special effort to spend time with your children during this difficult time. Give them your full attention. Reassure them that both parents love them, and give them extra love now. They need it.

—3—

IMPORTANT FIRST STEPS

If you are served with legal documents, arrested, or your children's mother abruptly leaves or wants you to move out, then you have an emergency on your hands. This calls for prompt and aggressive action. In case of an emergency, use the tools provided to you in this chapter to protect your interests and those of your children as well. It covers moving out, access to children, domestic abuse, finances, and related matters. Use it as a checklist at the beginning of your case so you do not miss any important details.

MOVING OUT

Do not move out just because your children's mother asks you to. Stay put. You do not have to move out just because she wants you to. If you both own the house or you both lease an apartment, you have as much right to be there as she does. Tell her that you are staying. She cannot force you to leave without a court order. In fact, moving out can be hazardous to your legal case. It can have an adverse effect on divorce, alimony, property division, custody, visitation, and child support.

If you move out, your children's mother can use it against you later in a divorce or custody complaint to claim you abandoned or deserted her, the marriage, or the children. Desertion or abandonment is grounds for divorce in most states.

Fault or misconduct can be a factor in alimony. The divorce court might determine that your leaving caused the breakup of the marriage. This might justify a judge awarding your spouse more alimony. In many states, the divorce court can consider fault or misconduct when dividing marital property. If the judge finds that your leaving was desertion or abandonment and the cause of your estrangement, he or she can award your spouse more than half of the assets you owned together.

You will have a hard time convincing a judge to give you custody if you left the children with their mother in the marital residence. Although the phrase *possession is nine-tenths of the law* applies to property law, the same could be said for children. If you leave, you may be setting yourself up for less visitation. Once a pattern is set, it is hard to change visitation. If a certain arrangement seems to be working for the children, it has its own inertia and judges will not want to tinker with it.

If you have already made the mistake of moving out, you can correct it by simply moving back in. Nothing prevents you from living in your own house or apartment. If your wife has changed the locks, you can hire a locksmith and change them again. You can also break into your own house or apartment. If you have an alarm, your spouse may have changed the code, so you might want to explain to the alarm company or police what you are doing ahead of time.

If the situation has become so tense that you cannot stay and you absolutely have to leave, try to get your wife to sign a *move out agreement*. This can be used to show that you did not desert or abandon the family, if litigation follows later. The move out agreement is proof that a separation is mutual and voluntary.

A move out agreement is a simple agreement that covers the most important issue, namely that the move out is not desertion or abandonment. You can include more, such as who makes the mortgage payments or the car payments during the separation. However, it is often easier to get a simple agreement signed. In states where separation is one of the grounds for divorce, this agreement can also be used as evidence of the date of separation. A sample move out agreement follows.

Move Out Agreement

THIS AGREEMENT is made as of the 16th day of JUNE, 2007, by and between John Doe and Jane Doe .

WHEREAS, the parties were married on MAY 27, 1995 in Anytown, Anystate ; and

WHEREAS, 2 children were born of the marriage, who are minors; and

WHEREAS, certain differences have arisen between the parties and they wish to enter into a temporary separation agreement;

NOW, THEREFORE, in consideration of the mutual promises, agreements, and covenants expressed herein, it is hereby covenanted and agreed by each party hereto and with the other hereto as follows:

1.   The parties agree that they wish to live separate and apart from each other, in separate abodes, without cohabitation, until such time as they may reconcile or enter into a permanent separation agreement.

2.   In accordance therewith, John Doe shall vacate the marital home at 123 Easy Street , promptly after the execution of this Agreement.

3.   It is agreed by the parties that John Doe 's departure from the marital home is mutual and voluntary, and shall not be construed as desertion or abandonment.

IN WITNESS WHEREOF, the parties hereto have hereunder set their hands and seals the date and year first above written.

_*John Doe*_____   [Seal]

_*Jane Doe*_____   [Seal]

You can have the move out agreement notarized if you think your spouse will later dispute her signature, but it is not required. It is usually easier to get it signed if you do not have to do it before a notary. (The word *seal* at the end harkens back to the day when legal instruments had to be sealed with a stamp and wax to be official. Today, your signature is your seal.)

If you absolutely have to move out without an agreement, you can help your custody case by coming back each evening to have dinner with the children, help them with their homework, and put them to bed.

ACCESS TO CHILDREN

If your partner threatens to leave and take the children, let her know that she can go, but the children are staying. She does not have the right to remove the children from the family home. If she takes the children anyway, you can bring them back by asking the court to order her to return the children. If she leaves and takes the children with her, you have the right to know where they are.

Until and unless a court orders otherwise, you have joint legal and physical custody of your children with your spouse under the common law. Anything less than this takes your rights away. Many fathers opt for less than joint custody, and in some cases, joint custody may not be in the best interests of the children. But you have the right, if you wish to exercise it, to insist on joint custody from the outset. In cases in which the mother is an unfit parent, you can ask the court to award you sole custody.

If the mother denies you access to the children, you can ask the court to order her to let you see the children. You are entitled to half of the time with your children if you want her to let you see the children. There is nothing in the law that says you are an incompetent parent because you are a father, and there is nothing that says the mother is a better parent than you.

The court will tend to keep the *status quo* (existing situation) by leaving the children where they are from the beginning. This is to avoid more disruption in the children's lives than the divorce or separation of their parents is already causing. That is why it is important that you set the precedent of equal time from the beginning of your case.

There are many equal time-sharing arrangements. The simplest is alternating weeks with each parent, also called *week on/week off*. This minimizes the number of transfers and problems, like lost clothes and homework assignments. It also makes it easy for the children to know where they are going to be each week. Other equal time-sharing arrangements are discussed in Chapter 6.

If you and your spouse have arguments or other difficulties during transfer of the children from one parent to the other, you can arrange the transfer at a public place or you can stay in the car and both watch the children from car to front door. Set up a weekly time to only discuss parenting issues by telephone. It is usually a bad idea to pass messages back and forth through the children.

If you are concerned that your spouse will run off with your children, you can ask the court to prohibit this by issuing a *temporary restraining order* or a *preliminary injunction*. These are orders of the court that are issued to prevent harm pending further hearings. You can ask the court for an order prohibiting your spouse from taking the children out of the state. You would do this by filing a petition for a *ne exeat order* with the court. If your wife does take the children to another state, you can ask the court to order her to bring them back. Judges look with disfavor on a parent who takes the children out of school and moves them to another state.

At most courthouses there is a *duty judge*, whose job it is to hear walk-in or emergency motions. An *emergency motion* calls attention to your case and might help expedite it within the legal system. You should be aware, however, that every Friday the court is flooded with emergency motions about weekend visitation disputes. It is important for you to show that a real emergency exists or the judge will deny your motion. You will also be required to give notice of your motion and the emergency hearing to the other side.

DOMESTIC VIOLENCE

Domestic violence is a serious problem and no one should tolerate it. However, there are many cases in which a father is accused of domestic violence and the woman either struck first, made the first threat, or lied about the abuse. You must know how to protect yourself against false claims of domestic violence and how to avoid responding to provocation.

Do not let a woman provoke you into an argument, threats, or violence of any kind. Restraining her—even if she is hitting you—or using harsh words will be construed against you by her and maybe by the court. Your best bet is to walk away.

Your wife's attorney will tell her the only way to force you to leave the house is if you abuse her or the children, or make threats against them. Unfortunately, this encourages a number of women to provoke a fight or falsely allege domestic violence. It becomes a tactic for starting a divorce or to gain an advantage in a custody dispute.

You can be put out of the house with an injunction or arrested by the police or sheriff on your wife's testimony alone. If this happens, contact your attorney at once, because you need to defend against these allegations. If you disobey an injunction, the court can put you in jail. Even if the judge does not put you in jail, you can be fined, and the judge will have a hard time trusting you later when you testify. Also, the court can refuse to hear anything you have to say if you are in contempt.

In a custody battle, you do not want to give the other side any excuse to make a complaint of child abuse. Then you will have to deal with Child Protective Services, the court, and the police, all at the same time. Therefore, it is a bad time to use corporal punishment to discipline the children, even though it may be permitted by law in your state. Be careful how you deal with unruly children. If the children will not get out of their mom's car for visitation, do not pick them up, pry their hands loose, or physically force them to do so. Instead, get them into therapy or speak with their therapist about how to help them want to visit with you. You have to choose your battles right now and you do not have to win every one.

If your children's mother commits any domestic violence against you or the children, call the police first, and then your attorney. You are entitled to obtain a protective order if you or the children are in fear of harm. Sometimes the police will not get involved in problems between spouses or cohabitants, but if you show them an injunction they will often remove the other party. They have to act if you have a *protective order.*

FINANCES

There are a lot of important actions you need to take to protect your finances. Move your documents, records, and other papers somewhere else, like a friend's house or your attorney's office. You can expect that your children's mother will be going through your desk, briefcase, automobile, telephone records, bills, and computer looking for financial information and other evidence to use against you.

Go to the bank, divide the joint bank accounts in half, and deposit your half in your own name. You can put them all in your name, but sometimes this will make the judge angry with you. However, it is often easier to give money back than to get it back. If you are the breadwinner, do not put your children and their mother out in the cold without some money to get by. This will aggravate the judge, who will make you pay anyway. Make arrangements so that bills will be covered. Let your children's mother know what you have done, but not before you have done it. You do not want her to clean out the account first.

Call your broker and divide any stocks, bonds, or mutual funds that are held jointly with your children's mother. While this is not a taxable event, you will have to take future taxes into account if you want to be fair. Therefore, ask your broker to make sure the *tax basis* is equalized as well.

You do not want to wake up one morning and discover that your children's mother has charged $5,000 to your joint credit card while on a spending spree. You may be responsible for paying part or all of that $5,000. Close all joint credit or loan accounts, and notify the banks, charge cards, and others by a certified, return receipt letter that you are no longer responsible for the expenses of your children's mother. You may ask the company to reopen an account in your own name. This is a good time to make that request. Let your children's mother know so she is not caught by surprise at the gas pump when the credit card no longer works. If she has already started her spending spree, report the card as stolen. If she has charged her attorney's fees on the card, you can dispute the charges with the company.

If you cover your spouse or children on your insurance, do not drop them from the policy. Even after the divorce, you may want to keep your children covered. If you are paying child support, a large unexpected medical expense for the child could be assessed against the noncustodial parent as additional child support. The same could happen with alimony and an ex-spouse. Federal law allows most ex-spouses to be insured for up to thirty-six months after a divorce for a small additional premium.

Two cannot live as cheaply as one, especially if they are separated and trying to maintain two households. It is time to cut costs as much as possible. Cancel anything you do not need, like extra telephone lines or cable television. If there is any personal property you do not want or need, sell it. However, do not cut off the utilities on your children and their mother without giving them plenty of notice. Make sure you can prove this advance notice to the court, because leaving your children and their mother home without heat or light in December seldom sits well with the judge.

Retirement funds acquired during a marriage are marital assets that can be divided by the divorce court. Chances are good that your wife will share in anything you contributed to your pension plan at work or your Individual Retirement Account (IRA). Fill out the paperwork to have your employer stop your contributions to your 401(k) account or other pension plan. Do not make contributions to your IRA this year. This will keep your spouse from getting part of it, and chances are, you will be needing the money soon.

Make a list of everything in the house. Take pictures of or videotape everything. This way, if something turns up missing, you will have evidence of it. Be sure to date your inventory. Include furniture, appliances, clothing, and jewelry.

Move any valuables, like collections, jewelry, artwork, firearms, cash, and heirlooms, out of the house to a safe place. Anything with significant or sentimental value to you ought to be secured from your children's mother. You are not trying to hide things, but you do not want to come home from work and find that your valuables have been sold at a yard sale.

You can establish a safe-deposit box to store your valuables away from the house. If you already have a safe-deposit box and your children's mother has access to it, you will want to remove your items and store them somewhere else. Make a list, take a picture, or take a videotape of whatever is left in the box for proof later. The same goes for any storage unit you may have.

LEGAL MATTERS

Find a good family lawyer and set up an appointment right away. Some lawyers charge for an initial consultation and some do not. In the initial meeting, you will be able to get some good advice and strategy for your particular facts and circumstances. You will also be able to assess the attorney to see if he or she is a good fit for you. During this meeting, the attorney will discuss costs. Be aware that any estimate by an attorney is the roughest of all guesses and depends upon what your spouse and her attorney do.

Your attorney will probably tell you not to sign anything before he or she reviews it. This is a good rule. There are trips and traps in every legal document that can work against you in a contested custody or property case. If your children's mother asks you to sign a preliminary document, memorandum, or letter, explain to her that you will have your attorney review it first.

Your attorney may also ask you to begin keeping a daily log of important events in your case. Write down anything you think might be useful later. Include any discussions with your children's mother and time spent with the children. Always keep in mind that anything you write down, except communications with your attorney, may be obtained by the other side in a lawsuit during discovery.

Your attorney will advise you about other matters you will need to consider during this change in your life; for example, executing a new will and changing any powers of attorney.

−4−

THE LEGAL SYSTEM

The legal system is as confusing and confounding to you as Wonderland was to Alice. In order for you to know how to handle your case, first it will be helpful for you to know about the law that the judge will apply. This chapter tells you about the origins of our legal system, its limitations, how laws are made, and where to find the law. It also tells you how to find, hire, and fire a lawyer, and describes the roles of lawyers, judges, and the various other participants in a custody case.

ORIGINS OF OUR LEGAL SYSTEM

Our legal system has its roots in England from about four hundred years ago (with the exception of Louisiana, which follows the *Napoleonic Code* of France). The church's courts of *equity* handled divorces and the government's courts of *law* handled matters such as property, estates, contracts, and torts. Today, we have merged the courts of equity and law, meaning that the same judge may hear a divorce one day and a contract case the next.

Our law is based on an *adversarial model*. The theory is that each side marshals the facts, presents evidence, and argues the law most favorably to their side. In theory, the judge or jury is supposed to sort out the truth and render a just result.

The law was developed to codify and guide human behavior. It is supposed to be logical and rational. The rules of law fall into the following three general categories.

1. *Substance.* This is the basic substance of the law, such as how the judge is supposed to decide custody.
2. *Procedure.* These are the rules for dealing with the court. For example, what pleadings are to be filed by what dates.
3. *Evidence.* These are the rules for how facts are presented at trial.

LIMITATIONS

Since human beings are imperfect, and our legal system was designed by human beings, it has some major flaws. Realizing that may save you some frustration in dealing with your case. Several people, when dealing with the courts for the first time, develop many false assumptions about the legal system. You might assume that you will win your case because of one or more of the following statements.

◆ You are right and your children's mother is wrong.
◆ The judge is fair, impartial, wise, and all-knowing.
◆ The judge will see immediately that you are telling the truth and your children's mother is lying.
◆ Two lawyers and a judge will certainly arrive at a fair result.

However, the realities of the legal system are quite different. Trying to solve modern family problems with a four-hundred-year-old system is like forcing a square peg into a round hole. The legal system was designed by lawyers, not psychologists. It is slow. It is expensive. It is an adversarial model that does not work very well when there are families and children involved. It is regrettable, but people can and do cheat the system.

There are some things for which the law has no remedies. The law cannot make the mother of your children into a better person. Lawyers and judges do not have magic wands. They must work within the confines of the law and the procedures the system has in place.

HOW LAWS ARE MADE

In family law matters, there are essentially three ways that laws are made—by the legislatures, by the courts, and through rules. Each affects you and plays a role in how your case will proceed and be handled.

Legislatures are bodies of elected officials who meet and make most of our laws. Legislatures are constantly making new laws. They are supposed to represent the will of the majority. The laws they pass should then reflect what most people in your state want. Laws are usually general and prescriptive in nature.

The courts interpret the laws passed by the legislature. When you cannot settle a dispute, you may ask a judge to decide it at a trial. The courts decide disputes on a case-by-case basis. They are supposed to protect the minority from the majority when a law does not apply in a certain case or violates the constitution.

There is also a *Rules Committee* in each jurisdiction that passes rules for the court. The parties and their lawyers must follow these rules. These are generally the rules regarding procedure for how matters are presented to the court and the manner in which evidence is used.

WHERE TO FIND THE LAW

The law used to be the province of lawyers and judges only, who, like oracles or wizards, deciphered the writings for the benefit of their clients. Now the law is freely available to the public on the Internet and in law libraries. Every law school and most courts have law libraries. The following describes where you can find the law.

The United States, as well as each state, has a written *constitution* that sets forth essential rights of the people. This is the supreme law of the land and provides the framework for all other laws passed.

The legislature, elected by and representing the people, passes laws, called *statutes*, each year. These are published in books for each state called *codes*. Laws are meant to codify human behavior and they reflect the will of the majority in our society. They are intended to be logical and practical, but you may not always find them to be so. Laws are supposed to be consistent with the constitution of your state and of the United States.

The manner in which a law applies to a specific set of circumstances is usually decided by the courts. The appellate courts for each jurisdiction review the record of trial courts on a case-by-case basis when appeals are brought by the parties. The appellate court either affirms, vacates, modifies, or reverses the trial court. It usually explains its decision in writing, and many decisions are published in books called *reporters* and summarized in books called *digests*. These cases form a *precedent* for later trials and appeals. The court can interpret or even invalidate laws if they are unconstitutional. While the legislature reflects the will of the majority in writing general laws, the court can look at the facts of individual cases and make exceptions for the minority when the law would work an unjust result.

The rules for court procedure are published in a book of *Rules* and must be followed. They are very detailed and cover time deadlines, how pleadings must be presented and signed, how information is obtained from the other side, how evidence is to be presented at trial, and many other subjects. In addition, some courts and some judges publish what are called *local rules*, which may be available only on a memorandum from the court clerk. There are also what lawyers refer to as *unpublished rules*—the local customs and practices of various courts and judges that you can only know from experience.

There are various legal encyclopedias, digests, treatises, practice manuals, and other books available at the library to help you sort out and make sense of the law.

NOTE: *Most court files are public records, and you can review and copy them at the courthouse. You can use them to see how lawyers* *draft pleadings. In addition, some courts provide forms, help desks, and seminars to assist you in your case.*

LAWYERS

As you can see, even though much of the law and court procedures are open to the public, there is a lot to know. Family law is complicated and many fathers want to have a lawyer represent them. A good lawyer can guide you through the process, help you avoid mistakes, save you time, and protect your interests. Any time you have a case that involves children, hiring a lawyer is highly recommended. While doing it on your own is possible, the system is complicated and one mistake, one missed date, or one wrong form could cost you your children. At the very least, think about getting a lawyer if:

- the case is contested and the stakes are high;
- your children's mother has a lawyer;
- you are stuck and you do not know what to do; or,
- you do not have the time, interest, or tolerance for the frustration and confusion sometimes encountered in the legal system.

If you represent yourself, you will be a *pro se* litigant. *Pro se* is Latin, meaning *by yourself* or *on your own behalf*. A number of cases involving fathers and custody of children are decided by the courts with no lawyers involved. It is up to you to decide, based on the circumstances of your case, if you need to hire an attorney to help you.

Usually, there is no right to counsel in family law like there is in criminal cases. The court will not appoint or provide you with an attorney. The court might appoint counsel, however, if you cannot afford one and are charged with criminal contempt for failing to pay child support, or if you are about to have your parental rights terminated. However, for other matters not involving the threat of jail or termination of parental rights, you are responsible for hiring your own attorney.

There are several advantages to having a lawyer represent you. If you have a lawyer, you can let the lawyer do all the worrying about your case. Lawyers have the training, skills, and experience for this job. Lawyers are used to dealing with the courts and they know the rules, the laws, and the cases in which the courts have interpreted the laws. When you represent yourself, the judge will not give you much leeway. You are expected to know the rules, the laws, and the cases.

Lawyers can efficiently and effectively negotiate and draft a parenting plan, and will guide you through the legal process. Lawyers know what to do when there are complications in your case (like not being able to serve the other side), or when difficult issues like custody, visitation, and child support arise. Along with the judges, they share a common language that contains lots of terms and jargon that are shortcuts for a body of law they understand. In part, because of this common jargon, the judge and the opposing attorney may give more consideration to you if you have an attorney. The opposing attorney is not permitted to give you advice or help you.

If you decide not to hire a lawyer to represent you, you may still want to engage one as a consultant on your case. Lawyers are permitted to enter into a *limited scope of engagement* with you. This means you can hire a lawyer to consult with you on an hourly basis, to answer your questions, plan strategy, guide you, and review your pleadings. However, the lawyer might not be your *counsel of record* or go to court for you.

When you hire a lawyer as a consultant, you can still tap into his or her expertise and knowledge. This will keep you on the right track. You will still have to do all the legwork yourself and be responsible for answering all pleadings sent by the other side. However, you will not have the expense of hiring a lawyer to handle the entire matter.

Finding a Lawyer

You may decide to hire a lawyer to represent you. In litigation, the lawyer will be called *attorney for the plaintiff* or *attorney for the defendant*. Lawyers are also sometimes referred to as *counsel* or *counsel of record*. That lawyer could be a sole practitioner or associated with a firm. If you decide to hire an attorney, there are resources available for finding a good family lawyer.

- Check the Internet.
- Ask your friends who have been divorced about their experience with their lawyer.
- Get recommendations from the county bar association or ask the chair of the family law section of the county, state, or American bar associations.
- Go to seminars on divorce.
- Ask your therapist.

Evaluating a Lawyer

There are several factors to consider when searching for a lawyer to hire. Evaluating your prospective attorney may be the most important thing you do to enforce and protect your rights as a father. Some considerations you want to research and questions you want to ask before hiring a lawyer are discussed in this section. You can learn a great many things about your prospective lawyer from the Internet, by being observant at your initial interview, and by asking direct questions of the lawyer.

Fathers' rights is so specialized and complex that you should try to hire someone who has practiced in this area for at least five years (ten to fifteen years is even better). However, you cannot assume that just because a lawyer has been in practice for fifteen years, he or she has the knowledge, skills, wisdom, and right experience that you need. You still have to investigate and interview the lawyer. It is preferable to find an experienced, recognized authority who is a full-time fathers' rights attorney. Ask the lawyer about his or her practice, experience, and percentage of cases on matters such as yours.

You want a lawyer who will settle or try your case in a professional, methodical, and workmanlike manner. Try to find someone with a reputation for taking a constructive approach toward the other side, opposing counsel, and the court. This is the best way to navigate the litigation process. That way, you can preserve the relationships you have built with your children, other family members, and friends.

Some specific things you may want to look for and ask include the following.

- Is the lawyer's office and desk neat and organized, or is it overflowing with case files?
- Does the lawyer have the time for your case, or does he or she seem overworked and not able to keep up?
- Will the attorney you are interviewing handle your case personally or pass it off to an associate or paralegal?
- Who covers for the lawyer when he or she is in trial or on vacation?
- Does the lawyer have so many cases that he or she cannot give you personal care, time, and attention?
- Does he or she limit services to a few select clients who receive the best legal care he or she has to offer?
- Do you feel that the lawyer is interested in your case and wants to provide you with the help you need?
- Do you get the impression that he or she is only in it for the money?
- What does the attorney do to keep costs down?
- Are there additional charges for things such as copies, faxes, filing fees, transcripts, process servers, or online research?
- Is the lawyer hidden behind a wall of secretaries, associates, paralegals, administrative assistants, and receptionists, or is he or she accessible?
- Does the lawyer return your calls promptly?

You want a lawyer who is readily available to you by telephone, fax, and email. You will not be the attorney's only client, but your case does need the attention it deserves. Ask yourself if the lawyer can provide that attention.

Look for stability—a lawyer who has been in the same place or with the same firm for some years. You do not want a lawyer who has been bouncing around from place to place looking for new practice areas and new opportunities.

It is of utmost importance that your lawyer have superior communication skills. Look at how the attorney communicates with you. The way the lawyer communicates with you will be similar to the way he or she communicates with opposing counsel and the judge. Make sure the lawyer you choose has a communication style you relate to.

Credentials of lawyers as rated by other lawyers and judges can be found in the publication *Martindale-Hubbel*. Its *AV* rating is the highest rating, and only about 10% of all lawyers have this rating. You can find this information on the Internet at **www.lawyers.com**.

Finally, look for lawyers who have a passion for their work—those who teach seminars, write articles, and publish books about divorce after their work day is done.

Traits to Avoid When Selecting a Lawyer

There are some undesirable traits you may find in a lawyer. When found, they should start your alarm ringing and you may need to run the other way.

If your research shows you that a lawyer has recently graduated from law school, the hourly fees he or she charges may be lower, but it may end up costing you a lot more in the long run. All lawyers have to start somewhere, but you do not want to be their practice case. The amount of money you pay for experience may end up saving you money, because of the experienced lawyer's efficiency in getting the job done.

Some lawyers are suffering from burnout and they no longer care about their work or their clients. They do not particularly enjoy practicing law and they are not very good at it. Lawyers who procrastinate, are disorganized, and cannot manage their cases are the ones most likely to neglect your case and possibly cause you to lose.

A lot of divorce lawyers are not good at returning telephone calls. They think you will see that they are very important and much in demand. However, at some point in your case, you will want to get in touch with your lawyer immediately and you will not want to wait two or three days. If you cannot get your lawyer on the phone, find another lawyer.

Finally, you will be making a big mistake if you hire a lawyer because of his or her reputation as a *shark* (also called *barracuda* or *bomber*). That is what many clients think they need or want, particularly when the other side has hired one. Although the legal system is based on an adversarial model, it functions most efficiently when opposing lawyers are civil and courteous with one another. Attorneys hurling insults at the other side in telephone calls, letters, and pleadings will not win your case. Judges are not impressed by this. It will increase your legal fees, prolong your case, and damage family relationships.

Hiring a Lawyer

You typically begin the process of hiring a lawyer by making an appointment for an initial office consultation. Consultations are normally about one hour. Some lawyers do not charge you for the initial meeting and some charge a reduced fee, but the lawyers that are in demand usually charge their normal hourly fee. During this consultation, the lawyer will interview you and you can ask the lawyer questions as well. Everything you say to the lawyer is confidential and cannot be disclosed to anyone else. At the end of the consultation, the lawyer will discuss fees with you.

Family lawyers usually require a *retainer* (an advance on fees) to accept your case and to begin drawing up the necessary papers. A typical retainer might be $2,000 to $5,000. When you retain the lawyer, you will sign a contract setting out the terms of representation in writing. The retainer is refundable to the extent not used.

If you are in a particularly difficult case, your retainer may be exhausted and the lawyer may ask for an additional retainer. If you cannot pay, the lawyer may withdraw from representing you unless you can work out other mutually agreeable payment arrangements. You should be aware, however, that the paying client is the client who gets the lawyer's time and attention first.

NOTE: Your lawyer probably has a secretary who can often answer your questions by telephone. The good thing about talking to your lawyer's secretary is that he or she does not charge you for the call.

Legal Fees and Costs

The important thing to know is that any discussion with a lawyer about the costs or attorney's fees is the roughest of estimates. There are many variables in every case, including some that your lawyer has no control over. Who your spouse will hire as an attorney, how complex the financial records are, or what mood the judge is in on the day of trial will all affect how your case is handled, and therefore, what it will cost you.

The largest expense in a custody case is usually the *attorney's fees*. This is what is charged for the work lawyers do on your case. Lawyers charge by the hour, typically at a rate of $150 to $300 an hour, depending upon their experience. The more experienced a lawyer is, the more likely he or she has handled a situation like yours before and can accomplish results in less time than the inexperienced lawyer. In contested cases, total attorney's fees are higher. Lawyers sometimes hire paralegals or legal assistants to help them. The time for paralegal and legal assistant work is billed at a lower rate than the lawyer, around $75 to $100 an hour.

You can expect your lawyer to do certain work for the money you pay, such as marshal the facts in your case, determine your objectives, advise you on the law, and develop a strategy for your case. Your lawyer will file pleadings with the court for you, interview witnesses, obtain information from the other side, and review and organize documents. Finally, your lawyer will negotiate and draft a settlement agreement, appear in court on your behalf, examine witnesses at trial, present documents in evidence, and argue to the judge why he or she should rule in your favor.

There are different types of expenses besides legal fees in custody cases. Court costs are the fees that are charged by the court for the filing of the papers in your case. There are other costs for things such as depositions, private investigators, expert witness fees, and psychological evaluations. These expenses can run into thousands of dollars. You must pay these costs, as lawyers are ethically prohibited from lending clients money.

Sometimes a father ends up paying not only his own legal fees, but also some portion of the mother's legal fees, as well as any children's legal fees, even when he is not at fault. This is for the purpose of permitting the economically dependent party to maintain their part of the lawsuit. If a mother has no money and the father controls all of the family finances, the judge will probably order the father to pay a portion of the mother's attorney's fees, based on need and ability to pay. The way to defend against this is to show the judge, if it is true, that the mother has access to assets or the ability to earn enough money to pay her own attorney's fees.

How to Increase Your Legal Fees

Contested custody cases are the most complex and costly of trials. The cost is comparable to buying a car or a year of college tuition. Legal fees will be measured in the thousands—not hundreds—of dollars. If, for some reason, you wish to increase your legal fees, then just follow these simple steps.

- *Lie to your lawyer.* Do not tell your lawyer about an affair. Keep some funds in a secret bank account that you do not disclose. Let this come out at the hearing as a surprise to your lawyer. Then, ask your lawyer to fix it after an adverse ruling from the judge.
- *Lose your temper.* Do something really reckless in your case out of anger or revenge.
- *Do not listen to your lawyer's advice.* Interrupt your lawyer when he or she speaks. If your lawyer tries to tell you about the law, tell your lawyer what you think the law ought to say.
- *Take unilateral actions.* Do not tell your lawyer or the other side in advance. Send email or letters to the other side without letting your lawyer read them first. Make agreements with the other side without telling your lawyer.
- *Be indecisive.* Wait until the last minute to make decisions or change your mind after you agree to something, then expect your lawyer or the court to rescue you.

Firing Your Lawyer

Firing your lawyer is pretty simple. You have the absolute right to fire your lawyer at any time, for any reason or no reason at all. You can expect your files and a prompt refund of the balance of your retainer. If you believe, after carefully thinking about the situation, that it is in your best interest to fire your attorney, send a dismissal letter in writing (by mail, hand delivery, fax, or email) as follows.

```
                                          June 1, 2007
    John Q. Attorney
    123 Somestreet Avenue
    Anytown, MD 55555


    Dear Mr. Attorney:
    I no longer require your services.


                                    Sincerely yours,
                                       Joe Client
```

Even though it is simple, the court will require this notice in writing. Keep a copy for your records. If litigation has already been filed, you will need to notify the court clerk, in writing, either that you intend to represent yourself or that you have new counsel. Even though you have fired a lawyer, he or she is still counsel of record for you in the litigation until the court approves the withdrawal or another attorney files an appearance with the court. Until then, all pleadings and letters will go to the lawyer you have fired.

NOTE: *There may be additional legal fees involved if you fire one lawyer and hire another, because the new attorney will have to review a lot of documents to get up to speed on the case. Most attorneys will reduce their charges for getting up to speed in a case like this, but only if you ask.*

JUDGES

A judge will hear your case and decide your divorce. The judge will control the courtroom procedure and make rulings on matters that are presented in *motions* or other pleadings. Judges are lawyers who have been appointed or elected to office. They are paid to make decisions when parties cannot agree. If you do not like the decision, there are appellate courts to review the judge's decision.

People think that judges are wise and knowledgeable, and that they always make the right decision. In reality, judges are human and they do not always get it right. That is why they have *appellate courts* looking over their shoulders. Remember, even though you may be telling the truth and the other side may not, there is no lie detector at the judge's bench.

There are more cases than there are judges. Your case is not the judge's only case. The judge has heard thousands of cases. Behavior by the other side that seems shocking to you may not seem so shocking to the judge, who has probably heard the same or worse before.

The judge is working on someone else's case right now, and he or she is not thinking about your case. To get the judge to pay attention to your case, you will have to file pleadings with court. Then you will have to compete with hundreds of other litigants to get in front of the judge for a hearing. While you may have lived with your case for years, you will only have a few hours to present your case to the judge, who may make a decision in five minutes.

OTHER PARTICIPANTS IN YOUR CASE

In your adventure with the legal system, you will meet a host of participants with different names. Some will be protagonists and some will be antagonists. Some can decide your future and your children's future. It is important for you to know the role each participant will play in your dealings with the legal system.

Parties

You and the mother of your children are the *parties* to the divorce, custody case, paternity suit, or other legal proceeding involving children. In the litigation, the person who files first is called the *plaintiff* (or sometimes the *petitioner*) and the other party is then the *defendant* (or *respondent*).

In certain types of matters, you might be referred to as *Husband* and *Wife*, or as with a parenting plan, *Mother* and *Father*. The plaintiff makes a claim and moves the case forward. The defendant opposes the claim and contends it. If the defendant files a *counterclaim* against the plaintiff, then the parties are more or less in equal positions.

NOTE: There is usually no advantage to being the first to file. The person who files first has to pay a filing fee to the court. In some cases, you will have to be the first to file in order to have the court enforce your rights, such as when the mother is denying you access to your children.

Children

The court makes its decisions regarding children based on what the judge believes will be in the children's *best interests*. Lawyers may be appointed to represent the children. Evaluators or assessors may be appointed to investigate and make recommendations to the court.

Masters, Magistrates, or Commissioners

Masters, magistrates, and commissioners are not quite judges, but they are appointed as special assistants to the court. They hear uncontested divorces and some contested divorces, and they make recommendations to the judge. The recommendations are usually adopted by the judge, unless one of the parties files an objection through a motion or some other form of appeal.

Courthouse Staff

The court hires *clerks* to take care of all paperwork. There are different clerks for different tasks at the court house. The first clerk you see will be the one that processes your *Complaint*, starts a court file, and assigns your case a number. There is also a *file clerk* who keeps track of all the files. The judge may also have a *courtroom clerk* at the hearing, a *law clerk* to help research the law, and a *secretary*. Clerks are not permitted to give you legal advice, but if you recognize they are overworked and underappreciated, they can be helpful in answering your questions or moving your case along. Conversely, if you pester or annoy them, they can move your file to the bottom of the stack.

Custody Evaluators and Assessors

Courts may hire social workers to make investigations, reports, and recommendations on issues of custody. The *evaluator* will interview you, your spouse, the children, and sometimes third parties, such as teachers and neighbors. The *assessor* usually only interviews the children and the parties involved in the case. The court places great weight on the recommendations of the evaluator or assessor when determining custody. If the evaluation is not in your favor, you may hire your own evaluator to give a different opinion to the court.

Children's Attorney (Guardian Ad Litem)

The court may appoint a lawyer, also known as a *guardian ad litem*, for the children if custody is in dispute. This lawyer can consult with the evaluator or assessor, and may also recommend which parent should have custody. Sometimes the court must appoint an attorney who can waive the child/therapist privilege. You will probably have to pay for a portion of this lawyer's fees. Usually, payment is required in advance.

In the beginning of the case, the guardian ad litem usually acts like another investigator for the court. After the trial, the guardian ad litem may stay on as a third-party decision maker for minor disputes between the parties.

NOTE: *The American Bar Association has issued guidelines for children's attorneys and recommends abolishing the term* **guardian ad litem** *because its use is confusing.*

Mediator/Alternative Dispute Resolution Facilitator

The court may order you to participate in *alternative dispute resolution* (ADR), which means settlement discussions with a neutral third party who acts as a mediator or facilitator to help you reach an agreement out of court. Usually, the court will not order ADR in domestic violence cases.

Process Server

Your *Complaint* can be served by mail. However, if your spouse does not sign or accept the mail, you must have it hand-delivered by someone other than yourself. You can hire a private *process server* or the local sheriff to perform this service.

Private Investigator

You can hire a *private investigator* to follow your spouse and try to prove misconduct. However, most times this is easier to prove through discovery. It is usually money better spent to hire a private investigator for finding witnesses, assets, and income instead of misconduct.

Witnesses

You need to prove facts in court. You can do this through the testimony of *witnesses*. You will probably want to *depose*—that is, examine under oath—some witnesses before trial. You can require witnesses to appear at a deposition or trial with a *subpoena*.

Expert Witness

An *expert witness* can give the court an expert opinion (unlike regular witnesses, who can generally only report facts). A therapist, for example, can be qualified to testify about custody and visitation.

–5–

CUSTODY

The care and control of a child is called *custody*. There are two parts to custody: *legal custody* and *physical custody*. (These will be discussed later in this chapter.) When you father a child, you start out with *joint custody*, meaning both parents make decisions together about the child. *Sole custody* means only one of the parents makes decisions. All fathers, separated or not, have joint custody of their minor children until and unless the court orders otherwise. However, the court can determine custody and issue a custody order in a divorce or other proceeding involving the children.

Mothers end up with custody in about 90% of all cases involving children. However, more than 90% of all cases settle by agreement before trial. That means most fathers are agreeing to let the mothers have custody. It may be because they are concerned about their careers, they are the support for the family, or they do not wish to have the responsibility for child rearing. It may be because they take the path of least resistance, give up, or think they cannot win. When fathers fight for custody, however, they actually win sole or joint custody in about 50% of divorces.

Before you get involved in a custody fight, however, be sure that the children would be significantly better off with you than the other parent. Disagreement over custody is almost guaranteed to put you right in the middle of a bitterly contested and expensive lawsuit. Custody cases are the cruelest and most destructive of litigations. They are expensive in both emotional cost and legal cost.

A custody case will automatically double your legal fees. The damage caused by winning a custody case is great, and the damage caused by losing is terrifying.

If mom has been the caretaker and you have been the provider, ask yourself if you really want to change those roles after you separate. While you will no longer be living together, you will still be in a long-term partnership in raising your children together. Frequently, the best partnerships are those in which the partners complement, rather than duplicate, the other's skills.

Moms sometimes complain that dads have all the fun time with the children while they do the real work of parenting, like changing the diapers, carpooling, helping with homework, bandaging the scratches, and kissing away the tears. Before you get in a fight over custody, ask yourself these questions. Are you ready for the hard part of parenting? Are you prepared to provide for child care while you are working? Does it make more sense for you to concentrate on your job and career, enjoy the play time with your children, and let their mother be the caretaker?

CUSTODY LAW

The legal standard in deciding who will get custody is what is in the *best interests of the children*. Certain doctrines, presumptions, and considerations govern the custody decision, but in the end it comes down to the judge's best guess. As stated long ago by one court:

> *The fact finder [judge] is called upon to evaluate the child's life chances in each of the homes competing for custody and then to predict with whom the child will be better off in the future. At the bottom line, what is in the child's best interests equals the fact finder's best guess.*

(*Montgomery County Dept. of Social Services v. Sanders*, 38 Md. App. 406 (1978).)

As a practical matter, every judge sees each situation differently. If the judge's father abandoned his family and the judge's mother slaved day and night to help her child through law school, then the judge will have a hard time understanding why a father should have custody.

Historically, children were considered by the law to be the property of their parents. Originally in the United States, fathers had the right to control their children; however, that changed during the Industrial Revolution. As men went to the factories, women were left in the home to care for the children. The courts responded with the tender-years doctrine.

Custody of children, particularly those under the age of eight, was usually awarded to mothers based on the *tender-years doctrine*. The theory was that mothers had a special bond with young children and only mothers knew intuitively how to care for young children. The primary considerations of the tender-years doctrine were the age and sex of the children. The only way to for a father to win custody under the tender-years doctrine was to prove that the mother was an *unfit* parent. *Unfit* meant that she was unable to care for the children properly, or abused or neglected them.

Ideals have changed again since then. More women are in the workforce. More homes have two working parents. More men are participating as primary caregivers or co-caregivers for the children. Research has shown that fathers make just as good parents for young children as mothers. The courts have acknowledged this and the tender-years doctrine has been eliminated in custody cases. Today, in theory, there are no courts where the mother has an automatic edge, because the law is supposed to be applied evenly without regard to gender. However, old beliefs change slowly.

The standard today for determining custody is best interests of the child. Mothers are no longer automatically awarded custody of young children. Under this standard, the age and sex of the children are factors to be considered by the court, but there are several other factors considered as well. There are also certain doctrines and presumptions (but not inflexible rules or requirements) that aid the courts in determining the best interests of the child. The factors the court will consider in determining custody are similar, but with slightly different nuances, in every state. (Appendix A tells you where to find the factors regarding legal custody in your state.)

In general, the court will look at the following factors in deciding who gets custody of the children.

- *Parental rights.* Parents must be shown to be unfit before the children will be given to someone else, such as grandparents. When a third party, such as a grandparent or stepparent, is trying to obtain custody, parents almost always win. Parents are always presumed to be the best caretakers for their own children. The presumption can be overcome by showing that the parent is unfit.

- *Continuity.* Children need stability and routine. If children are doing well where they are, the court will be reluctant to move them because of the risk of upsetting the *status quo.*

- *Children's preference.* A judge will consider who the children want to live with. The judge may talk to the children in private. The judge is not bound by what the children want. However, the older the children, the more weight the judge will give their preference.

- *Other factors.* The court can consider the custodian's age, health, wealth, religious beliefs, conduct, type of home, and psychological evaluations; the location of the residences of the children's siblings; the children's school performance; or, anything else the court considers important.

Some states have enacted *presumptions* in favor of joint custody. A presumption in favor of joint custody means that the court must find that joint custody is in the best interest of the child, unless the other party proves it is not. If you want to have the court award joint custody, a presumption shifts the burden of proof from you to the other side. Overcoming a presumption is a high hill to climb. However, the presumption does not apply in cases where there is domestic violence. (Custody presumptions for each state are detailed in Appendix A.) States that do not have a presumption look at the various factors discussed to determine the best interests of the child.

LEGAL CUSTODY

Legal custody means the ability to make long-term parenting decisions, such as educational, medical, disciplinary, and religious decisions. You have joint custody of your children under the law, unless a court rules otherwise. The court can continue *joint legal custody* or issue an order awarding *sole legal custody* to the mother or the father.

Joint Legal Custody

Legal custody can be joint, meaning both parents mutually make decisions about the care of their children. No one parent has the final decision-making authority. The parents share the responsibilities of raising their children, including decisions about education, religion, medical treatment, and where the children will live.

The end of your relationship with the mother of your children does not end the family. Just because you are terminating the relationship between two adults does not mean you are terminating the parental relationship. If you and the mother can agree on parenting or find a new way of working together to take care of the children, then joint custody is in the best interests of the children. The children will benefit if the parents can work together.

Parents bring different personalities, skills, and assets to the table. Joint custody can allow them to combine these for the benefit of the children. Joint custody permits real participation in parenting, so that one parent does not get burdened with all of the responsibilities for the children.

Sole Legal Custody

The court can also grant one parent *sole legal custody*, which means that parent makes the long-term parenting decisions, such as where the kids go to school, what religion they practice, what doctors they see, and where they live. That parent can also give consent for a child's marriage or enrollment in the armed services.

If a mother has sole legal custody, she can decide whether the kids go to private or public schools. She can decide if your children need braces, medications, therapy, or cosmetic surgery. If you are the one paying for all or part of these expenses, then you have to open your checkbook to her.

A father who gives a mother sole legal custody loses even the right to sue for his child in court. In *Elk Grove Unified School District v. Newdow*, a father sued a school for his daughter over the use of the phrase "under God" in the Pledge of Allegiance. The U.S. Supreme Court held that he lacked the ability to bring the suit on behalf of his daughter because the mother had sole legal custody.

PHYSICAL CUSTODY

Physical custody means where the children live most of the time. The parent who has physical custody, or care and control of the child on a day-to-day basis, makes the short-term parenting decisions (as contrasted with long-term parenting decisions that are the subject of legal custody). These are the everyday items, like deciding what television the children can watch, setting bedtimes, helping with homework, and bandaging scraped knees.

Physical custody is called by different names in different states. For example, it is sometimes referred to as *residential custody*. Until there is a court order, both parents have shared physical custody in law (*custody de jure*), even though they are separated and the children may be living with one of them in fact (*custody de facto*). The court can order that physical custody be shared, sole, or split.

Shared Physical Custody

Shared physical custody (sometimes called *joint physical custody*) is when the children will be living more or less equally at mom's house and dad's house—spending a substantial amount of time with each parent.

Sole Physical Custody

Sole physical custody is when the children live primarily with one parent. That parent is called the *custodial parent* and the other parent is called the *noncustodial parent*. The noncustodial parent has *visitation* rights. (see Chapter 6.)

Split Physical Custody

Sometimes one parent will take one child and the other parent will take another. Courts and child psychologists, however, are reluctant to split up children, because they want to preserve sibling relationships.

Deciding on Custody

Do not get stuck on the words themselves. A creative lawyer can write a document entitled *Joint Legal Custody Agreement* and then proceed to take joint legal custody away, paragraph by paragraph, until one party or the other has all the decision-making authority. Likewise, an agreement can give primary physical custody to one party and then take it away and give it to the other party with a visitation schedule.

For all practical purposes, a parent with sole physical custody and joint legal custody might as well have sole legal custody. If your wife decides the children need a psychiatrist, medication, or private schooling, then you may either have to pay for it or pay for a lawyer to fight it. Legal custody is very important in the legal world, and many hours and dollars are spent in trying to obtain joint legal custody or sole legal custody. In the real world, however, most decisions are made by the parent with physical custody of the child. For example, in a situation in which you have joint legal custody and your children's mother has sole physical custody (a typical arrangement), if she decides to take the child to a new pediatrician without telling you, are you really going to pay $5,000 to get a lawyer and take her to court?

In fact, a father can *lose* physical custody in court and end up getting more time through visitation than if he had won joint physical custody. You can see how easy it is to get confused about legal custody, physical custody, and visitation. So, instead of taking an inflexible position for *joint legal custody* or for *shared physical custody*, focus on what will happen to you and your children in real life. Look at how parenting decisions will be made. Focus on how much quality time you and your children will actually spend together.

Physical custody also frequently plays a role in the amount of child support you will have to pay. (see Chapter 7.) The judge will not look favorably on you, however, if he or she believes you are using a custody claim to try to obtain a more favorable financial settlement.

If you are trying to obtain approximately equal time with your children, there are several types of shared physical custody arrangements for you to consider, including the following.

- *Week on/Week off.* The children alternate weeks, usually Friday after school.
- *Nesting.* The children stay at the same place, and parents move in and out.
- *Three/Four.* The children are with one parent three days of the week, then with the other parent for four days, and then the schedule alternates.
- *School days/Summer vacations.* The children spend school days with one parent, and weekends, most holidays, and summers with the other parent.

CUSTODY EVALUATIONS

In custody and visitation cases, the court or either party may ask for a *custody evaluation*. The court may rely on this evaluation to determine child custody and visitation. The importance of the custody evaluation cannot be stressed enough. Custody cases may be won or lost on the evaluator's report.

The judge does not leave the bench and go investigate by visiting the homes of each parent and interviewing witnesses. Instead, the parties are expected to present all the evidence in his or her favor to the judge at trial.

However, most courts have an investigative arm for custody cases. That arm is the ability to order a custody evaluation. This is an investigation of each party's parenting skills. An evaluator, usually a social worker or other mental health professional, will conduct a comprehensive review of each parent's psychological makeup, parenting skills, and other factors. Based on this, the evaluator makes a report to the court on the best custody arrangements (which may include legal custody, physical custody, and visitation). Because the evaluator is hired by the court and not the parties, his or her report is very influential with the judge.

To prepare for the evaluation, make sure your home is clean, neat, and safe for children. Do not try to influence the children. Tell them to tell the truth to the evaluator. (Now is a good time to give up smoking, as secondhand smoke is harmful to children and it could count against you on the evaluation.) Do not have the television on when the evaluator is there.

When you are interviewed by the evaluator, be careful to focus on the children and what is best for them. This is not the time to point out the flaws in their mother. Instead, point out your own strengths as a parent.

The evaluator will come to your house to interview you. He or she will be observing your house and living arrangements to develop a written report to give the court about them. The evaluator will summarize all of the interviews and make a recommendation to the court about custody and visitation.

You may not see the report until a few days before trial, and the evaluator will not tell you the result if you call. That makes it difficult to correct any inaccuracies or to oppose the report. You will have a chance to call the evaluator to the witness stand and examine him or her at the trial. It is usually better to question the evaluator about your positive points than about the mother's negative points. You may also have your own private custody evaluator testify. The final decision is up to the court. It is possible, but very difficult, to convince the court to order something different than what the evaluator recommends.

The guardian ad litem may also make a recommendation to the court with respect to custody and visitation. The *guardian ad litem* is the children's attorney, whose job is to represent the children and further their best interests. The evaluator and the guardian ad litem are usually in contact with one another during the evaluation, and their recommendations are frequently the same.

It may be that you do not need a full custody evaluation in your case. In a custody evaluation, the evaluator interviews the parties, the children, and collaterals. *Collaterals* may include teachers, coaches, doctors, relatives, home workers, neighbors, and others. In a *custody assessment*, the assessor only interviews one or both parties and the children. A custody evaluator determines which parent is the best one to have custody of the children. A custody assessor recommends whether a parent is fit to have custody at all.

You want to have as many protagonists as possible in court. Therefore, you want to make the evaluator your ally, not your enemy. The same goes for the assessor, the guardian ad litem, the children's therapist, and the judge. More than one father has made the mistake of treating these people with hostility and anger. Instead of seeing them as obstacles to visitation and custody, try seeing them as doors to which you must find the key. This is where you might find the advice of your own private consultant helpful in custody evaluations.

–6–

VISITATION

Visitation is the time the children spend with each parent when physical custody is shared, or the time they spend with the noncustodial parent when one parent has physical custody. The word *visitation* may raise negative connotations. After all, why should you have to visit with your own child? Because of this, it is sometimes called *access* or *time-sharing*.

When you think about it, visitation is really a form of custody. The child is in your care and custody during visitation. When you lose custody at trial, you get visitation. However, it may be possible to negotiate even more time with the child if you call it visitation than you might get if you call it *shared physical custody*.

There is a correlation between visitation and child support. When the children are with you, you are paying directly for their expenses. When they are with their mother, you are paying indirectly, through her. So, the more time they spend with her, the higher your child support payments will be. Withholding visitation from the children or the noncustodial parent to coerce the payment of child support is illegal, and it never works. They are two separate issues. The court can find a parent in contempt for withholding visitation and even change custody to the other parent.

You can petition the court to establish *court-ordered visitation* for you. The law favors visitation and frequent contact with both parents, as long as there is no evidence of any danger or harm to a child. Therefore, the courts encourage visitation except in very extraordinary circumstances.

You may have to prove you are the father of the child before you can obtain visitation. The easiest way to do this is to sign an *affidavit of paternity*. If there is no dispute that you are the father, then you and the mother can agree on a visitation arrangement. When you cannot agree, you will have to ask the court for a visitation order. You will need to present a proposed visitation schedule to the court.

You have a fundamental right to parent your child in the way that you feel is best when the child is with you during visitation, as long as you act responsibly. This means you can go where you want to, do what you want to, and associate with anyone you want to, free from interference from the other parent. You can take the child to the church, synagogue, or mosque of your choice. However, you and your child's mother can agree to limit these rights by contract.

RON'S CASE

Ron and Cory agreed, in writing, that they would raise their son, Mitch, in the Southern Baptist religion. Further, they agreed that Ron would take Mitch to Sunday school and church every other weekend during his visitation. Ron missed a few Sundays and Cory took him to court on a motion for contempt to enforce the agreement.

Ron's attorney argued that Ron had an unfettered right, found in the U.S. Constitution, to the pursuit of happiness. The U.S. Supreme Court had ruled that the right of parents to raise their children as they see fit was implied in the right to the pursuit of happiness. In addition, the attorney argued, Ron was guaranteed freedom of religion by the U.S. Constitution, which included the right to choose his own religion or no religion at all. The judge found that this was not a constitutional case, but a contract case. He ruled that Ron had limited his constitutional rights when he signed the agreement.

VISITATION SCHEDULES

If you are able to handle visitation without dispute, sometimes an agreement will just say that the father has *reasonable* or *liberal* visitation, and you will not have a specific schedule. However, many parents feel more comfortable with a detailed visitation schedule. That way, they can avoid any disputes about visitation in the future.

A visitation schedule will cover weekly routines, summers, and holidays. If you are in negotiations with the mother of your children over visitation, you will want to prepare a proposed schedule. Attach or incorporate the final schedule in your settlement agreement. If you cannot settle and have to go to court over visitation, attach your proposed schedule to your Complaint.

Weekly Visitation

In preparing a visitation schedule, start with the regular weekly schedule. Even if it is one of the arrangements described in Chapter 6 on physical custody, like week on/week off, the basic schedule should be set forth in detail. Be sure to put down drop-off and pickup times and places to avoid confusion and dispute later. If travel expenses are involved, like airplane tickets, you will have to agree on who pays what expenses. Here are some examples of weekly visitation schedules.

Alternating Weekends
The Father will have time-sharing with the children every other weekend from Friday evening at 5:00 p.m. through Sunday evening at 7:00 p.m., and Wednesday evening of each week for dinner from 4:00 p.m. to 8:00 p.m.

Week On/Week Off

Each party will have time-sharing with minor children on alternating weeks from 6:00 p.m. Sunday until 6:00 p.m. the following Sunday. The noncustodial party, according to the foregoing schedule, will also have time-sharing with the minor children on Wednesday from after work or school until 7:30 p.m.

Another Equal Time Arrangement

The Father will have time-sharing with the children every other weekend beginning Friday after school and ending Monday when school resumes. The Mother will have time-sharing with the children every other weekend beginning Friday after school and ending Monday when school resumes. The children will be in the Mother's care overnight on Wednesday and Thursday. The children will be in the Father's care overnight on Monday and Tuesday.

School Year/Summer Break Arrangement

During the school year, the children will reside primarily with the Mother, and the Father will have time-sharing with the children (a) every other weekend from Friday morning through Monday evening and (b) Wednesday evening of each week.

During summer break, the children will reside primarily with the Father, and the Mother will have time-sharing with the children (a) every other weekend from Friday evening through Monday morning and (b) Wednesday evening of each week. In lieu of using a third-party day care provider during the summer, the Father will leave the children with the Mother for day care, if her schedule permits. Notwithstanding the summer schedule, each party will be permitted to spend at least two uninterrupted weeks

of vacation time with the children each summer. The par-
ties will coordinate their vacation schedules with each
other. The parties will discuss parenting issues and day
care schedules each Monday night by telephone from
7:00 p.m. to 7:15 p.m.

Summer Visitation

The summer school vacation is about ten weeks. You can divide that in any way that makes sense based on your work and vacation schedule. The following is an example of a summer schedule.

Summers

The Father shall have time with the children for up to four
weeks during the summer months. During this four-week
period, the Mother may have access to the children from
time to time as agreed between the parties. In addition, by
mutual agreement, either party may also take a vacation
with one or more of the children. This particular summer
time-sharing schedule shall supersede the regular time-
sharing schedule and holiday schedule set forth in this
agreement. The exact summer time-sharing schedule shall
be established by the parties before March 1ˢᵗ of each year
to avoid conflicts with summer camps. If the parties are not
able to agree on the summer time-sharing schedule in any
given year, then the Father shall have first choice in even-
numbered years, and the Mother shall have first choice in
odd-numbered years.

Holidays and Other Events

Most people prefer to alternate holidays and other events. An example provision follows.

Alternating Holidays

In even-numbered years, the Mother has the children for Memorial Day, Labor Day, Halloween, Christmas Eve, and Christmas Day until noon for the Winter School Break. The Father has the children for President's Day, Easter, Spring Break, Fourth of July, Thanksgiving, and Christmas Day from noon through New Year's Day for the Winter Break. The schedule is reversed in odd-numbered years.

Birthdays and Other Events

The children are also with the Mother on her birthday and with the Father on his birthday. The children alternate spending their birthdays with each parent. The children are with the Mother on Mother's Day and the Father on Father's Day. The holiday schedule overrides the normal weekly schedule, which resumes after the holiday.

Making it Work for You

Each case and each child is unique. You are trying to arrange visitation to maximize the time spent with each parent, while at the same time minimizing the transfers for the child from one residence to another. This calls for some creative thinking, as Tony's case shows.

TONY'S CASE

Tony wanted 50% of the time with his 5-year-old son, Chris. Beth, Chris's mother, wanted Chris to be with her during the school year. During mediation, Tony and Beth compromised with the following creative visitation schedule:

Weekly Schedule
The Father will have liberal time-sharing every fourth week of the month from 8:00 p.m. Friday until 2:00 p.m. the second Sunday following.

Weekend Schedule
In addition, the Father will have liberal time-sharing for the weekend that is between the week-long visitations from 8:00 p.m. Friday until 2:00 p.m. on Sunday.

DIFFERENT TYPES OF VISITATION

Usually, visitation includes overnights. It is unsupervised and voluntary. Once established, it usually remains unchanged during the child's minority (until the child is a legal adult). However, that is not always the case. There are different types of visitation that may be appropriate in certain cases.

Visitation usually includes *overnights*, but there are some situations in which it may not. The judge might not approve of overnights or the parties might agree to no overnights in cases when a very young child is still breastfeeding, the father does not have appropriate living facilities, the father has spent little or no time with the child, or the father is just not interested in having overnights.

Supervised visitation, whether by agreement or by court order, means a third party is present during visitation. The court can order supervised visitation when the judge believes that the visiting parent may cause some harm to the child. Visitation may be supervised by the other parent, a social worker, or another third party, such as a friend or a relative.

If you are required to have supervised visitation, your objective will be to restore unsupervised visitation as soon as possible. It is not an easy task. You will have to convince the judge that you pose no threat to the child. It takes time and money. Your best bet is to hire a mental health professional with experience in this area to advise you. Together, you can devise a long-term plan to restore unsupervised visitation. It may require therapy for you and the child. When you are in a position to have the decision reconsidered, you will file a motion with the court. Your adviser will serve as an expert witness at the hearing.

Graduated visitation means that visitation increases over time. This might be a good arrangement if you need to establish a relationship with a child after a gap in visitation, or for very young children. The following is an example of a graduated visitation schedule.

> *For the first three months, the child will spend from 12:00 noon on Sunday until 4:00 p.m. on Sunday with the Father, every other week.*

> *For the next three months, the child will spend from 8:00 a.m. on Sunday until 4:00 p.m. on Sunday with the Father, every other week.*

> *For the next six months, the child will spend from 5:00 p.m. on Saturday until 4:00 p.m. on Sunday with the Father, every other week.*

> *Thereafter, the child will spend from 5:00 p.m. on Friday until 4:00 p.m. on Sunday with the Father, every other week.*

Age and needs appropriate visitation makes a lot of sense. Visitation might vary according to the age and developmental needs of the children. Infants need feeding, bathing, and changing by a parent on a regular schedule. Toddlers need routines and consistency. School-age children have school schedules and activities. Preteens still have school and more extracurricular activities. Teenagers have school, peers, and employment schedules.

Sometimes the parents will decide that the children will stay in the home and the parents will move in and out. This is called a *nesting* arrangement. An example of a nesting arrangement follows.

Both parties acknowledge that it is in the children's best interests and future welfare that the parties have shared physical custody. The parties have decided and agreed that the Father and the children will reside in the former family residence, and each party will have liberal time-sharing with the children. The Mother will have full and daily access to the former family home to feed the children, help them with their homework, put them to bed, and perform other related parental acts. The parties may agree between themselves from time to time that the Father will vacate the former family residence so that the Mother may have overnight time-sharing with the children in the former family residence.

If you can agree on visitation, the courts will usually approve your schedule. There is a widely held belief that every other weekend is the *usual visitation schedule*. In truth, there is no typical schedule or default schedule in the law. There are many other schedules that work just as well, and courts order different schedules every day. If you present an equal schedule to the court that has the children staying with you one week and mom the next week, that is a perfectly acceptable schedule. There is no single best plan or typical plan that suits every family. A good visitation arrangement takes into consideration work, school, social, and family schedules.

VISITATION DISPUTES

If you cannot agree on a schedule, you have a visitation dispute. Visitation disputes can arise from various circumstances. The following describes some of the more common disputes and what to do about them.

Sometimes, when parents fight about visitation, they are very upset about something else that they do not believe they can fight about. It may be because they feel angry at the other spouse for leaving or it may be that they feel they gave up too much in the divorce agreement. For whatever reason, they are involved in an argument about the children. It is frequently the mother wanting to restrict the father's visitation. Usually, the problem is that the mother does not want the father to visit. In some cases, the problem is that the mother wants the father to visit and he will not do it because she is trying to force him to visit with the children. First, try to talk these problems over between yourselves. If you cannot resolve them, next try a counselor, parenting coordinator, or mediator before you take your dispute to court.

When the children say they do not want to visit with you, you are between a rock and a hard place. If you drag them kicking and screaming from the car, you are forcing them to visit, and they may dig in their heels even more. That does not help your relationship with the child and it could lead to allegations of abuse. On the other hand, if you let the children run visitation, they will become negatively empowered to resist visitation. Children do not determine visitation—adults do. If you do not enforce visitation, you are losing valuable time with your children.

You should try not to overreact. Focus on what is causing the children to have this reaction and not your dispute with their mother. Remember what it was like to be a child. Dads are big and loud and scary. There must be a reason for the breakdown in your relationship with your children (besides or in addition to any influence from the mother). You will have to give it time and try to restore your relationship. Counseling might be required to identify and solve the problem.

The traditional approach of winning at all costs and fighting until the other side loses or gives up is often destructive in visitation disputes. Unfortunately, many dads get stuck in this mode. In cases with children involved, a victory that destroys family relationships is no victory at all. A different approach is called for. Sometimes you have to give up visitation for awhile to get more visitation. Think about judo, in which you first give in to your opponent's strength, and then turn that strength back against your opponent. Rather than attack, you must attract.

When there has been some serious rift or breakdown between a father and a child, the court favors *reunification*. Reunification means to restore and reestablish a normal parent/child relationship. This is usually accomplished through therapy, which can either be court-ordered or agreed to between the parents.

Other visitation disputes center around the school week. In order to defeat a father's claim for equal time, mothers sometimes argue to the court that they are more disciplined than the father in making sure the children do their homework each night, and take the right books and supplies to school. Another similar argument is that the children need the routine of staying in the same house, especially if the mother is in the family residence, during the school week. Transitions involve clothes, homework, and school books, and are too disruptive.

Your reply to this argument should be that you are quite capable, and a competent human being and parent. You are both organized and disciplined. You are able to organize homework, books, clothes, and supplies for children going to school. The courts appreciate a father who wants to participate in parenting on an equal basis. In a lot of cases, the court cannot even find the father, or the father just wants the good times, like weekends, to play with the children. Mom gets to do all the hard work as the caretaker parent. A father who wants to do the hard work of parenting will be given the opportunity by the courts.

Third Parties

Sooner or later, you and your children's mother will begin to form new relationships. This raises the question of how and when third parties will be introduced to the children. Can your new girlfriend stay overnight when you have visitation? Can the new boyfriend of the children's mother stay overnight when the children are with her? While visitation is generally controlled by the parent having visitation, you can agree to certain restrictions, such as those involving third parties. A provision for an agreement that a third party will not stay overnight when the children are present follows.

> *The parties agree that neither will have overnights with members of the opposite sex, unless that party is remarried, when the children are present.*

The following is a different provision for the gradual introduction of third parties.

> *Although the Father and the Mother both understand that neither may dictate to the other the way in which the other conducts his or her life, the Father and the Mother recognize that each of them will enjoy a social and dating life. It is important to both parents that the children are comfortable with the concept before another adult is introduced into their lives. Accordingly, the parties shall only introduce members of the opposite sex (not related by blood or marriage) to the children on a gradual basis.*

Interfering with Visitation

If the children's mother wrongfully withholds visitation from you, in violation of a child custody order, you can file a petition to hold her in contempt of court. There may also be criminal penalties for abducting the children. There is a narrow exception if it was necessary for the abducting parent to keep the child in order to avoid danger to the child from the other parent. The abducting parent must prove this danger to the court. It may take several petitions and trips to court before a judge will take action to enforce visitation. As you might imagine, judges are reluctant to put mothers in jail.

A visitation dispute may involve *parental alienation*. This means one parent is sabotaging the children's relationship with the other parent. This can be intentional or not, and it can be overt or covert. Children sense hostility or fear between parents even if nothing is said. Judges do not like a parent who interferes with visitation or actively encourages the children not to visit with the other parent. If a judge finds that one parent is alienating the children from the other parent, the judge may take custody or visitation time away from the alienating parent.

If you are in a dispute over visitation with the children's mother, you may hear the term *reactive attachment disorder*. It means that the child has so bonded with the mother that separation will cause psychological harm to the child (and separation equals visitation with the father). The problem with the theory is that it is sometimes used as code for *mom gets custody*. It can be used as an argument to deny visitation to the father. The argument on the other side is that some visitation with the dad would cause the children to bond with him, too, and that would be beneficial to them also.

Court Order

The end result of litigation over visitation disputes is an order issued by the judge. It will probably not be as detailed as what you could do by agreement. A court-ordered visitation schedule looks similar to the sample on the following page. Review it so that you know what to expect and what you are trying to obtain.

IN THE CIRCUIT COURT FOR GREEN   COUNTY, MONTANA

Jane Doe	)
Plaintiff	)
vs.	) Case No. 1234
John Doe	)
Defendant	)

<u>ORDER</u>

This cause having come on for a custody hearing before the Court on __JUNE 16__ , 2007, both parties present and represented by counsel, and testimony heard and considered, it is this 23rd day of _JUNE_ , 2007, by the Circuit Court for GREEN   County, __MONTANA__ ,

ORDERED, that the parties be, and hereby are, awarded joint legal care and custody of their minor children; and it is further

ORDERED, that the parties consult one another regarding long-range decisions involving education, religious training, discipline, medical care, and other matters of major significance concerning the children's lives and welfare; and it is further

ORDERED, that each of the parties be, and hereby are, entitled to receive copies of all reports concerning the minor children, including without limitation, grade cards, school reports, medical, dental, and psychological reports; and it is further

ORDERED, that the parties be, and hereby are, awarded joint physical care and custody of their minor children; and it is further

ORDERED, that the parties be, and hereby are, awarded time-sharing with their minor children on alternating weeks from 7:00 p.m. Sunday until 7:00 p.m. Sunday; and it is further

ORDERED, that the noncustodial party according to the foregoing schedule, shall also have time-sharing with the minor children on Wednesday from after work or school until 8:30 p.m.; and it is further

ORDERED, that parties will alternate time-sharing on federal holidays and the following holidays with the minor children; the holiday schedule will have precedence over the weekly schedule; and after the holiday visitation, the weekly schedule will resume at the point where it was interrupted; and it is further

ORDERED, that in odd-numbered years, the children will spend the first half of Spring Break with the Plaintiff, and the second half of Spring Break with the Defendant; and vice versa in even-numbered years; and it is further

ORDERED, that in odd-numbered years, the children will spend the first half of Christmas Break, from the end of school until noon on Christmas Day, with the Plaintiff, and the second half of Christmas Break, from noon on Christmas Day until 8:00 p.m. the day before school starts, with the Defendant; and vice versa in even-numbered years; and it is further

ORDERED, that the children will spend Mother's Day with the Plaintiff, and Father's Day with the Defendant, specific times to be decided at least seven days before the occasion; and it is further

ORDERED, that the parties each be able to spend time with each child on the child's birthday, specific times to be decided at least seven days before the occasion; and it is further

ORDERED, that the issue of child support be, and hereby is, set for a hearing before a Family Law Division Master on ___JULY 1___ at ___4 P.M.___ .

Fair M. Partial
_____
JUDGE

Seen and Agreed:

John Z. Attorney
_____
Attorney for Plaintiff

Joseph A. Lawyer
_____
Attorney for Defendant

Jane F. Child
_____
guardian ad litem

cc: Counsel of Record

VISITATION RIGHTS CHECKLIST

Visitation disputes are sometimes settled on the courthouse steps right before the trial. Agreements or orders are hastily scribbled on legal pads and read into the record. The transcript then becomes a binding agreement and order of the court. In the rush and pressure of court proceedings, it is easy to overlook something important. For example, the sample might contain no provisions for visitation by telephone. Here is a checklist of visitation rights that you should try to include in any agreement or court order.

- ❑ Regular telephone conversations with the child.
- ❑ Unopened and uncensored mail to the child.
- ❑ Prompt notice of hospitalization, major illness, or death of the child.
- ❑ Access to school records.
- ❑ Access to medical records.
- ❑ No derogatory remarks by either parent in the presence of the child.
- ❑ Notice and participation in extracurricular events.
- ❑ Itinerary and contact numbers if the other parent leaves the state with the child.
- ❑ Access to school for lunch and other activities with the child.

CHANGING VISITATION

Because of your job or other events in your life, you will want to change visitation dates from time to time. For the most part, however, you will want to follow the visitation schedule as much as possible, not cancel at the last minute, and be on time. If you continually miss scheduled visitations, the mother could petition the court to decrease visitation or custody, and increase your child support. The court can change visitation—and even custody—upon the mother's request if you do not show an interest in having visitation.

If you do need to change the overall visitation schedule, you can petition the court for a modification. Whenever you agree to change the terms of a court order regarding visitation, that change needs to be commemorated with another court order.

If you need to change visitation, you can petition the court for a change. If you show a *change of circumstances*, then the court may modify the current visitation order to accommodate the new set of circumstances.

Relocation

Sometimes one parent or the other will want to move with the children to a distant location. A move might be for the purpose of accepting better employment, or it might be to live closer to friends and relatives. The mother of your children has the right to live anywhere she chooses, but unless she has sole custody, she cannot automatically take the children with her. The court can decide whether or not it is in the best interests of the children to relocate.

Relocation is a change of circumstances. That means either party can petition the court for a change in custody or visitation arrangements. Some states have a tendency to permit the children to relocate, some tend to prevent it, and others look at it on a case-by-case basis.

If the children's mother is threatening to move, you can file a petition to stop the move. If she has already moved, you can ask the court to order her to bring the children back. The court will usually set a hearing. Be prepared to show the court that the children have strong attachments to their home, friends in the neighborhood, school, doctors, teachers, and coaches. You can also compare educational, social, economic, and cultural opportunities in your location and the new location to persuade the judge that it is in the best interest of the children to stay in their original location.

It is always better for the parents to agree, preferably in advance, on relocation provisions. If not, you will have to litigate custody in court. In an agreement, you will need to cover when each of you will spend time with the children, the methods of travel between homes, costs, communications, and holiday plans. The following is an example of a provision that permits relocation and sets up visitation arrangements in advance.

> *The parties have the right to move to any location in the United States. The moving party shall provide the other party with at least ninety (90) days' written notice.*
>
> *In the event that one or both parties move, the parties will still share legal custody, and the Father shall still have primary physical custody. The time-sharing shall be the same as what is set forth above, if the parties reside within one hundred (100) miles of each other.*
>
> *If the parties reside more than one hundred (100) miles from each other, time-sharing shall be changed to the following: The Mother shall have time-sharing for up to eight (8) weeks summer vacation, to be determined by the parties by May 1 of each year. The Mother shall also have visitation for either (a) the Christmas break or (b) the Easter and Thanksgiving breaks, to be decided by the parties each year. If considered appropriate, the parties shall negotiate as to whether the children will be permitted to be kept out of school for one additional day at the end of a holiday, to permit additional time-sharing on the part of the Mother.*
>
> *The parties shall share equally in the cost of transporting the children back and forth for visitation.*

This is an alternate provision that prevents relocation unless both parents consent or, if they cannot agree, then the court makes the decision.

> *A party planning to relocate away from the metropolitan area shall give not less than one hundred twenty (120) days' written notice of such plans to the other party, setting forth the date of the intended move, the destination, and the reasons for making the move. In no event shall a child of the parties be removed from the metropolitan area until*

the parties have reached a revised agreement relative to custody and visitation, or failing such agreement, until a final determination of custody and visitation has been made by a court of competent jurisdiction.

If you have custody and the children's mother files to prevent your move, then you will have to marshal the evidence you need to show that the move is in the best interest of the children. You will need to prove to the court there is a good reason for the move, such as a better job, and not just to prevent visitation. Also, be prepared to show that the schools, doctors, and cultural opportunities are better where you plan to move.

It is possible for you to remain in frequent contact with the child even though you are separated by a great distance. You can use regular mail service to send letters, cards, pictures, and gifts. You can have conversations by phone and send text messages, video, and pictures. The Internet allows you to exchange emails, chat, build a Web page, play games, and Web-conference.

THIRD-PARTY VISITATION

Grandparents and stepparents can also petition the court for visitation. Many courts will grant reasonable visitation with related third parties if it is in the best interest of the children. However, if the parents have a different visitation schedule, the United States Supreme Court has ruled there is a presumption that the parents' schedule is in the best interest of the child. This presumption can be overcome in certain circumstances, such as when a parent is refusing any visitation with the grandparents at all.

Grandparents can offer special relationships, opportunities, and extended roots to children that should not be overlooked. One study indicated that many gifted children have had a third-party caretaker in their lives who helped them with their homework, self-esteem, and emotional well-being.

−7−

CHILD SUPPORT

Whether you are a father by biology or by law, you are required to provide financial support for your children. This chapter explains the basics, history, and theory of child support, as well as how to calculate child support.

Both parents are required to support their children. The law presumes that the parent who has the child living with him or her most of the time—the *custodial parent*—pays child support by paying for food, shelter, clothing, medical care, education, day care, summer camp, and other expenses of the child. The other parent, called the *noncustodial parent*, pays a monthly child support amount to the custodial parent.

A parent, or any third party with custody of a child, is entitled to ask the court for a child support order. Usually, the court orders the noncustodial parent to pay the custodial parent a specific sum. It can be paid monthly, twice a month, every week, or every two weeks, depending on how the payor gets paid. The court can issue an earnings withholding order to have your employer deduct child support from your paycheck. The court also has the power to order the noncustodial parent to pay the mortgage, utilities, and so forth, instead of a monthly amount. However, child support is usually a set amount each month.

The time that the children spend with each parent during the year is taken into account in calculating monthly child support.

The child support stays the same even when the children are visiting during summer vacation or otherwise spending time with
the noncustodial parent.

Fathers who pay child support sometimes complain that the
children's mother is not using the child support for the benefit of
the children. However, as long as the children are being fed, clothed,
and sheltered, the court is not likely to require the custodial parent
to account for how child support is spent.

CHILD SUPPORT MODELS

To establish child support obligations and enforce child support,
Congress established the *Office of Child Support Enforcement* in
1975. It is a government agency within the Department of Health
and Human Services. In 1988, Congress made child support guidelines mandatory and required the states to adopt child support
guidelines. In response, the states have adopted different methods
for calculating child support. There are three different models for
determining child support.

A majority of states use the *income shares model*, which is a
formula based on the relative and combined income of the parties,
the number of children, and the time each parent spends with the
children. Child support is calculated based on an estimate of how
much of each parent's income was used to support the child when
the parents were living together. The idea behind the model is that
the children should not be harmed financially by the breakup of
their parents. Income may be based on *gross income*, *adjusted gross
income*, or *net income*, depending upon the state. The income shares
model has been adopted by the following states.

- Alabama
- Arizona
- Colorado
- Connecticut

- Florida
- Idaho
- Georgia
- Indiana
- Kansas
- Kentucky
- Louisiana
- Maine
- Maryland
- Michigan
- Missouri
- Montana
- Nebraska
- New Hampshire
- New Jersey
- New Mexico
- New York
- Ohio
- Oklahoma
- Oregon
- Pennsylvania
- Rhode Island
- South Carolina
- South Dakota
- Tennessee
- Utah
- Vermont
- Virginia
- Washington
- Wyoming

The second most popular model is the *percentage of income model*. It calculates child support based on a *fixed percentage of income* of the noncustodial parent. The percentage of income model has been adopted by the following states.

- Alaska
- Arkansas
- District of Columbia
- Illinois
- Mississippi
- Nevada
- North Carolina
- North Dakota
- Wisconsin

The third model is the *Melson model*. It allots a subsistence level to each parent for basic needs, then a subsistence amount of child support for the children's basic needs. The formula starts at 15% for the first child. If the parent has income beyond these two amounts, the children are awarded a percentage of the excess as a *standard of living* allowance. The Melson model is followed in Delaware, Hawaii, Minnesota, and West Virginia. Minnesota plans to change to the percentage of income model in 2007.

CALCULATING CHILD SUPPORT

Although the child support models use different calculations and variables, a rough rule of thumb is that you probably will not have to pay more than half of your take-home pay in *family support* (combined alimony and child support).

In determining the amount of child support, the court looks at the needs of the children and the financial resources available to the parents to pay child support. The court can also consider the lifestyle of the children during the marriage, any special needs of the children, and any financial resources available to the children. Misconduct is not a factor in determining child support.

Most states have either a chart, table, or formula in their statutes that predicts what the parents would pay for a child if they were still together, based on their respective incomes. These are called *child support guidelines*. They are presumptively correct, so the court must have good reasons to deviate from them. There are also worksheets in most states that take you through the calculations and that you present to the judge.

Disputes can arise over the correct amount of income to use for the calculations. If you are self-employed and set your own salary, the court can look behind that number and determine a different income. The court can also impute income to a party who is voluntarily underemployed or unemployed. If you have lost your job, you want to show the judge that you have made efforts to find new employment. If you are trying to prove the mother is underemployed, you need a *vocational rehabilitation expert* to give an opinion as to what she could be earning.

The procedures for determining child support under the percentage of income model and the Melson model are fairly straightforward and can be done by using the tables provided by your state's laws. The court can usually provide the tables for you. Calculating child support under the income shares model can be a little more tricky.

The procedure for determining child support under the income shares model is as follows.

◆ First, determine each parent's gross income. This includes every source of income, including wages, earnings from self-employment, interest, dividends, rents, gifts, capital gains, and inheritances. If you have what the IRS calls a *pass-through entity*, your gross income is what the business earns, not what you have paid yourself in salary or draw. When a parent is unemployed or underemployed voluntarily, the court can impute income to that parent for purposes of determining child support.

- Next, specific deductions, such as health insurance premiums, child support for previous children, and alimony are then taken from gross income. Your particular deductions depend on your state.
- The two incomes are then added together for a combined income.
- The combined income amount along with the number of children are used to look up the needs of the children as presented in your state's statutory table or chart.
- Each parent's share of the combined income is calculated as a percentage. For example, if the father's income is $60,000 per year and the mother's is $40,000 per year, then their combined income is $100,000, of which the father has 60% and the mother has 40%.
- Each parent's percentage is multiplied by the amount from the chart or table to determine the child support obligation of each parent.
- Various adjustments are made for day care, extraordinary medical expenses, and other special circumstances (described in the next section).
- The custodial parent is presumed to pay child support directly to third parties. The noncustodial parent pays his or her share to the custodial parent as monthly child support.

There are several sites on the Internet that will calculate child support for you. Put in the income of each party, the number of children, and the time spent with each parent, and the program will quickly give you a child support calculation. One of these is www.alllaw.com, which has child support calculators for every state.

Perfect accuracy is not guaranteed, but it is a good starting point for roughly determining what you may have to pay. Also, it is easy to run different scenarios. For example, you can easily see the difference it makes in child support for different alimony amounts. You can try different time-sharing arrangements. You can see if it makes more sense for a parent not to work, or to work and have day care costs.

ADJUSTMENTS

Even though the states use one of the three models previously discussed, the guidelines vary greatly from state to state. Various adjustments can alter the amount of support by several hundred dollars a month. Some of these adjustments include costs for:

- second families and new children;
- shared visitation;
- custody;
- health insurance;
- medical expenses;
- day care;
- education; and,
- other extraordinary expenses for the children.

Remarriage

When parents remarry and have children in their new families, some states do not permit judges to take new children into account for changing child support. Others say this is a change in circumstances that may be taken into account in modifying child support. Similarly, some states permit a judge to take into account children of a previous marriage when setting a child support amount for children of a second marriage, and some do not.

Visitation Schedule

Some states permit the judge to multiply the child support by the percentage of time the child spends with each parent during the year. In those states, one extra night every other week or extra time on holidays and during the summer can make a big difference in child support. Others do not permit the judge to include this as a factor. In cases of split custody, when each parent has one child, the judge can calculate child support for each parent and award the net amount as child support.

Day Care

Some states require child care to be added to the basic child support amount and allocated between the parents. Others require the parties to pay day care in addition to child support on a *pro rata* basis according to incomes. A few leave it to the discretion of the judge whether to deviate from the guidelines to take child care into account. Some do not include child care expenses at all. If you are in a state that includes day care in child support, only work-related day care expenses are counted.

Health Care

Some states only consider health insurance premiums in calculating child support, others only uncovered medical expenses, and others include both. Some states incorporate these costs into the guidelines, others add it to the child care support, and some leave it to the judge to consider as a deviation from the guidelines.

DEVIATIONS FROM GUIDELINES

Child support guidelines will usually be followed by the court, unless you can persuade the judge that there is a good reason for deviation from them to allow you to pay less child support than they indicate. Some states require the judge to set forth and explain in writing the reason for the deviation.

Some of the reasons that have justified a deviation from the guidelines follow.

- ◆ One parent is responsible for paying a high amount of debt incurred during the marriage for the benefit of the children.
- ◆ One parent has extraordinary capital gains.
- ◆ One parent receives the tax benefits of the exemptions for children and child care expenses.

- ◆ One parent receives a larger share of the marital property.
- ◆ A child has a physical or mental disability.
- ◆ The children have independent financial resources.
- ◆ The needs of the children are exceptional and require more than average expenditures.
- ◆ The parents have substantially different incomes.
- ◆ The *Marital Settlement Agreement* provides resources readily available for the support of the child in an amount at least equivalent to the formula amount.
- ◆ There are other children from previous or subsequent marriages to support.

EDUCATION EXPENSES

A frequent dispute is whether a parent must pay extraordinary costs for a child to attend a private school when that parent thinks the child should be attending a public school. A few states allow judges to deviate from the guidelines for this expense, in situations when the child has been in private school by agreement of the parents until the divorce or when it is shown that the child has special needs that are best met by a private school or educational program.

Some states will require a parent to pay for college expenses, but many states will not require a parent to put a child through college. (see Appendix B.) In those states that do not provide for college, you can still do so by private agreement. Even though the court may not have the power to award college support, it will enforce college support when it is by agreement and not by law.

The following is one provision for an agreement to provide support for college.

> *It is the intent and desire of the parties that their children graduate from college. The parties agree that they will confer with each child, as he or she becomes eligible to attend college, in the selection of the school. The parties will take into account the child's particular talents and abilities, the cost of*

the school that is under consideration, any financial aid that is available, and any factor deemed relevant to such decision. Upon selection of said school by all concerned, the parties hereto will each pay a pro rata portion for said education, based upon the relative income of each party.

If you want to put a cap on college costs or include an *escape clause* if the costs would become a financial hardship, you can use a provision like this one.

The parties agree that they will pay, in proportion to their respective incomes, for up to four years of in-state college for each of their children. This will include tuition, room, board, books, fees, reasonable transportation costs, and allowance, unless such payment would work a financial hardship on either party. Said obligation shall not run beyond the school term in which the child has his or her 22nd birthday.

NON-GUIDELINES CASES

Most cases are decided by using the guidelines for the state. However, the guidelines only go up to a certain amount of combined income. When the guidelines do not apply or would not result in a fair amount of child support, the court can look at the needs of the children, as well as the financial assets, earnings, and needs of each parent. As a result, even a simple child support case can become complicated. Darryl's case is an example of what can happen to you in a non-guidelines child support case.

DARRYL'S CASE

Darryl and Tonja, the parents of two young children, both worked for the federal government, so their incomes were relatively straightforward. Darryl earned 60% of the combined income and Tonja earned

40%. The two children spent an equal amount of time with each of them.

However, they could not agree on child support—Darryl offered $300 a month and Tonja demanded $600 a month. So they had a four-hour hearing on child support before a family law master. Tonja's lawyer showed that Darryl had omitted some stock dividends from his income statement, and Darryl's lawyer showed that Tonja omitted some overtime pay from hers. As a result, the Master decided that neither income statement was credible and he threw them both out.

The Master then used child support guidelines to determine that Darryl should pay Tonja $375 a month in child support. The Master had to extrapolate, because together they made over $120,000 a year and the guidelines did not go that high.

Tonja took exception and another one-hour hearing was held before a judge. The judge accepted the income statements, but then she revised them to reflect what she thought were the reasonable needs of the children. Based on this analysis, the judge increased the child support to $425 a month.

MODIFICATION

Child support always remains subject to the court's jurisdiction to modify it. However, some states require that a certain amount of time pass before you can petition the court for a modification (usually two years). Others require a *material change in circumstances*.

Many things can amount to a material change in circumstances. A common change occurs when one child reaches the age at which support ends and there are still other minor children at home.

NOTE: *When one child reaches emancipation, child support is some-times not reduced proportionately. You have to recalculate based on the formula or tables.*

Other changes in circumstances include a child changing resi-dences from one parent to the other, a substantial decrease in one parent's income, or the custodial parent moving to an area with a substantially higher or lower cost of living.

Past child support cannot be modified. There is a federal law against this. Only child support going forward may be modified.

Your child support order does not change automatically when an event occurs that would otherwise justify a change. You need to *petition the court* to change the prior child support order for it to be effective.

Try to obtain agreement to the modification with the children's mother before filing your request with the court. Even if the modi-fication is agreed to, it should be put in the form of a *Consent Order* and filed with the court.

TERMINATION

Child support runs until emancipation, death, or termination of parental rights, whichever occurs first.

Emancipation

Child support terminates when a child is *emancipated*. Emancipation usually occurs when the child reaches the age of 18, but each state sets the age of majority (for example, it is 21 in the District of Columbia). If you have a child with a mental or physical disability, it may be possible to have support continue past the age of majority (emancipation).

In all but a handful of states, child support will continue past 18 if a child is a full-time student in high school. In that case, child support terminates on the earlier of graduation from high school or the child's 19th birthday.

Some states will provide for college support, or you can provide for college expenses by private agreement. (See Appendix B for your state's age of majority and laws regarding college expenses.)

Actions by the minor could also lead to emancipation. *Marriage* of a child, while still a minor, is an emancipation event and will terminate child support. If a child, while still a minor, enlists in the *armed services*, it is considered an emancipation event that will terminate child support. If a child becomes *self-supporting* while still a minor, it is also considered an emancipation event that will terminate child support.

Death

The death of a child terminates child support. However, if you die, your estate will be liable for any past-due child support. A claim may also be made against your estate for future child support. You may provide, by agreement or otherwise, for life insurance to pay your child support obligation in the event of your death.

If the child's mother dies, you will most likely become guardian of the child and pay the expenses of the child directly.

NOTE: *While the court cannot require you to obtain life insurance, it is usually a part of negotiated settlement agreements to provide for the children in the event of your death, especially when you already have a policy or your employer provides one. You can provide that the amount of insurance should decrease each year by the amount of your payments. You may also want to think about the expenses you would incur for caretaking in the event of the mother's death and provide for some insurance on her life.*

Termination of Parental Rights

Adoption by a stepparent or another court order that terminates your parental rights also terminates child support. However, you will still be liable for any past-due amount.

Inability to Pay

If you become unable to pay child support, for example, through disability, involuntary unemployment, or incarceration, your obligation does not terminate automatically. Child support will continue to accrue until you obtain a court order modifying your support.

AVOIDING PAYMENT

As long as the custodial parent does not request or sue for child support, you do not have to pay. However, you are taking a chance. Your child's mother may ask for more money later, and child support may be retroactive in your state. You could end up with a judgment against you for thousands of dollars.

If the custodial parent does sue for child support in a divorce or paternity action, there is no way to get out of paying child support. Intentionally impoverishing yourself, hiding assets, or not paying can have dire consequences. If a parent fails to make child support payments as required by law, the party entitled to that child support has several options to enforce payment.

First, every state has a *child support enforcement agency* that will attempt to collect child support for a nominal fee. A list of state agencies and their contact information is included in Appendix E.

If you owe child support, your children's mother can obtain a *wage withholding order*. This requires child support to be deducted from your paycheck and paid directly to the court.

The usual way to enforce a child support order is for a parent to file a petition asking the court to hold the paying parent in contempt. The petition is filed with the court where the original child support order was entered. The court will then set a hearing to determine whether the parent failed to make those payments.

The way to defend against a contempt petition is to prove to the court that you were not able to make the payments because you did not have the money. If you win, however, you will still owe the child support. If you do not show up for the hearing, the judge can issue a bench warrant for your arrest.

At the hearing, the judge will order you to begin making payments immediately. The court has the power to enforce its order. For example, a judge might take away your driver's license or professional license. The judge could also put you in jail. A typical order might sentence a delinquent payer to two months in jail, commencing in thirty days, with the sentence purged if the debtor pays the child support due before it starts.

If you owe child support, the children's mother can also freeze and seize your assets, such as your bank accounts, automobiles, or furniture, with a *writ of attachment*.

You can also be prosecuted criminally by your *state's attorney* for failing to pay child support. A conviction could result in a criminal record, incarceration, or supervised probation.

In addition, the court can order you to pay the attorney's fees the other spouse incurred to enforce child support, as well as interest on child support arrears.

CHILD SUPPORT AGREEMENTS

You can settle child support by agreement, just like custody and visitation. The court will approve your agreement, as long as it is consistent with the guidelines, it meets the needs of the children, or there is a good reason for deviation. The following are some sample provisions from a child support settlement agreement.

> *Commencing and accounting from January 1, 2007, the Father shall pay to the Mother, for the support and maintenance of the parties' children, the sum of eleven hundred*

*ninety-five dollars ($1,195) per month, in two equal install-
ments on the first and fifteenth of each month by mail,
directly to the Mother. Said child support payments shall
continue until the first to occur of the following: the death of
a child, the death of the Father, a child's marriage, when a
child enters the armed forces, when a child no longer has his
or her principal residence with the Mother, a child obtains
full-time employment (other than employment during school
recesses), or when a child attains the age of eighteen (18). If
a child has not graduated high school by his or her 18th
birthday, child support shall continue until graduation or
the 19th birthday of that child.*

*The parties agree to recalculate child support every two
years from January 1, 2007, based on a ten percent (10%)
extrapolation of the Child Support Guidelines for combined gross incomes in excess of $120,000. The parties
agree to exchange tax returns every two years in September
in order to recalculate child support.*

*The Mother agrees to continue the health insurance cov-
erage for the children until age 22 or for as long as she is
able to obtain such insurance through her employment. The
parties agree that the children will use those physicians
that participate in the Mother's insurance plan.*

*The parties agree to share, in proportion to income, all
unreimbursed medical expenses incurred on behalf of each
child until age 18, including orthodonture and psychotherapy
if recommended by a child's primary care physician. The
Mother agrees to provide full receipts for all such costs to
the Father so they may be submitted to the insurance
company, whether covered or not. Before either party may
be liable for such expenses that constitute elective procedures,
such as cosmetic surgery, both parties must agree to the
expense in writing.*

BANKRUPTCY AND TAXES

Child support is not an obligation that can be discharged in bankruptcy. Child support is not tax deductible. If you try to make it deductible by disguising it as alimony, it will not work. Any alimony that ends on a date tied to the age of majority of the children—for example, alimony that ends six months after the child turns 18—is not deductible. You can, however, ask the judge to deviate downward from the guidelines because you are paying alimony in an amount greater than or equivalent to what the guidelines would indicate for child support.

The general rule regarding claiming exemptions for dependents on your income tax return is that if you pay more than half of the living expenses of a child for a calendar year, then according to the Internal Revenue Code, you are entitled to claim that child as a dependent on your tax returns. However, for divorced parents, the rule is that the parent with custody for the greater part of the year gets to claim the exemption. If the divorce decree does not say who gets the exemption, the custodial parent wins. More details can be found in IRS Publication 504, "Divorced or Separated Individuals," available free from the IRS or on the Internet at **www.irs.gov**.

Divorced or separated parties may, by agreement, switch the exemption to the noncustodial parent by filing IRS Form 8332. The form is signed by the custodial parent and attached to the tax return of the noncustodial parent. Switching is not available if the parties were never married.

Being able to claim the exemption can have a serious impact on a person's tax return. While the amount changes every year, you can subtract $3,300 (2006 amount) from your income for each exemption claimed. The exemption begins to be phased out for certain high-income taxpayers (for example, starting at adjusted gross income of $150,500 for single taxpayers in 2006). If you are in a 28% tax bracket, that saves you $924 in taxes per child. In addition, the exemption can open the door to other valuable tax benefits, namely the *Child Tax Credit*, the *Dependent and Child Care Credit*, and *Educational Credits*.

The *Child Tax Credit* is a maximum of $1,000 per child for 2006 through 2010. It is available if you have a dependent who is under age 17. For example, you may be able to claim this credit if you are filing as single or head-of-household, and your annual income is less than $75,000. There is a phaseout above that income level. The credit reduces your tax dollar-for-dollar down to zero. Some taxpayers may qualify for an *Additional Child Tax Credit*. With this credit, taxpayers can receive a refund (not just a reduction in tax owed) for the amounts that your tax obligation falls below zero, up to the maximum of $1,000 in combined child tax credits. This credit is attached to the child dependency exemption and cannot be allocated to the other parent. You can use IRS Publication 972 to calculate your Child Tax Credit.

The *Dependent and Child Care Credit* is a credit to offset baby-sitting and day care costs, after-school care, or recreation programs incurred to permit a custodial parent to work or look for work. It is applicable if you have a child under 13 or a disabled dependent child. The amount is 20% to 35% of child care expenses between $3,000 and $6,000. This equals a tax credit of $600 to $1,050 for one child or $1,200 to $2,100 for more than one child. This credit reduces your tax bill dollar-for-dollar, but like the Child Tax Credit, it cannot reduce your taxes below zero. There is a phaseout of the credit at higher incomes. Unlike the child care credit, this credit can be detached from the dependency exemption. If you have custody of the child for most of the year and have assigned the exemption to the mother with IRS Form 8332, you can still claim the Dependent and Child Care Credit. For more details, see IRS Publication 502.

The *Hope Credit* is worth up to $1,500 per student for the first two years of education after high school. The *Lifetime Learning Credit* is worth up to $2,000 per family after the first two years of higher education. This benefit is also phased out based on your income level and filing status. The income levels start as low as $43,000. For more information, see IRS Publication 970, "Education Benefits."

It pays to try to reach an agreement over who will take the exemptions and associated credits. Otherwise, if you file conflicting returns, the IRS will simply disallow both exemptions until the conflict is resolved. If you are in a higher tax bracket than your children's mother, then the dependency exemptions and the associated tax credits may be more valuable to you than to her. You may be able to compromise by paying her some portion of your tax savings. In that way, both parties will be better off than if she got the exemptions instead of you.

−8−

FEDERAL AND UNIFORM LAWS

State laws are used to decide who gets custody and visitation, and how much child support will be paid. However, there are special federal statutes and uniform laws that tell the states how to handle various special cases involving children and their fathers. It is important that you have some familiarity with these federal and uniform laws, because they may well affect the outcome of your case.

CHILD SUPPORT

About a third of all contested child support cases involve parties living in two different states. Before the *Uniform Reciprocal Enforcement of Support Act of 1950* (URESA), a mother seeking child support had to travel to the father's state to file for child support. Now, a parent may file in the state where he or she lives (the *initiating state*). The order is then sent to and enforced in the state where the payor lives (the *responding state*).

In 1968, certain revisions to URESA were made and the *Revised Uniform Reciprocal Enforcement of Support Act* (RURESA) was drafted. Some form of URESA or RURESA has been adopted by every state. However, problems of interpretation arose under both acts, resulting in multiple state orders and lengthy proceedings.

To solve these problems, the *Uniform Interstate Family Support Act* (UIFSA) was drafted. It has been adopted by over half the states, and replaces URESA and RURESA. It creates *continuing exclusive jurisdiction* in the first state that issues a child support order, as long as one of the parties or the children reside in that state. No other jurisdiction can modify the child support order. Jurisdiction may be transferred to another state by agreement of the parties.

The Uniform Interstate Family Support Act also permits a payee to send an income withholding order directly to an employer in another UIFSA state and have it enforced. Each state has a *central registry* for the reception of interstate documents. You can find the central registry under "child support" in your state government telephone directory, or contact the Office of Child Support Enforcement in the Department of Health and Human Services in Washington, D.C.

HEALTH INSURANCE

Either parent may ask the court for a *Qualified Medical Child Support Order* (QMCSO). Congress, by amendment to the *Employee Retirement Income Security Act* (ERISA) provisions, guaranteed the right of children to receive benefits under their parents' group health insurance plan.

A QMCSO allows a child or the child's custodian to work directly with the insurance company for benefits and payments. The plan administrator gives the child an insurance card, a list of providers, and an explanation of benefits and procedures. The child can then select the plan options that best suit his or her needs. The insurance company will reimburse any expenses paid by the child or his or her custodian. The child is called an *alternative recipient* and is both a participant and beneficiary under the plan, with rights and remedies that are independent of the insured parent.

A QMCSO can be any order, judgment, or decree, including the approval of a settlement agreement, from a court of competent jurisdiction pursuant to state domestic relations law. After the court issues the order, it is sent to the plan administrator for qualification. To qualify, the order must contain all of the following:

- ◆ a specific provision for health coverage for the child of a participant enrolled in a group plan;

- the name and last known mailing address of the participant;
- the name and mailing address of each child covered by the order;
- a reasonable description of the coverage to be provided under the plan or the manner in which such coverage is to be determined;
- the period to which such order applies; and,
- each plan to which such an order applies.

The order cannot require the plan to provide any type or form of benefit or option not otherwise provided under the plan. While costs of insurance premiums are not required to be part of the QMCSO, it is a good idea to address the issue in the order. You can address who pays for the insurance, increased costs due to options selected by the child, uninsured costs, deductibles, coinsurance, and costs for care outside the plan.

SCHOOL RECORDS

The *Family Educational and Privacy Act* (FEPA) (Title 20, United States Code, Section 1232(g) (20 USC Sec. 1232(g))) requires any school receiving federal funds to give parents the right to inspect and review the education records of their children. Many states also have passed laws giving parents access to school records.

CHILD SNATCHING

What do you do when mom takes the kids and leaves the state? If you file for custody in your state and she files for custody in her state, the result can be a complex and expensive custody battle in two courts across state lines with conflicting orders. In an attempt to resolve some of these conflicts between states, certain federal laws have been passed by Congress and uniform acts have been adopted by the states. In the event the children are taken out of the country, the *Hague Convention* and other laws may apply.

The *Parental Kidnapping Prevention Act* (PKPA) (28 USC Sec. 1738A) is a federal law that tells states how to resolve custody conflicts that arise in different states. (see Appendix C.) The PKPA provides that the state where the child lives is the *home state*. The home state is the only jurisdiction that can enter a first-time custody order. The home state retains continuing exclusive jurisdiction over custody as long as one of the parties or the child remains in that state. Other states must give *full faith and credit* to the custody order of the home state, and may not attempt to overrule or modify it. Litigants must go back to the home state to change the custody order.

Like the PKPA, the *Uniform Child Custody Jurisdiction Act* (UCCJA) is designed to bring some semblance of order into multiple-state custody proceedings. It has been adopted in one form or another by every state. The UCCJA establishes custody jurisdiction in the *home state*—where the child had his or her home for the last six months, or where there are other strong contacts with the child and his family. It provides for the recognition of out-of-state custody decrees. It limits jurisdiction to modify decrees of other states by giving a jurisdictional preference to the prior court. It denies access to a court to petitioners who have engaged in child snatching or similar practices. The UCCJA also encourages courts of different states to communicate with each other in interstate custody cases.

However, problems arose with the UCCJA. It provides four different ways to obtain jurisdiction but no priority among them, so more than one state still ended up asserting jurisdiction. Different courts also interpreted their power to make modifications of custody decrees of other states differently.

Therefore, the *Uniform Child Custody Jurisdiction Enforcement Act* (UCCJEA) revised the UCCJA and attempted to clarify its provisions. It is gradually replacing the UCCJA, and a majority of states have adopted it. The UCCJEA fixes clear priorities for initial custody jurisdiction, with the home state having the highest priority. It also eliminates *best interests* as a basis for custody jurisdiction (reserving that to the decision on the merits of who should have custody). For modification of custody orders, it clarifies continuing exclusive jurisdiction. It distinguishes among initial orders, modification orders, temporary emergency orders, and enforcement orders. Finally, the UCCJEA provides expedited procedures for registering and enforcing out-of-state orders.

The *Violence Against Women Act* (VAWA) (18 USC Sec. 2266) is a federal law that provides for the enforcement of protective orders of other states. However, the VAWA does not establish custody jurisdiction. Also, if the custody provisions of a protective order are obtained *ex parte*, that is, without notice and a full hearing with both sides present, the order will not be entitled to full faith and credit under the UCCJEA.

The *Indian Child Welfare Act* (ICWA) (25 USC Sec. 1901) is a federal law that recognizes tribal jurisdiction over certain custody proceedings involving Indian children residing on a reservation. For the ICWA to apply, the child must both reside on a reservation and either be a member of an Indian tribe or eligible for membership. The ICWA applies to adoptions and terminations of parental rights, but it does not apply to custody awards in divorces.

In the event the mother leaves the country with the children, fathers have several remedies available to them. The United States and other countries that signed the *Hague Convention of Civil Aspects of International Child Abduction* have pledged to resolve international custody disputes in a summary fashion. (see Appendix C.) A wrongfully removed child is to be returned immediately to the country of habitual residence without a determination of best interests first. That determination is reserved to the country of habitual residence. Certain defenses are permitted, such as the petitioner had no custody rights to begin with, or the petitioner's country is not the child's country of habitual residence. The Hague Convention only applies to children under age 16.

Congress enacted the *International Child Abduction Remedies Act* (ICARA) (42 USC Secs. 11601–11610) to implement the Hague Convention in the United States. (see Appendix C.) The International Child Abduction Remedies Act provides that Hague Convention cases may be brought in either state or federal court, and that state court custody proceedings are stopped until the issue of summary return is decided under the Hague Convention. In the case of child abduction to a foreign country, you can file a Hague petition with the U.S. State Department. The State Department is made the central authority to deal with other governments by ICARA. Although the Hague Convention is supposed to be stream-lined and simple, international cases often become tied in up in foreign courts.

If your child is abducted to a foreign country, you may also file a criminal complaint with the U.S. Justice Department under the *International Parental Kidnapping Crime Act* (IPKCA) (18 USC Sec. 1204). The child must be under age 16, have previously been in the U.S., and have been removed from or retained outside the U.S. with the intent to obstruct the lawful exercise of parental rights that flow from a court order or an agreement. The abducting parent's passport or foreign visa can be revoked by the court. Defenses include a custody order or allegation of domestic violence.

GAY DADS

Fathers' rights issues may arise when gay men marry heterosexual women and have children. They may hope this will end their attraction to others of the same sex. They may want to have children. They may feel pressure to conform to social norms. No matter what the reason, gay men can be excellent, caring fathers.

People have different views about homosexuality. Many believe that homosexuality is naturally occurring and biological. Others disapprove. Vermont and Connecticut have approved civil unions between homosexuals. The Massachusetts court had this to say about children of gay parents when it legalized gay marriages.

> *No one disputes that the plaintiff couples are families, that many are parents, and that the children they are raising, like all children, need and should have the fullest opportunity to grow up in a secure, protected family unit. Similarly, no one disputes that, under the rubric of marriage, the State provides a cornucopia of substantial benefits to married parents and their children. The preferential treatment of civil marriage reflects the Legislature's conclusion that marriage "is the foremost setting for the education and socialization of children" precisely because it "encourages parents to remain committed to each other and to their children as they grow." In this case, we are confronted with an entire, sizeable class of parents raising children who have absolutely no access to civil marriage and its protections because they are forbidden from procuring a marriage license. It cannot be rational under our laws, and indeed it is not permitted, to penalize children by depriving them of State benefits because the State disapproves of their parents' sexual orientation.*
>
> *Goodridge vs. Dept. of Public Health,* 440 Mass. 309,
> 798 N.E.2d 941 (2003).

However, there are still laws on the books of some states that describe homosexuality as a crime against God and Nature. These laws make it difficult for a gay father to win custody and impose harsher visitation restrictions than for heterosexual fathers.

Theoretically, gay fathers have equal protection under the law, and they should not be discriminated against. However, when gay fathers divorce, they may run into judges who have an unfavorable view of their role as parents. In contested custody cases, it may be hard to get a fair hearing.

A young child probably does not know that his or her father is a homosexual. This is an adult issue. The key to raising children in any family is the love of both parents. If the two parents can agree on time-sharing, things will go much better. If the heterosexual partner can manage to overcome her hurt upon discovering her spouse is homosexual, then the parties can have a parenting agreement. When no one makes homosexuality an issue, then it will not be an issue before the court.

PHYSICALLY OR MENTALLY IMPAIRED DADS

Many state laws prohibit discrimination on the basis of physical or mental impairment. The mental and physical state of the parties may be a factor in custody determinations, but only if it affects the ability to parent. Henry's case shows what might happen in a case involving a father with a mental impairment.

HENRY'S CASE

Henry suffered from bouts of depression and had been diagnosed with several other mental disorders. He had voluntarily committed himself for a period of time and let his wife, Claire, have custody of their 12-year-old son, Alex, for the past three years. Henry was now under a physician's care, taking his medication, and able to conduct a normal life. He wanted more time with Alex and asked the court to change custody. Claire was concerned about another relapse.

The parties put on their case. Claire showed that she had done a good job of caring for Alex under extreme circumstances when Henry abandoned them. She presented email in which Henry wrote to Alex and told him he had a safe place if he wanted to run away.

Henry gave evidence that Alex had bonded with him, confided in him, and wanted to spend more time with him. Alex was having anger management problems at school and his grades were suffering. Claire was having trouble disciplining Alex, sometimes grounding him and sometimes spanking him, to which Henry objected.

The judge told the parents that she was not going to take Alex away from either one of them. Although they had each tried to show the other was a fault, the judge said sometimes the parents are not at fault. She denied Henry's request to change custody, but she did give him additional time-sharing with Alex. She said she would consider increasing this in the future if Henry stayed in counseling. She also ordered a psychological-educational assessment for Alex and family therapy for the parents.

MILITARY DADS

The *Servicemembers Civil Relief Act*, formerly known as the *Soldiers' and Sailors' Civil Relief Act* (50 USC Secs. 501–591), suspends enforcement of civil actions against active duty military personnel so they can devote their time and attention to defending the United States. The suspension is not automatic. Section 521 provides that the court may stay the proceedings on its own or the military member may request a stay. The court may deny the stay if military service has no material effect on the service member's ability to prosecute or defend the action. The duration of the stay is at the court's discretion, so the military member needs to present a reasonable timetable to the court for resolving the issue, taking into account the military obligation and family needs.

—9—

ALTERNATIVES

You do not want to have a contested custody trial if you can help it. A trial is the last place you want to be, since you might lose. Half of the people that go to court lose. In every case, there is a winner and a loser.

Regardless of whether you win or lose, trials are expensive. They involve enormous expense, time, and uncertainty. Lawyers and expert witnesses may cost thousands of dollars, and the other costs, like hurt feelings and damage to relationships, can come at a great price.

The system is slow. It takes a long time to get to trial, and the judges do not always rule at the end of the case. They may take a case under advisement at the end of the trial, which means they want to think about it. Then you may not get the result for weeks or months. Appeals can drag the matter out for years.

Judges are not trained in human behavior. Mental health professionals have expertise in custody evaluations. Judges, on the other hand, are lawyers. They are strangers to your life and marriage. They are called upon to make a decision after hearing only a few hours or days of testimony about a marriage that may have lasted for years. Judges are not perfect and the winning party is not always the deserving party.

Judges are limited in what they can do. They are also limited in how they must rule by the legislature. Private agreements between the parties are not so limited. You can be much more creative than the judge can.

Although the court will usually uphold an agreement by the parties with respect to child custody, visitation, and support, it must make an independent decision that this is in the best interest of the child. The court can consider the opinion of the parties and third parties, and often follows these recommendations, but it cannot delegate this authority to the parties or a third-party mediator or arbitrator. However, using mediation, arbitration, or other form of alternative dispute resolution (ADR) can have tremendous benefits, both emotionally and economically.

Less than 10% of custody cases actually go to trial. However, when a lawyer takes your case, they spend 90% of their time preparing for trial. That means spending a lot of money on a long shot. Fortunately, there are several alternatives. These are presented in order from the least expensive to the most expensive.

WORKING IT OUT

You and your children's mother can try to work out an agreement. If you try to work something out yourselves, meet on neutral ground—not at your office or at her mother's home, but some place where both parties will feel comfortable.

A reasonable amount of time should be set aside to deal with the issues. If you leave to answer a telephone call just as you almost have things worked out, you may find that things have fallen apart when you get back. On the other hand, do not leave the meeting time open-ended. A meeting without a deadline will drag on and issues will not get resolved.

Set an agenda. Decide what will be dealt with at the meeting. For example, set an agenda that says, *this week we will decide on custody and child support, and next week we will decide on who is going to live where and what to do about the house.*

Talk about what you agree on. No matter how bad it is, there are some things you agree on (e.g., the marriage stinks or the kid is cute).

If you hit a point that gives you trouble, move on to something else and come back to the problem after you have resolved some other issues.

Reschedule as needed. If things start to turn nasty, if someone gets angry, or if you are losing everything, reschedule the meeting for another time. It is important that both of you feel that the agreement is a good thing.

Keep the kids out of it. Your children do not need to be involved in this. Do not have them around. They will interrupt you and it will upset them. Do not discuss or complain about the case to the children. Reassure them that they will be provided for—even if you are worried about it.

Start talking early. Cases usually settle at one of two times—early on when both parties feel guilty and are not locked into a position, or after much litigation when the parties are too exhausted to fight anymore. Sometimes you can get more with guilt than you can get at a trial.

It is good to know what you want. Write down your objectives before you start negotiating. Then, assign priorities to your objectives so you can make sure you get what you really want and can forgo something that just does not matter as much to you. You also need to ask questions and learn what the other side wants and what her priorities are.

Sometimes you have to be flexible, especially on items that are a strong priority for your spouse and a weak priority for you. A good settlement is where each side gives up 60%.

If you and your children's mother work something out, make notes and sign them. This could be considered an agreement. If it is not correct legal language, you may be bound by something other than what you thought you agreed to, so you may want to have a lawyer review it at this point.

PARENTING COORDINATOR

In cases in which the parents are constantly arguing over small details, like visitation arrangements, it is too expensive and time-consuming to ask a judge to resolve these fights. Therefore, some parents will agree to use a *parenting coordinator* to referee minor disputes.

Anyone willing to serve in the capacity may be a parenting coordinator, but it is usually best to find a therapist or social worker who can be impartial and make sound decisions based on what is best for the children.

The parties agree on a mechanism for submitting disputes to the parenting coordinator—for example, by email, telephone, fax, or otherwise—and the parenting coordinator issues a decision. The parenting coordinator will usually charge by the hour, typically about $100 to $150.

MEDIATION

Mediation uses a trained, neutral third party who attempts to help the parties resolve their disputes through special mediation techniques, like *interest-based bargaining*. The mediator does not represent either party, but guides the discussions, explores and offers options, explains the law, and facilitates an agreement. John's case shows how mediators use interest-based bargaining to resolve disputes.

JOHN'S CASE

John and Judy, a couple in their thirties, had been married for three years when they decided to separate and get a divorce. Judy would be moving to a new job about two hours away. They had a two-year-old son. They decided to mediate.

John told the mediator, "I want 50% of the time with the child."

Judy said, "I want the child with me during the school year."

The mediator recognized those statements as *positions*. Traditional negotiation proceeds with position-based bargaining. However, the mediator knew that he would be hitting his head against a brick wall by trying to negotiate positions. So, the mediator interviewed John and Judy separately and asked questions to try to ascertain the *interests* underlying those positions. It was not easy, and the parties kept restating their positions. But the mediator was persistent and kept asking why until he got at the reasons that the parties were taking their respective positions.

John had a child from a prior divorce that he saw only every other weekend. He felt guilty for settling for that schedule in his first divorce and he was determined not to let it happen again in this divorce. He also felt that his son could benefit by having him as a male role model and that he could impart things of value to his son.

Judy felt that John had a quick temper and she thought the less exposure the child had to John, the better. She also wanted to reduce the number of transfers between houses to minimize the child's disruption.

Now the mediator could use *interest-based bargaining* instead of position-based bargaining. He had moved the issue in dispute from school year and 50% to the real interests of the parties. He called the parties together again. The mediator explained the interests of each party to the other and invited them to try to come up with a visitation schedule that took those interests into account.

> **Working with interests instead of positions, both parties were able to compromise on their positions. John agreed to continue in counseling. They agreed that John would have time-sharing every fourth week and every weekend between the weekly visitations. They would also alternate holidays and John would have an additional five weeks with his son in the summers.**

Mediators can be lawyers, psychologists, accountants, ministers, or anyone else with proper training. You can hire a private mediator. They are listed in the telephone book and on the Internet. Often the court will require litigating parties to go to mediation. The reason for this is that there are more cases filed than there are judges to hear them, so the judges count on most cases settling.

Mediation has a high success rate (about 85%) for settling cases. *Court-appointed mediators*, sometimes called *facilitators*, can recommend solutions and do a little more *arm-twisting* than their private counterparts.

Mediators charge around $150 to $200 an hour, split evenly between the parties. Payment is expected at the end of each session. Sometimes it will only take one meeting of two or three hours to reach a mediated agreement. More frequently, you will have several meetings with the mediator and your children's mother until you reach an agreement.

The objective of mediation is to end up with an agreement, but it is not required. You do not have to agree with the mediator. You can always try your case. At the conclusion of a successful mediation, however, the mediator will prepare a *Memorandum of Understanding* or *Separation Agreement*, in writing, for both parties to sign. You are encouraged to have this document reviewed by a lawyer before you sign it. It will be too late to change your mind afterwards.

PARENTING PLANS

Although you may be ending your relationship with your spouse, you will still be partners in the business of raising your children for the next several years. Just like any other business, you need a plan.

Parenting Plans are an infinitely better resolution of custody disputes than a custody trial. Parenting Plans provide much more detail than a custody order from the court. Because they are designed by the parties and not the judge, they can be much more specific about plans for parenting the children.

Parenting Plans cover the basic matters that would be decided by the judge in a custody trial, namely legal custody, physical custody, visitation, and child support. However, you can add many more details about how you will coordinate parenting with a Parenting Plan. The essential provisions included in a Parenting Plan are:

- legal and physical custody of the child;
- where each parent lives currently and intends to live (relocation);
- where each parent works and the hours of employment;
- who will provide any necessary child care when the parents cannot and who will pay for the child care;
- where the child will go to school;
- what doctor or health care facility will provide medical care for the child;
- how the child's medical expenses will be paid;
- what the child's religious commitment will be, if any;
- who will make decisions about the child's education, medical care, choice of child care providers, and extracurricular activities;
- who will have access to school and medical records;
- how the holidays will be divided;
- what the child's summer schedule will be;
- whether and how the child will be able to contact the other parent (telephone and email visitation);

- ◆ how the parent proposes to resolve disagreements related to matters over which the court orders joint decision-making;
- ◆ what child support and family support there will be; and,
- ◆ how the child will be transferred between the parties.

You can use the Parenting Plan on pages 121–126 as a guide for drafting your own.

THIS PARENTING PLAN, the original of which being executed in quadruplicate, is made this __3rd__ day of __August__, 2007, by and between Jane Doe, hereinafter referred to as "Wife" and John Doe, hereinafter referred to as "Husband."

WITNESSETH:

For good and adequate consideration, and the mutual promises contained herein, the parties hereby agree as follows:

Custody

1. The parties shall have joint legal custody and shared residential custody of their minor children. The Wife and the children shall have exclusive use and possession of the family home, the furnishings therein, and the family automobile from the date of this agreement until three years from the date of their divorce unless agreed otherwise by them. The parties acknowledge that the welfare and best interest of their minor children are the paramount consideration of each of them. Toward this end, the parties shall confer with one another, and jointly make decisions affecting their children's lives, including but not limited to health, education, religious education, summer plans, and disciplinary and developmental matters. It shall be, at all times, the objective of both parties to discuss all matters affecting the children so as to promote the children's welfare, happiness, growth, and well-being. Each party shall make every effort to promote the relationships between their children and the other parent, and neither party shall act or speak disparagingly of the other parent to or in the presence or hearing of the children.

Access to Records

2. Each of the parties shall be entitled to receive copies of all reports concerning each child, including without limitation, school records and reports, and medical and psychological reports. If either party meets with a doctor, dentist, psychologist, therapist, teacher, or other professional and a written report of such meeting is not created, then the party who met with such professional shall provide the other party with an oral report of the meeting. In the event that the school shall refuse to provide the Husband or the Wife with school records or reports, each parent shall be under a duty to inform the school that the other parent is entitled to and should be provided with such information, but if the school should continue to refuse, each shall then be under a duty to notify the other of any and all teacher conferences or meetings involving the children, and both parents shall have the right to be in attendance at such meetings so that there may be unanimity with regard to a course of action designed to nurture the development and growth of the children.

Information

3. The parties shall keep each other informed of the children's schedules so that each parent can participate in scheduled activities whenever possible. Each parent shall provide the other with a copy of the children's school calendars, sports schedules, and the like, as soon as he or she receives them. The parties shall

notify each other as soon as possible of any illness, emergency, accident, etc., concerning the children; provided, however, that the parent having responsibility for the children at the time of such illness, emergency, or accident may make medical decisions on behalf of the children.

Time-sharing

4. The parties shall make every effort to work with each other concerning arrangements for the time that the children are to spend with the other party. The parties shall be flexible in scheduling their time with the children so as to coincide with the children's interests consistent with their schedules and notify the other party when time with the children is desired or is required. Each party shall be respectful of the needs and schedule of the other by providing as much advance notification of that request for a change in schedule, if any, as is possible under the circumstances.

5. The Husband will have timesharing with the children every other weekend beginning Friday after school and ending Monday when school resumes. The Wife will have timesharing with the children every other weekend beginning Friday after school and ending Monday when school resumes. The children will be in the Wife's care overnight on Monday and Tuesday. The children will be in the Husband's care overnight on Wednesday and Thursday. The parties will select and agree on summer camp or a third party day care provider, which agreement shall not be unreasonably withheld. During evenings and weekends, the other parent will be the preferred day care provider. Notwithstanding this schedule, each party will be permitted to spend at least two uninterrupted weeks of vacation time with the children in the summer.

Extracurricular Activities

6. The Husband and the Wife shall jointly decide, with input from the children, the extracurricular activities in which the children shall participate. The children shall have the opportunity to have both parents present at any games or activities to which parents are invited. Neither party shall schedule activities for the children during those times when the children are scheduled to be with the other parent without that parent's consent.

7. The children also shall have the opportunity to have both parents present at all secular and religious school activities including back to school night, shows, and other events to which parents are invited, as well as all such events at summer camp.

Medical Care

8. Either parent may initiate emergency medical care for the children. The Wife and Husband shall coordinate who will make the regularly scheduled medical and dental appointments for the children. Both the Wife and the Husband shall make every effort to keep the other informed of any prescription and/or nonprescription medications that the children may be taking or illnesses that the children may have. Ultimate responsibility

rests with each party to maintain communication with the medical professional working with the children.

Privacy

9. Although the Husband and the Wife both understand that neither may dictate to the other the way in which the other conducts his or her life, the Husband and the Wife recognize that each of them will enjoy a social and dating life. Accordingly, the parties shall only introduce members of the opposite sex (not related by blood or marriage) to the children on a gradual basis. It is imperative that the children are comfortable with the concept of another adult.

10. Neither party shall inquire of the children information concerning the other party. This shall not preclude either party from asking questions such as "How was your day/weekend?" The children should feel free to speak openly and honestly concerning activities in "Mom's house" and activities in "Dad's house."

Routines

11. Both parties agree to establish similar routines for the children, i.e., bedtimes, finishing homework, television access, etc. Both parties will insist on proper hygiene for the children. Neither party will permit the use of foul language by the children.

Religious Faith

12. The children shall continue to be raised in the Jewish faith and shall attend appropriate religious training. Each of the children shall have a Bar or Bat Mitzvah. The parties shall cooperate with one another and communicate regarding the nature of the party, celebration, or other means of recognizing such an event. If the Husband and the Wife jointly decide that a party or celebration is appropriate, they shall cooperate and communicate with one another regarding the planning of each child's Bar or Bat Mitzvah party. Each party shall invite their immediate families and the parties shall jointly determine the other guests to be invited to the children's Bar or Bat Mitzvah.

Relocation

13. Neither party shall relocate outside of the metropolitan area without either prior written agreement of the other or an order of a court of competent jurisdiction. A relocation by either party outside the metropolitan area shall be deemed to be of a material and substantial change in circumstances with regard to the time spent by both parties with the children. To this end, both parties shall notify each other as soon as practicable of such intended relocation. In addition, so long as the children of the parties are under the age of 18 years, the parties shall be under a duty and obligation to notify the other of any change of their residence address and telephone number within three (3) days of such change.

Decision Making

14. The parties shall make every effort to agree on decisions or scheduling matters concerning the children. In the event they are

unable to reach a consensus, then the rights, privileges, duties, and powers of a parent shall be determined as set forth below.

Duties and Powers of Each Parent
15. During any period that the children are with a parent, shall have the following duties and powers:

(a) the duty of care, control, protection, and reasonable discipline of the children;

(b) the duty to support the children, including providing the children with clothing, food, and shelter;

(c) the power to consent to medical, dental, and surgical treatment during an emergency involving an immediate danger to the health and safety of the children.

Rights and Powers Reserved to the Husband
16. At all times, the Husband shall have the following rights and powers:

(a) the right to access medical, dental, psychological, and education records of the children;

(b) the right to consult with any physician, dentist, or mental health professional of the children;

(c) the right to consult with school officials concerning the children's welfare and educational status, including school activities;

(d) the right to attend school activities;

(e) the right to be designated on any records as a person to be notified in case of an emergency;

(f) the right to manage the estate of the children to the extent that the estate has been created by that parent or the family of that parent;

(g) the power to determine the necessity for and course of: (i) medical, dental, and surgical treatment involving invasive procedures; and (ii) nonemergency, noninvasive medical care, medication, and procedures.

Rights and Powers Reserved to the Wife
17. At all times, the Wife shall have the following rights and powers:

(a) the power to represent the children in any civil legal action and to make other decisions of substantial legal significance in that matter concerning the children;

(b) the power to represent the children in any criminal legal action and to make other decisions of substantial legal significance in that matter concerning the children, after consultation with an attorney and a therapist;

(c) the authority to make all decisions regarding the children's education, including the decision whether to enroll the children in private or public school, after consultation with an appropriate expert if such expert is chosen and paid for by the Husband;

(d) the power to determine the necessity for and course of psychiatric, psychological, or mental health treatment for the children, after consultation with a mental health professional.

Rights and Powers to be Exercised Jointly

18. The Husband and Wife each shall have the following joint rights and powers:

(a) the power to consent to or forbid marriage;

(b) the power to consent to or forbid enlistment in the armed forces of the United States; and,

(c) the power as an agent of the children to act in connection with the children's estate, in the event of the death of the child, if such action is required, after consultation with an attorney and a therapist.

Parenting Discussions

19. The parties agree that when either parent wishes to discuss with the other important issues concerning the children's health, education, religion, recreation, and welfare, they will communicate out of the presence or hearing of the children, and may communicate by letter or telephone with one another for this purpose.

20. The parties agree that they will not discuss their marital or financial situation or parenting decisions yet to be reached, in the presence of or within the hearing of the children. They agree not to have the children deliver messages either written or verbal to the other parent. They agree that neither of them will say, by word or gesture, anything that would diminish the children's love, respect, or affection for the other parent, nor will they allow their friends or relatives to do so.

21. The parties agree to nurture and assist in the proper development of the children's emotional state. They agree to support and encourage their children. The parties agree that neither of them will say, by word or gesture, anything that would diminish the children's self-respect.

Dispute Resolution

22. In the event a dispute arises under this Agreement, the parties shall first consult a mutually agreed-upon experienced mental health professional or trained mediator who shall assist them in mediating any disputes. If the parties are unable to reach agreement after consultation with the mental health professional, either party may petition the court to decide the outstanding issue.

Death or Disability

23. On the death or disability of either parent, the other parent shall have absolute and superior rights to the custody and guardianship of the parties' children against all other persons, and both parties' rights are deemed to be paramount over all other persons, entities or agencies. The parties unequivocally and mutually agree that this Agreement is not to be deemed a surrender by the Husband or the Wife in and to any parental right with respect to the children.

24. The parties further agree that in the event of the death of either parent, the grandparents, siblings, aunts, uncles, and cousins shall have the right to meaningful access to the children

in order to preserve and foster any relationship they had with the children prior to the death of such parent.

Name Change

25. The Wife and the Husband covenant, represent, and warrant that they will not, at any time or for any reason, cause the children to be known by any surname other than "Doe."

IN WITNESS WHEREOF, the parties being fully advised as to the matters herein set forth, have set their hands and affixed their seals on the date set forth below.

WITNESSES:

_____*Mark Smith*_____   _____*Jane Doe*_____ (SEAL)
                              JANE DOE

_____*Mary Smith*_____   _____*John Doe*_____ (SEAL)
                              JOHN DOE

COLLABORATIVE LAW

In *collaborative law*, each party hires a lawyer trained in collaborative law to be their advocate, with a focus on settlement and not on the trial. From the beginning, the lawyers and parties sign an agreement that both lawyers must withdraw if the case does not settle and goes to litigation. Everyone is committed to settle the case and not litigate it.

Collaborative family law works through a series of four-way meetings, with you, your spouse, and the two lawyers. You are a full participant in the settlement process. You can speak face-to-face with everyone involved instead of having to communicate with your spouse through your lawyer, who speaks to your spouse's lawyer, and vice versa.

The lawyers and parties also agree to provide full and early disclosure of all issues, such as income and assets.

The parties may agree to hire experts to express opinions for both sides (instead of the litigation model, where each party hires competing experts). For example, the parties would hire one appraiser to value the house, one expert to value the business, one financial planner to analyze financial issues, or one therapist to design a parenting plan.

Collaborative lawyers can and do place value on long-term relationship issues. These are often overlooked in the litigated divorce, where only financial and legal issues are considered. A traditional lawyer might tell you that 90% of what is important to you is irrelevant, because it is not important to the trial judge. That 90% is as important to the collaborative lawyer as it is to you.

The two lawyers usually charge their normal hourly rates, which can range from about $150 to $300 an hour or more for experienced attorneys.

NEGOTIATION THROUGH ATTORNEYS

You can hire attorneys to try to work out an agreement. The classic negotiation style is when one party makes a proposal in writing (*offer*) covering all issues of the dispute. The other party then responds in writing to the offer with his or her proposal (*counteroffer*) or with *specific objections* to identified provisions of the offer. These writings go back and forth, with compromises being made by both sides to narrow the gap until a final agreement is reached. Telephone calls and face-to-face meetings help answer questions or break an *impasse* during these negotiations.

Two good attorneys can negotiate and draw up an agreement fairly quickly and inexpensively. A bad attorney can waste a lot of time and money over whether visitation is going to be on Tuesday and Thursday or Monday and Wednesday.

Using this alternative can cost somewhere around $1,500 to $3,000 each for the negotiation and drafting of a *Separation Agreement*.

ARBITRATION

The parties can agree to submit their dispute to a third party for a decision through a process called *arbitration*. The third party, an *arbitrator*, can be a mediator, a lawyer, a retired judge, or any other party. Each party presents their best case to the arbitrator and the arbitrator decides who wins.

The decision is issued in writing and it can either be *binding* or *nonbinding*. Even a binding decision can be appealed to the court in some circumstances, unless appeals are waived. The parties might ask for a nonbinding or an *advisory decision* to test their theories of the case or to facilitate a settlement.

Arbitration has the advantage of speed and less expense over a trial. It can also be used to decide limited issues when negotiation, mediation, or collaborative law reaches an impasse. However, the parties may prefer the case be decided by the judge with all of the formality, procedural safeguards, and rules of the court.

–10–

FILING A LAWSUIT

If you cannot reach an agreement on the issues of custody, visitation, and child support, then you can ask a judge to hold a trial to make a decision. This is called *litigation*. You begin litigation by filing a *lawsuit* at the county courthouse. Filing a lawsuit does not have to stop settlement negotiations. Litigation and settlement often proceed on parallel tracks.

THE THREE PHASES OF A LAWSUIT

A lawsuit, like a chess game, has three phases—a beginning, middle, and end. Phase one, the beginning of your case, consists of *preliminary legal procedures*. These include meeting *threshold requirements*, filing *pleadings*, giving *notice* to the other side, appearing at a scheduling conference, and appearing at other various conferences and hearings. This chapter covers the first phase.

Phase two is *discovery*. These are the rules and methods by which you discover information about your opponents case and vice versa. The purpose of discovery is to avoid surprises at trial and to encourage settlements. Discovery is covered in detail in Chapter 11.

Phase three is the *trial*, which is the dramatic climax of a lawsuit. Chapters 12–13 are devoted to the trial.

THRESHOLD LEGAL REQUIREMENTS

Before you can file a lawsuit and ask a judge to make a decision in your case, you must meet some preliminary legal requirements.

The power and authority to decide matters concerning your children is called *subject matter jurisdiction*. The court has jurisdiction over a marriage and divorce as long as one of the parties meets the residency requirements set forth in the law. In some states, the court can also obtain jurisdiction if the grounds for divorce arose within the state. (There are certain special laws that apply to establishing jurisdiction for custody and visitation issues. These are described more fully in Chapter 4.)

The court must also have the power to bind the parties to its decisions. This is called *personal jurisdiction*. There are various ways to obtain personal jurisdiction. The court has jurisdiction over any person living in the state or served with *process* in the state. The court can also obtain personal jurisdiction over a nonresident in certain circumstances by serving process outside the state (known as *long-arm jurisdiction*).

A person may also submit to jurisdiction of the court by appearing in court or filing a pleading in the case. Some states will permit you to appear in court to contest personal jurisdiction without your appearance being considered as submitting to jurisdiction. That is called a *special appearance*.

Venue means the jurisdiction where you file suit has some connection to the lawsuit. For example, you can usually file suit in the county where you live or where the defendant lives. While any court in your state may have jurisdiction to hear your case, the court located in the county in which you live may be the only one with proper venue. The parties may consent to a different venue. If you file in the wrong county and the defendant challenges it on the basis of venue, you may simply ask the court to transfer venue to the right county.

You or the defendant have to meet the requirements for *residency*. This means you have to live in a jurisdiction for a certain period of time in order to use the courts of that jurisdiction. However, you can file for emergency relief, such as custody or support, before the residency requirement has been met. If the defendant contests your residency, you can prove it with items like a lease, utility bills, driver's license, or voter registration card. Once you establish your home in a jurisdiction, it stays there, even if you temporarily move elsewhere, as long as you have the *intent* to remain a permanent resident in that state.

It is only necessary that you meet the residency requirements at the time of filing. Neither party has to be a resident at the time of the lawsuit. More than one jurisdiction can have jurisdiction and venue in a case, so you may have a choice as to where to file your complaint.

If you are filing a lawsuit for a divorce, you must have *grounds*—good reasons for a divorce. You have to prove these grounds to the court at your divorce trial. You must plead and prove your grounds even if your divorce is uncontested.

It used to be that the only grounds for divorce were *fault grounds*, like desertion or adultery. Now most states have added *no-fault grounds*, such as separation or irreconcilable differences, while keeping the old fault grounds as well. Some states have abolished fault grounds altogether and only have no-fault grounds. Even in no-fault states, fault is still considered sometimes in setting alimony and dividing property.

There are certain defenses to the various grounds for divorce that may be raised by your spouse. For example, renewing physical relations starts the separation period over again. Another example is *condonation* as a defense to the claim of adultery. Condonation means forgiveness, and is usually shown by sexual relations between spouses after the adultery is disclosed.

While fault may play a role in grounds, alimony, and property distribution in a divorce, it has little to do with custody, visitation, or child support. Adultery makes you a bad spouse—it does not necessarily make you a bad parent. The court will usually not deny custody because a parent has committed adultery. The exception is if the other man or woman poses some threat of harm to the child.

BEGINNING THE LAWSUIT

Once you meet the preliminary requirements, you begin a case by filing a *Complaint*. It might be called a *Petition, Motion for Judgment*, or some other name, depending upon the custom of your jurisdiction and the type of case you are filing. After the Complaint has been filed, you must give *notice* to the other side, by serving her with a *Summons* and a copy of the Complaint. She has a certain amount of time to file an *Answer* or other responsive pleading to your complaint, or she will be in default and judgment will be entered for you. When an Answer has been filed denying all or some of the allegations of the Complaint, the case is said to be *at issue*.

Your attorney will file your Complaint and related papers with the clerk's office at the courthouse in the county where you live or where the defendant lives. As discussed in Chapter 4, matters like these are best handled with the assistance of an attorney. However, it is helpful to your case and to your own peace of mind to understand these documents and the processes that will be occurring. This material will also help you should you decide not to use an attorney, which again, should be given some serious thought.

If you decide to file your own Complaint, call the clerk's office first and ask how many copies the clerk requires and what the filing fee will be. The clerk's office is usually clearly marked at the courthouse. Sometimes family law cases are filed in a different place than other cases, so ask the clerk. Clerks are prohibited from giving legal advice, but they are able to tell you what forms are required with your Complaint, and they may be able to tell you what to fix if there is something wrong with your pleadings.

There is a filing fee to file a Complaint or similar pleading, typically $100 or less. If you truly cannot afford the filing fee because of poverty, you can ask the clerk about procedures for filing without a fee.

The clerk will start a court file and put the Complaint in it. The jacket of the court file will have an index of pleadings filed by the parties and orders of the court.

The clerk will stamp the date and case number on the Complaint, put the original in the file, and give you a copy with some attachments. Besides the original Complaint for the court file and a copy to serve on the defendant, have the clerk stamp an extra copy for your file.

NOTICE

You have to give the other side *notice* that you have filed a lawsuit. Notice gives the defendant an opportunity to defend and be heard, which is required by the due process of law. It also gives the court personal jurisdiction over the other party. In some cases, you will have to notify other interested parties, such as a *guardian ad litem* for the child, if one has been appointed.

Summons

A *Summons* is an official court form that tells the other side that you have filed a lawsuit. It also instructs her that she has to file a response within a certain time, or be held in default and lose the case. In most jurisdictions, the clerk will give you a Summons when you file your Complaint. In others, you will have to prepare the Summons yourself. An example of a blank Summons from the state of Montana is provided on the following page.

Plaintiff/Plaintiff Attorney

Address

Plaintiff/Plaintiff Attorney telephone number

IN THE JUSTICE/CITY COURT OF_____ COUNTY, MONTANA
BEFORE _____, JUSTICE OF THE PEACE/CITY JUDGE.
            * * * * * * * * * * * * *

_____,	)	
Plaintiff,	)	
	)	Civil Case_____
vs.	)	
	)	SUMMONS
_____,	)	
Defendant.	)	

THE STATE OF MONTANA TO THE ABOVE-NAMED DEFENDANT, GREETINGS:
You are hereby summoned to answer the Complaint in this action
which is filed in the office of the above-entitled Justice of
the Peace/City Judge, a copy of which is herewith served upon
you. In the event that you deny any or all of the material
facts stated in the complaint, you must file your written
answer together with a $15.00 answer fee for each Defendant
with the above-entitled Court, and serve a copy of your answer
upon the Plaintiff or attorney at the address as shown on the
Complaint.

The answer must contain a denial of any or all of the material facts stated in the Complaint that the Defendant believes
to be untrue, and also a statement, in plain or direct manner, of any other facts constituting a defense. Any matter not
denied shall be deemed admitted. If you fail to answer or
assert a counterclaim within twenty (20) days after service of
the Complaint and Summons, the Plaintiff may request entry of
default judgment against you for the relief demanded in the
Complaint.

GIVEN under my hand this _____ day of , 200_____

JUDGE/CLERK OF COURT

SERVICE OF PROCESS

Service of process means delivering the Complaint and Summons to the defendant. You cannot personally serve the defendant. You must have have a friend, the sheriff, or a professional *process server* do it. The average cost of a process server is about $35. You can help the sheriff or process server find the defendant by providing all the information you have about her, such as a description, a picture, where she lives, where she works, her schedule, and what kind of car she drives.

Once the Complaint is served, the sheriff or process server files an *Affidavit of Service* with the court. You will usually receive a copy to let you know the defendant has been served. Sometimes they send you the original to file with the court yourself. Some states will also permit you to effect personal service by leaving the papers with a person of suitable age and discretion at the home of the defendant.

Some states permit service by certified mail. If the defendant signs for the mail, attach the return receipt to an *Affidavit of Service by Certified Mail* and file it with the court.

Sometimes service is easy. You just call the defendant up and ask her if she can make an appointment with your process server to accept service. If you know the defendant has an attorney, an attorney can accept service for a client if he or she has the client's authority to do so. The defendant can voluntarily submit to jurisdiction of the court by filing an Answer, and then the plaintiff may not need to serve the Summons and Complaint or file an Affidavit of Service.

If the defendant is actively avoiding service or cannot be found, you can ask the court for *service by alternative means*. First, you have to try all reasonable means to serve her. A process server can give you an *Affidavit of Efforts and Unsuccessful Attempts to Serve*. If you do not know where the defendant is, you must make a diligent search to find her. That includes:

- ◆   contacting her relatives, friends, and old neighbors;
- ◆   contacting her last known employer;
- ◆   conducting a search on the Internet;
- ◆   calling directory assistance;
- ◆   asking the post office for a forwarding address;
- ◆   checking military listings to see if she is in the armed forces;
- ◆   inquiring at the state agency for her driver's license, registration, and traffic records; and,
- ◆   checking the courthouse files for civil and criminal records.

Next, file a *Motion for Alternative Service* with the court, accompanied by the *Affidavit*. The court will give you an *Order for Alternative Service*.

Typically, the alternative means will be publishing a notice in the newspaper or posting a notice on the courthouse bulletin board. Your court will have specific rules regarding the size, number, frequency, and days of publication. After posting, file a *Motion for Default* with the court, together with your Affidavit of Service or a copy of the published notice, depending on your local rules.

PLEADINGS

Pleadings are a way of telling the judge your side of the story. A pleading is essentially a letter to the judge, but it follows certain formal rules. If you hire a lawyer, he or she will prepare pleadings for you. However, if you represent yourself, then you will have to prepare and file pleadings.

Fortunately, a lot of courts have developed forms for family law pleadings that are available at the courthouse or on the Internet. You can also look at the case files at the courthouse to see how lawyers have prepared pleadings in other cases.

Almost all courts require that pleadings be on letter size (8.5" x 11") white paper. Typing is usually required, or at least preferred. If you need to fill out the form by hand, ask the clerk first if it will be accepted.

Every pleading starts with the *caption*, also called the style of the case. It identifies the court, the names and addresses of the parties, and the case number assigned by the court clerk. The party that files the initial pleading in the case is shown as the *plaintiff* (or sometimes complainant, petitioner, or movant). The other party is shown as the *defendant* (or respondent). The pleading also has a title. The first pleading in a case has the address of the parties. In later pleadings, it is only required that you list the names of the parties. The following is an example of a caption and title for a pleading.

```
           SUPERIOR  COURT  OF  GREEN
                 FAMILY COURT
JOHN  DOE            )
  Plaintiff          )
                     )
  v.                 )      Civil Action No. 07-0001234
                     )
JANE  DOE            )
  Defendant          )


     MOTION  FOR  TEMPORARY  PROTECTIVE  ORDER
```

All pleadings must be signed. An original signature is usually required. If you sign in blue ink, it will be easy to tell it is an original. Most courts require your name, address, and telephone number under your signature. If you are representing yourself, sign your pleadings like this:

```
                        Respectfully submitted,
                              John Doe
                                John Doe
                           Plaintiff pro se
                           123 Easy Street
                          Anytown, MD 55555
                            (777)333-8888
```

Some pleadings, like a Complaint, must be *verified*. Verification is a statement that you know the contents of the pleading are true or believe them to be true. It is signed before a notary public, making your pleading a statement made under oath and subject to penalties of perjury if you knowingly make a false statement. The following is an example of a Verification.

SUPERIOR COURT OF GREEN
FAMILY COURT

JOHN DOE	)	
Plaintiff	)	
	)	
v.	)	Civil Action No. 07-0001234
	)	
JANE DOE	)	
Defendant	)	

<u>AFFIDAVIT SUPPORTIVE OF PETITION (FATHER)</u>

I,___JOHN DOE_____, say upon oath that I am the Petitioner herein above, and the natural father of ___JAMES DOE_____ and that the allegations contained in said Petition are true to the best of my knowledge, and that this Petition is presented in good faith, and that there is no known opposition to this Petition.

Respectfully submitted,

John Doe

John Doe
Plaintiff pro se
123 Easy Street
Anytown, MD 55555
(777)333-8888

```
COUNTY: GREEN
STATE: MARYLAND ss:

Subscribed and sworn to before me this  16 day of
____JUNE_____, 2007

Joseph Schmoe
_____
NOTARY/DEPUTY CLERK
```

The first pleading to start a case has to be served in a special way, as previously discussed. However, all subsequent pleadings may be served by regular mail or hand delivery. You only need to attach a *certificate of service* to the pleading, stating that you have caused a copy to be mailed or hand-delivered to the other side. The following is an example of a certificate of service.

```
                CERTIFICATE OF SERVICE
I HEREBY CERTIFY, that on this  16th  day of  JUNE ,
2007, I mailed a copy of the foregoing by first-
class mail, postage prepaid, to the defendant.
                                        John Doe
                                        John Doe
```

COMPLAINT

A lawsuit starts with a *Complaint*. Sometimes this is called a *petition* or a *motion*, depending on the state or the type of case. A Complaint will contain certain statements, called allegations, to the court. For example, in a divorce complaint, first you state the jurisdiction of the court; then, facts about the parties, the marriage, and the children; and, finally, the grounds for divorce. The Complaint will set forth the facts that entitle you to the relief you are asking for.

The court may require attachments to the complaint, such as an information cover sheet, affidavit, financial statement, or a child support guidelines worksheet.

The Complaint is sometimes accompanied by an *information form* for the clerk, which provides names and addresses of the parties, the type of case, the issues that are being disputed, and the estimated time required for a hearing or trial.

For a Complaint seeking custody or visitation, you are required, by the *Uniform Child Custody Jurisdiction Act* (UCCJA), to give certain information to the court about the children by affidavit. (see Chapter 8.) This includes where the children have lived for the past few years and whether there are any other cases filed that might affect custody or visitation in this case. Your jurisdiction may require a separate affidavit for this, or it may require that the information be included in the Complaint itself.

If child support or other financial issues are in dispute, you will usually have to attach a *Financial Statement* on the court's form, listing assets, liabilities, income, and expenses for you and your children. You will also have to file a *Child Support Guidelines Worksheet* on the court's forms, indicating your income, the other parent's income, certain expenses, and proposed child support payments. For an uncontested case, you may attach a copy of the *Settlement Agreement* to the Complaint.

ANSWER

Once served with a Complaint, the defendant is required to file some kind of responsive pleading within a certain time period set by the rules. The usual response is an *Answer*, but it may also be some other pleading, such as a *Motion to Dismiss the Complaint*, raising a legal issue that must be decided before an Answer is due.

The answer must address the allegations of the Complaint by admitting or denying each one made or by admitting in part and denying in part the allegations made by your spouse. It is also permissible to neither admit nor deny because you lack sufficient knowledge or information.

If you are the one served with a Complaint, the following is an example of how you could answer, demonstrating the various ways to respond to allegations.

SUPERIOR COURT OF _____GREEN_____ COUNTY
FAMILY COURT

JANE DOE
Plaintiff   )
)
   v.   ) Civil Action No. 07-0001234
)
JOHN DOE   )
Defendant   )

ANSWER

Comes now the Defendant, and for his Answer to the Plaintiff's Complaint, states as follows:

1. Defendant admits the allegations of paragraphs 1-7 of the Complaint.

2. Defendant denies the allegations of paragraphs 8-12 of the Complaint.

3. Defendant does not have sufficient knowledge or information to admit or deny the allegations of paragraph 13 of the Complaint.

4. Defendant admits the allegation of paragraph 14 of the Complaint that the children are currently residing with the mother, and denies the rest of the allegations therein.

5. Defendant denies any and all allegations of the Complaint not specifically admitted.

Respectfully submitted,

John Doe
_____
John Doe
Plaintiff pro se
123 Easy Street
Anytown, MD 55555
(777)333-8888

Put the caption of your case at the top, sign the Answer, and attach a certificate of service. The Answer may also be accompanied by an Information Cover Sheet, as well as a Financial Statement and Child Support Guidelines Worksheet, if there are financial issues in dispute.

The defendant may file a *Counterclaim* with the Answer, and must do so if the counterclaim arises from the same facts and circumstances as the Complaint. For example, if you file a Complaint for divorce against your spouse, she may Counterclaim for divorce against you. Then you have to file an Answer to the Counterclaim.

If the defendant fails to file an Answer or other pleading within the required time (twenty to thirty days in most states), or after the time passes that is set forth in the judge's order for alternative service, you may seek entry of a default order in your favor. You will still have to put on your evidence at an *ex parte* hearing (meaning one-sided), but since the defendant will not be there, the judge will probably give you everything you ask for (within reason).

PRETRIAL PROCEEDINGS

Once the case is at issue, the court will usually send you a notice of a *scheduling conference*, at which the judge will set various dates for your trial. The court will not hear arguments about your case at this conference, but it is important to know what you are doing. For example, the court can set a hearing for temporary visitation to your children and temporary child support. The court can appoint a *mediator*, a lawyer for the children, and a custody evaluator. However, if you do not ask for these services at the initial conference, you may have waived them. The scheduling conference will result in a *scheduling order*, with the deadlines for various actions in your case.

If custody is disputed in a divorce, the court may divide the case into two trials at the scheduling conference and give you two schedules. The first trial will be the *custody trial*. It will determine all issues related to the children, such as custody, visitation, and support. The other trial, called the *merits trial*, will determine everything else, including the remaining financial issues, such as alimony, property division, and grounds for divorce.

Some family law courts will order co-parenting classes in contested custody cases. These are usually given by therapists or social workers. The court can order custody mediation. Custody mediators are usually mental health professionals, and they have a high rate of success in settling custody cases.

The court may also require you to participate in *alternative dispute resolution* (ADR) on the other issues in your case. Facilitators are experienced family lawyers who will attempt to help you settle the financial issues in your case, such as child support. (See Chapter 9 for more information on ADR.)

If you need temporary custody or access to the children, you will need to ask the judge for a *pendente lite hearing*. The lawyers and judge may refer to this as a *P.L. hearing*. Be sure to tell the judge the temporary relief you need, such as access to your children or a time-sharing schedule. At the end of the scheduling conference, read the scheduling order before you leave the courtroom to make sure that everything you asked for is listed.

The *pretrial conference* is where the judge makes sure that everyone is ready for trial and sets the trial date. The parties may be required to present pretrial statements that inform the court about such matters as mediation, discovery, pending motions, disputes, agreements, trial exhibits, and trial witnesses. The judge will also usually ask about the possibility of settlement.

In most jurisdictions, the court clerk controls the calendar. You and your opponent will receive a notice of your hearing or trial date in the mail from the clerk. In others, the parties themselves set up the hearing dates by calling the court clerk or the judge's secretary. If you are in a jurisdiction where the parties set the date, you are required to file a notice of hearing with the date you wish to set and serve a copy on the other side, as well as on other interested parties, such as the guardian ad litem (if one has been appointed). Your lawyer will handle these notices, and will discuss with you the preliminary hearings and conferences. Make sure you ask him or her what you need to be doing for each of these steps.

HOW LONG DOES IT TAKE?

It takes about a year or more to litigate a case to completion. Add another six months if there is an appeal. A sample trial timeline is displayed on page 146.

HOW MUCH DOES IT COST?

It costs a lot to try a case. That is one of the reasons most cases settle somewhere along the trial timeline. Assuming your lawyer charges $200 an hour for his or her time, the sample trial budget provided below shows you an estimate of the cost for a contested custody case. (Your mileage may vary.)

Legal Services	Hours	Fees
($200/hour)		
Initial Office Conference with Client	1	$200
Prepare Complaint & Related Documents	5	$1,000
Information Cover Sheet Child Support Guidelines		
Scheduling Conference	1	$200
Facilitation	2	$400

Discovery
    Expert Witness Statements
    Interrogatories
    Request for Documents
    Request for Admissions
	15	$3,000

Respond to Other Side's Discovery
    Interrogatories
    Request for Documents
    Request for Admissions
	5	$3,000

Telephone Conferences & Letters	10	$2,000
Prepare for and Appear at Hearing on Temporary Support	15	$3,000
Conferences with Witnesses and Expert	20	$4,000
Prepare for and take Depositions	40	$8,000
Legal Research	20	$4,000
Prepare Pretrial Statement	3	$600
Pretrial Settlement Conference	3	$600
Trial Preparation	60	$12,000
Trial (two days @10 hours/day)	20	$4,000
Total:	230	$46,000

In addition to legal fees, you will have to pay costs as follows:

Filing Fee	$100
Process Server	$35
Expert Witness	$5,000
Deposition Transcripts	$2,500
Copies, Faxes, Postage, Courier, Etc.	$500
Total:	$8,135

Date	Event
January 1, 2007	Plaintiff's Motion for Temporary Protective Order
January 10, 2007	Defendant's Opposition to Motion
January 11, 2007	Hearing on Motion and Order
February 11, 2007	Plaintiff's Complaint for Divorce
February 28, 2007	Affidavit of Plaintiff's Process Server
March 28, 2007	Defendant's Answer
April 18, 2007	Scheduling Conference and Scheduling Order
April 18, 2007	ADR Facilitation
May 15, 2007	Custody Mediation
May 18 & 25, 2007	Parenting Classes
May 30, 2007	Temporary Support Hearing and Order
June 30, 2007	Plaintiff's Discovery
July 15, 2007	Defendant's Discovery
July 31, 2007	Plaintiff's Responses to Discovery
August 15, 2007	Defendant's Responses to Discovery
September 15, 2007	Defendant's Deposition
September 15, 2007	Plaintiff's Deposition
September 30, 2007	Witness Depositions
October 1, 2007	Plaintiff's Motion to Compel Discovery
October 18, 2007	Defendant's Opposition
October 19, 2007	Defendant's Motion to Compel Discovery
November 10, 2007	Plaintiff's Opposition
November 30, 2007	Hearing on Discovery Motions and Order
December 1, 2007	Pretrial Conference
December 31, 2007	Trial and Order
January 5, 2008	Plaintiff's Exceptions
February 5, 2008	Hearing on Exceptions and Order
February 27, 2008	Plaintiff's Notice of Appeal
March 25, 2008	Plaintiff's Brief
April 24, 2008	Defendant's Brief
May 5, 2008	Plaintiff's Reply Brief
May 30, 2008	Hearing on Appeal
July 1, 2008	Order

–11–

DISCOVERY
AND
PRETRIAL PROCEDURES

Victory at trial goes not to the most glib, the most aggressive, or the most persuasive, despite what you have seen on television. Victory goes to the most prepared. This chapter tells you about *discovery* and other ways to prepare for trial. Discovery is phase two of a lawsuit. This chapter discusses discovery procedures and the various means you and your attorney have available to find information about the other side's case so you can settle or get ready for trial.

You may discover any matter relevant to the Complaint, defense, or Counterclaim in your case. That includes the existence, description, nature, custody, condition, and location of any books, documents, or other things. It also includes the identity and location of persons having knowledge of any matter related to your case. You can even discover something that would not be admissible at trial, as long as it is relevant to your case.

Discuss options with your attorney to see what you can and should be doing to help your case. The formal discovery methods discussed in this chapter will be prepared by your attorney, but the actual gathering of the information will fall on your shoulders. Reviewing the questions and materials that the other side will be seeking, as well as what you will be looking for, will help you set your case in order.

Once you gather your discovery, you will want to review it, organize it, and use it to assist you in your pretrial and trial preparations. In addition to what you receive in discovery, there are other pretrial matters that you may want to do or the court may require you to do.

INVESTIGATION

The court discovery rules provide abundant opportunities to obtain information ahead of the trial. However, there is a lot of information you can collect through your own research and investigation even before you begin using the court's discovery rules.

You may wish to hire a *private investigator* if you want to try to prove something like adultery or hidden assets. Private investigators advertise in the telephone directory and on the Internet. They charge by the hour, usually around $150, and depending on what you want done, fees may run from five hundred to a few thousand dollars.

You can do a reasonable amount of investigation about a case on your own. After all, nobody knows as much about the case as you do. You had a relationship with the mother of your children, so you know a certain amount about the case already.

It is fairly easy to research the judge in your case, the other side's attorney or expert, and the guardian ad litem on the Internet. Just put their names in one of the search engines. (The most popular one is **www.google.com**.)

Your attorney will interview the potential witnesses. Your list of witnesses may include teachers, coaches, neighbors, relatives, nannies, housekeepers, doctors, social workers, and others. You will also want to interview any witnesses identified by the other side, including any experts.

Gather as many documents as you can. If financial issues are in dispute, you will want pay stubs, tax returns, deeds, mortgages, leases, pension plan documents, and the like. If your opponent leaves these in plain sight, they are fair game. The same holds true for a shared or family computer.

It helps to read as much as you can about cases similar to yours.

That will show you what is important as far as the court and the law are concerned. The cases will also discuss and probably recite applicable statutes and rules that may govern in your case. The easiest place to start researching is the Internet.

You can also use *informal discovery* to obtain information about the case. This means you just exchange information with the other side without regard to the rather complex court rules for discovery. If you have cooperation from the other side, informal discovery is not a bad way to start. However, if you rely solely on informal discovery, you take the chance that not all information will be produced. Remember, litigation is an adversarial process.

Discovery is the process by which each side learns about the other side's case before trial. The purpose is to avoid trial by surprise and to encourage settlement. The court's discovery rules provide for written *Interrogatories*, *Requests to Produce Documents*, *Requests for Admissions*, and *Depositions*. Although not required, it is usually a good idea to send discovery requests as early as possible. If your court rules permit, consider sending them with the Complaint.

INTERROGATORIES

Interrogatories are written questions that must be answered in writing under oath. Interrogatories should be sent to the other side, and usually the sooner the better. They could be included with the Complaint, or with the Answer if you are the defendant. In a custody case, the children's mother will be asked questions like why she does not want joint custody and what her plans are if she is awarded custody. When child support is an issue, questions about employment or efforts to find employment are appropriate. Other information that is important to your case and should be asked include what evidence she intends to use at trial and what expert witnesses she plans to call. Since the number of interrogatories is usually limited, questions should not be wasted on information you already know, like her name and address.

If you receive interrogatories, you only have a short time to answer, so it is best to attack them quickly. They will usually be accompanied by a request for documents, so you will have a lot to do in a short amount of time. You can expect to be asked how many parent/teacher conferences, medical appointments, and soccer games you have attended. Of course, you also will be asked about money—how much you make, how much you spend, and how much you save. You can object to interrogatories if you have a good reason for doing so, but this will lead to suspicion and extra costs, so it is usually easier just to answer them.

Most court rules limit the number of interrogatories you can ask, and require the answers be preceded by the questions. If the other side asks more than the limit, you can just answer the ones up to that number and object to the rest. You can ask the other side for a disk or email with the questions to save typing time. Usually, you mail signed interrogatories or answers to the other side with a certificate of service attached. You do not file them with the court, but instead file a statement with the court that you have sent or answered interrogatories on a certain date. (Sample Interrogatories are included on page 151.)

IN THE CIRCUIT COURT FOR GREEN COUNTY

JOHN DOE   )
Plaintiff   )
vs.   )   Family Law 1234
JANE DOE   )
Defendant   )

FIRST SET OF INTERROGATORIES

TO: JANE DOE, Defendant
FROM: JOHN DOE, Plaintiff

The following Interrogatories are propounded pursuant to the Rules of Procedure, Rule 2-401. These Interrogatories are <u>not</u> filed with any Court, but copies are served on all other parties. A <u>Notice</u> is being filed with the Court pursuant to Rule 2-401(c)(2). The original of these Interrogatories is in the file of the party generating them and is available for inspection by any other party. These Interrogatories must be answered, setting forth the Interrogatory and the Answer thereto, in full, under oath, or the grounds for refusal must be stated in full.

INSTRUCTIONS

a.   Your Answers are due within thirty (30) days after service of these Interrogatories or within fifteen (15) days after the date your initial pleading or Motion is required, whichever is later.

b.   These Interrogatories are continuing in character, so as to require you to file supplementary answers if you obtain further or different information before trial.

c.   Where the name or identity of a person is requested, please state full name, home address, and also business address, if known.

d.   Unless otherwise indicated, these Interrogatories refer to the time, place, and circumstances of the occurrence mentioned or complained of in the pleadings.

e.   Where knowledge or information in possession of the party is requested, such request includes knowledge of the party's agents, representatives and, unless privileged, his attorneys. When an answer is made by a corporate Plaintiff, state the name, address, and title of the person supplying the information and making the Affidavit, and the source of his information.

f.   The pronoun "you" refers to the party to whom these Interrogatories are addressed and the persons mentioned in clause (d).

INTERROGATORIES

1.   If you are presently employed, state your workdays and hours and whether you are required to put in overtime.

2.   State in detail what you consider to be the best custodial arrangements for your children and why.

3.   Have the children expressed a preference to live with you? If so, state:

    a. Each date such preferences were expressed.

    b. The circumstances giving rise to each expression.

    c. The words used by each child in expressing such preference.

4.   State the address at which you and the children would reside if you were granted sole or joint physical custody and describe with specificity the children's proposed living quarters.

5.   Would you be able to devote yourself full-time to the children's care and upbringing if you were granted custody? If not, state:

    a. The proportion of each day you intend to spend with the children.

    b. How you intend to provide for the children's care when you are unavailable (name each person and/or institution that will be hired for this purpose).

    c. Why you are unable to devote yourself full-time to the children's care.

6.   If you are not granted sole physical custody, state with specificity the visitation time that would be appropriate.

7.   If you are granted sole physical custody, state with specificity the visitation time that would be appropriate.

8.   State whether you and your spouse have any major disagreements concerning the children's education, religious upbringing, discipline, health care needs, and/or extracurricular activities, and if so, detail the nature of each disagreement and each party's position as you perceive it.

9.   List the name, address, telephone number, and dates of contact for each mental health professional or social worker who has been involved with the children or either parent during the last five years.

10. List the name, address, telephone number, and dates of contact for each physician to whom you have personally taken the children for evaluation or treatment during the last five years.

11. List the name, address, and telephone number of each person who has knowledge or relevant facts concerning the issues of custody and visitation in this case, and for each, state the nature of the knowledge.

12. List the dates since your separation from your spouse when the children have physically resided with you,

and for each period of time, state whether any other person or institution has cared for the children and, if so, provide their names, addresses, and telephone numbers, the circumstances warranting this care, and the dates and times during which this care was provided.

13. Is there anything about the plaintiff that renders him unfit to have sole physical custody of the children? If so, describe with specificity this unfitness.

14. Describe your current state of health and provide the name, address, and telephone number of each physician, medical clinic, or nurse practitioner you have consulted during the past eighteen months. State the date of each consultation, its purpose, the diagnosis, and the treatment.

15. List any current medications you are taking, the dates from which you have taken them, and their purposes.

16. Describe your plans for the children's educational development and how you intend to implement these plans.

17. Describe your plans for the children's religious education and development and how you intend to implement these plans.

18. Describe your plans for the children's extracurricular activities and how you intend to implement these plans.

19. Describe with specificity why you would be a better custodian than your spouse.

20. State with specificity your greatest strengths and weaknesses as a parent.

21. State with specificity your spouse's greatest strengths and weaknesses as a parent.

22. Describe how you discipline your children.

23. State any difficulties your children are having and how you are equipped to deal with these difficulties.

24. Do you have plans for remarriage? If so, describe with specificity the relationship between the children and the future stepparent.

25. Do you have plans to relocate? If so, describe your relocation plans.

26. Do you object to your children being removed from the immediate geographical area? If so, state your objections.

27. State the names, addresses, and telephone numbers of all experts whom you propose to call as witnesses in this proceeding; specify the field of expertise, the subject matter on which the expert is expected to testify, the substance of the facts and opinions upon which the expert is expected to testify and a summary of the grounds for each opinion.

28. If you propose to rely on documentary evidence, set forth the nature and contents of each document, together with the names, addresses, and telephone numbers of the custodian(s) thereof.

Respectfully submitted,

John Q. Attorney
_____
John Q. Attorney
Attorney & Attorney
Attorney for Plaintiff
123 Easy Street
Anytown, MD 55555
777-333-8888

CERTIFICATE OF MAILING

I HEREBY CERTIFY that on this __10__ day of ___August___, 200_7_, a copy of the foregoing Plaintiff's First Set of Interrogatories was mailed to Joseph A. Lawyer, Esquire, Attorney for Defendant, 456 Noname Avenue, Anytown, MD 55555.

John Q. Attorney
_____
John Q. Attorney

NOTE: *These Interrogatories are a slight modification of those recommended by the Family Law Section of the American Bar Association.*

REQUESTS FOR DOCUMENTS

You can ask that your children's mother produce, for your inspection and copying, documents related to the issues in your case. Likewise, she can make the same request of you. Usually, each side will ask the other to produce emails, letters, telephone records, canceled checks, bank statements, and credit card statements.

You can object if a request is unduly burdensome, but full disclosure is usually the best policy. The best procedure is to make a copy of everything and deliver it to the other side. If you have a lawyer, make a copy for your lawyer, and let him or her review your documents first. You can organize and number the documents according to the request, or you can produce them in the same order that you keep them in your own records. After your document production, you may receive a letter from opposing counsel saying that your disclosure is inadequate or deficient in some respect. If this happens, answer it as best you can, and always end your response with *Please let me know if there is anything else I can provide.* This will stand you in good stead if the other lawyer tries to claim that you are not cooperating.

A signed response is due a short time after the requests are served. A response is not the same as producing the documents themselves. They are usually delivered at the same time, but there is no requirement to do so. The response and documents go to the other side—not the court—and a *Notice of Discovery* is filed with the court. Again, time is short, and nobody likes to take time to gather and copy old documents. Act fast when you receive a request to avoid complications and increased legal fees. There is usually no limit on the number of requests. A sample *Request for Production of Documents* is on page 156.

IN THE CIRCUIT COURT FOR GREEN COUNTY

JOHN DOE   )
Plaintiff   )
vs.   )   Family Law NO. 9930
JANE DOE   )
Defendant   )

REQUEST FOR PRODUCTION OF DOCUMENTS

Plaintiff, John Doe, by his attorneys, pursuant to the Rules of Procedure 2-422, requests that the Defendant, Jane Doe, produce and permit the Plaintiff to inspect, copy, and photograph all documents and things in the Defendant's possession, custody, or control which embody, refer to, or relate to in any way the following subject, other than written materials prepared in anticipation of litigation or for trial.

As used herein, documents and things shall include all types of recorded information, including but not limited to writings, drawings, graphs, charts, photographs, phonorecords, computer disks, and other data compilations from which information can be obtained, translated, if necessary, through dictation devices into reasonably usable form.

1. Your federal and state income tax returns for the last five years, W-2 forms, 1099s, and all other documents showing savings, income, or other funds received by you for the past five (5) years. The word "funds" is all inclusive, including but not limited to, earnings, income, gifts, nontaxable earnings, and every form of deferred compensation.

2. All documents related to savings, investments, pension funds, retirement funds, profit-sharing arrangements, retirement agreements, and deferred compensation of any kind, in which you have or have had an indirect or direct interest for the past five years.

3. All records and documents related to savings, checking, credit union, and any other accounts, including all business accounts, whether presently open or closed, in which you have or have had a direct or indirect interest and/or on which you have been a signatory for the past five years, including signatory cards, deposit slips, passbooks, ledgers, check stubs, canceled checks, and monthly and periodic statements.

4. All signatory cards, deposit slips, passbooks, ledgers, check stubs, canceled checks, monthly and periodic statements and any other documents related to any checking, savings, investment, credit union, and other accounts opened by you jointly or separately, for the benefit of another, whether said accounts are now open or closed, for the past five years.

5. All records, minutes, resolutions, seals, stock certificates, contracts or other indicia of ownership or interest in any trust, corporation, partnership, joint venture, or any other business venture in which you have or have had a direct or indirect interest since the beginning of your current marriage.

6. All deeds, deeds of trust, mortgages, deed of trust notes, purchase contracts, settlement sheets, leases, tax assessments and bills, checks related to purchase, rental and mortgage payments, checks and receipts related to all repairs, furnishings, decorating, all communications with tenants, and any other documents related to purchase, ownership and leasing, for any and all real property in which you have, or have had, any legal or equitable interest, whether direct or indirect, for the past five years.

7. All certificates and documents related to stocks, bonds, mutual funds, or any like asset in which you have, or have had, any interest, direct or indirect, for the past five years.

8. All instruments, documents or records illustrating indicia of ownership or any other interest of yours in any other item of property, real or personal, not heretofore mentioned.

9. All instruments, documents or records evidencing purchase, sale, or other disposition, of any item of property, real, personal, or mixed, valued in excess of $200, in which you have or have had an interest for the past five years.

10. All receipts and billings for credit cards that you have used, illustrating each particular charge, and monthly statements, for the past five years.

11. All documents related to any current debts that are yours personally or joint debts.

12. All statements, not privileged, prepared by you involving any matter that might relate to the facts of this case.

13. All written reports made by an expert hired by you, or any agent for you, whom you propose to call as a witness.

14. Any and all documents reflecting an appraised fair market value obtained by you or any agent for you with regard to any item of real or personal property in which you have or have had any interest, whether direct or indirect, said appraisal having been obtained within the past five years.

15. All financial statements, written applications, balance sheets, income statements, and other documents you, your current wife, or any business entity in which you have or have had at least a one percent (1%) interest during the

past five years, have presented to any bank, lending institution, partnership, corporation, insurance company, or other business entity for the purpose of obtaining a loan or refinancing a loan.

16. All IRS Forms 1099 that in any way relate to you in the past five years.

17. All documents sent to or received from any stockbroker in the past five years.

18. Title documents and settlement sheets for any asset and item of property in which you have or have had any interest, legal or equitable, direct or indirect, within the past five years.

19. All documents currently held, and which were at any time held, in any safe-deposit box under your control or to which you have, or have had, access within the past five years.

20. Copies of all documents relating to your and/or your current wife's ownership or tenancy interest in your current residence.

21. Copies of all documents showing monies expended by you or your current wife for hobbies in the past five years.

22. A copy of your marriage certificate for your current marriage.

23. Copies of any and all documents showing travel outside of the Washington Metropolitan Area made by you or paid by you for someone else in the past five years.

24. All documents evidencing support by you for your children from May 2, 2002, to present.

25. All documents relating to any property or asset that you claim is nonmarital property.

26. All cell telephone records for the past three years.

27. All diaries, calendars, or appointment books maintained by you for the last three years.

28. Your current financial statement on the form provided by the court.

The Plaintiff requests that the documents and things herein requested be produced at the offices of the Plaintiff's attorneys, ATTORNEY & ATTORNEY, 123 Main Street, Anytown, Maryland 55555.

John Q. Attorney
_____
John Q. Attorney
Attorney & Attorney
Attorneys for Plaintiff
123 Easy Street
Anytown, MD 55555
(777) 333-8888

CERTIFICATE OF MAILING

I HEREBY CERTIFY that on this _____4_____ day of __September__ , 200_7_ , a copy of the foregoing Plaintiff's Request for Production of Documents was mailed to Joseph A. Lawyer, Esquire, Attorney for Defendant, 456 Noname Avenue, Anytown, MD 55555.

John Q. Attorney

John Q. Attorney

REQUESTS FOR ADMISSIONS

An often overlooked discovery tool is a *Request to Admit* certain facts. You can ask your children's mother to admit statements that you make. For example, "Admit that you took the children from the marital residence and did not give me contact information for two weeks." Admissions can focus the issues sharply and save time at trial, and there is usually no limit on the number of admissions you can request.

The responding party has to admit or deny your statements within a short period of time, or they will be deemed admitted. Conversely, if you receive a Request to Admit, you will want to answer it immediately. Do not put this aside. Contact your lawyer immediately. A sample *Request for Admission of Facts and Genuineness of Documents* is found on page 160.

```
            IN THE CIRCUIT COURT FOR GREEN COUNTY
JOHN DOE                      )
Plaintiff                     )
vs.                           )          Family Law 1234
JANE DOE                      )
Defendant                     )
```

REQUEST FOR ADMISSION OF FACTS
AND GENUINENESS OF DOCUMENTS

John Doe, Plaintiff, by his attorney, pursuant to Rule 2-424 of the Green Rules of Procedure, requests the Defendant, Jane Doe, within thirty (30) days after service of this Request, to make the following admissions:

1. That the automobile in the possession of the Defendant was acquired subsequent to the marriage of the parties.

2. That the Defendant is in good health.

3. That the Defendant is employed full-time.

4. That the Plaintiff is unemployed.

5. That the Defendant owns a condominium in her name acquired during the marriage.

6. That the Defendant was not in fear of Plaintiff when she applied for a Civil Protective Order.

7. That the Defendant provoked the Plaintiff to say the words that resulted in the Civil Protective Order.

8. That the Defendant filed for a Civil Protective Order to gain an advantage in her divorce from the Plaintiff.

9. That the Defendant has committed adultery during the marriage.

10. That the Defendant called Plaintiff's prior employer and demanded his last paychecks be sent to her instead of him.

11. That the Defendant asked the car dealer to repossess the automobile in Plaintiff's possession.

12. That no grounds for divorce exist based on cruelty or excessively vicious conduct.

13. That no grounds for divorce exist based on constructive desertion.

Respectfully submitted,

John Q. Attorney
John Q. Attorney
ATTORNEY & ATTORNEY
123 Easy Street
Anytown, MD 55555
(777) 333-8888

```
CERTIFICATE OF MAILING
I HEREBY CERTIFY that on this  5  day of   October   ,
200 7 , a copy of the aforegoing Plaintiff's Request for
Admission of Facts, Etc., was mailed to Joseph A.
Lawyer, Esquire, Attorney for Defendant, 456 Noname
Avenue, Anytown, MD 55555.
                               John Q. Attorney
                               John Q. Attorney
```

STIPULATION

A *stipulation* is a statement to the court that the parties have agreed on certain facts, for example, their ages, occupations, health, income, and children. This is an underused tool that can save time and expense at trial.

DEPOSITIONS

If your case involves the use of depositions, you need an attorney. If, however, you decide to conduct a deposition without the assistance of an attorney, this section discusses some things you need to know. You can send a *Notice of Deposition* requiring your children's mother to appear and answer questions under oath. At a deposition, a reporter will be present to prepare a transcript for use in court. It is common courtesy to ask the lawyer on the other side for some convenient dates, even though courtesy may not always be reciprocated. It is up to you to provide the place for the deposition and to order the reporter. Reporters advertise in the telephone directory and charge by the page. A one-hour deposition will cost between $100 and $200.

Do not let a lawyer on the other side intimidate you. If he or she asks for the *usual stipulations*, ask what he or she means. There are no usual stipulations.

Some lawyers will go through a lot of preliminary questions at the beginning of a deposition. They ask, "Are you comfortable? Did you receive the subpoena? Do you understand why you are here today? Do you have any questions? Do you want to take a break?"

You, on the other hand, should not do any of this. Get right to business and start asking the real questions about your case.

Use the pleadings and written discovery responses for your outline of questions to ask. For example, you could pull the following question from the Complaint: "What did you mean when you said in your Complaint that I am an unfit father?"

To further develop the answers given to your questions, ask open-ended questions, like "What happened next?" or "Please explain."

Control the deposition. It is your deposition, not the other lawyer's, so do not let him or her go off the record without your permission. The deposition is being recorded so you can use what is said in court. It is much harder to get things said off the record in front of the judge.

If the other lawyer makes an objection, ask the deponent to answer the question anyway. If the lawyer advises the deponent not to answer, stay calm, and keep asking questions. Don's case is an example of how to use a such a deposition at trial.

DON'S CASE

At Don's trial, his lawyer questioned his wife in the following manner.

Q: Do you remember the deposition you took in my office on January 10, 2007?

A: Yes.

Q: Here's the transcript. Read along with me here. When I asked you how much you earned, you said "I refuse to answer." Did I read that correctly?

A: Yes.

Q: And isn't it true that you refused to answer the next sixteen questions I asked you?

A: Yes.

The judge, addressing the wife's lawyer, asked why she didn't answer the questions.

> **Wife's lawyer: We objected to her deposition being taken before the husband's deposition, so I advised my client to refuse to answer any questions about her income.**

> **Judge: So it was strategy?**

> **Wife's lawyer: Yes.**

The judge ordered the wife to pay $10,000 of Don's legal fees for refusing to answer questions at the deposition.

When you are the party being deposed, prepare before you give your deposition. Read the pleadings and your written discovery responses.

Answer each question by turning it into a declarative sentence, like this:

> Q: *Where were you on the night of January 17th?*
> A: *On the night of January 17th, I was with my friends Paul and Tom.*

This will give you time to think of an answer and will also keep you from talking too much.

The deposition is not the trial. No deponent ever *won* a deposition, so do not try.

Do not give the other side a road map. If they do not ask you the right question, then do not answer it. Your job at a deposition is to answer questions truthfully, not to explain the case to the other side. Do not guess. Do not hypothesize. Do not try to answer a question if you do not know the answer.

SUBPOENAS

You serve a witness with a *subpoena* to make sure he or she shows up for trial or deposition. A *subpoena ad testificandum* orders a witness to appear and testify at a deposition or trial. You can request a subpoena for witnesses from the court clerk. The subpoena will help the witnesses get time off work to appear in court. If the witnesses do not appear in court, and you did not subpoena them, you cannot necessarily have the case put off until you can get them to appear in court. Your case could be dismissed.

A *subpoena duces tecum* requires a witness to bring documents as well. You can send a subpoena to the defendant to bring income tax returns, pay stubs, or other records to trial. You can subpoena bank, business, telephone, or other records from third parties if you need to.

EXPERT WITNESS STATEMENT

You are usually required by the discovery rules to identify your expert witnesses to the other side. This is usually done by sending the other side a pleading called an *expert witness statement*. The statement identifies the expert by name, address, and telephone number. It provides a brief description of what the expert will testify about.

The court will usually give you a deadline for identifying expert witnesses in your *scheduling order* that is early in the case. Mark it on your calendar. If you fail to file a statement, you may not be able to use your expert at trial. If the other side has an expert and you do not, they will have a big advantage. If the other side fails to file an expert witness statement, then you can object to any expert they try to put on the witness stand at trial.

Expert witnesses may be desirable in many contested cases. For example, a vocational expert can testify about the potential earning ability of a spouse seeking child support. An appraiser may testify about the value of a house, furniture, or a business. An appropriate mental health professional may give an opinion about custody and visitation. A financial planner or accountant may testify as to financial needs.

LIMITATIONS ON DISCOVERY

You cannot discover something that is *privileged*. The law provides that certain communications, such as those between a lawyer and client or a doctor and patient, are privileged and cannot be discovered.

There are several exceptions to the rules of privilege. If a third party is present during a conversation between a lawyer and a client, such as a parent or a paramour, then the conversation is not privileged and can be discovered. If a parent puts his or her mental state at issue in a custody lawsuit, then medical records for that parent can be discovered. You can also waive privileges, as illustrated in Joe's case.

JOE'S CASE

Joe filed a petition to modify visitation to expand time with his son. His son's mother, Shirley, countered in her response that Joe had abandoned the child for six months. Joe countered that he had suffered a period of depression.

Shirley's lawyer subpoenaed all of Joe's medical records, claiming that Joe had put his mental state in question when he raised depression in his pleadings. Joe's lawyer filed a motion to prevent this.

At the hearing, the judge said she was inclined to grant the motion to stop the medical records from being discovered, and then order a mental examination of Joe. A medical examination would delay the hearing on visitation for another six months. To avoid that, Joe's lawyer and Shirley's lawyer agreed that Joe would waive his privilege on a limited basis and disclose his medical records related to his depression.

MAKING THE OTHER SIDE RESPOND

The court can grant an order compelling discovery for failing to respond to discovery or for responding inadequately. The court can also grant sanctions for disregarding its discovery orders. Usually, you have to try to work out discovery disputes with the other side before asking the court to intervene. Keep track of these attempts and cite them to the court when you file for sanctions. *Sanctions* can include striking pleadings or payment of attorney's fees. Since the other side has the same sanctions available if you fail to respond to discovery, be sure to respond when you receive interrogatories, document requests, requests for admissions, or deposition notices.

The court can also grant protective orders limiting discovery that is unduly burdensome or is being used to harass, vex, or annoy a party or other witness.

PRETRIAL PREPARATION

Before trial, there are several things you need to do to get prepared. Organizing your discovery material is one of those things. To use all the material you have gathered, you will need to prepare a trial notebook. Additionally, during the months leading up to an actual trial, the judge may require the parties to undergo certain evaluations, especially if custody or visitation are at issue. The results of these evaluations all add to the factors the judge will look to when he or she makes a decision, and should be considered by you when deciding whether to settle.

Trial Notebook

At the end of discovery, you will have generated a lot of papers. Discovery responses can be used at trial as exhibits to prove your case. How do you organize them? What do you do with them? It is time to get ready for trial.

The trial accounts for only about 10% of the time spent in a case. The other 90% is spent in more mundane trial preparations, such as investigation, discovery, and pretrial motions. The trial is important, and it is the dramatic climax of a litigated case. But trials are, more often than not, won or lost in pretrial preparation.

The best way to prepare for trial is to make a *trial notebook*. This can be a three-ring binder with tabs. Make tabs for your opening statement, each witness you are going to present, the defendant, the defendant's witnesses, and your closing argument. Also have tabs for discovery responses and any rules, statutes, or cases that might apply to your case. You can use the trial notebook at trial to guide the presentation of your case to the judge.

Start at the end—that is, what you will be trying to prove to the judge at trial. You will find most of the elements of your case, as well as the facts you have to prove, in your Complaint.

Your main evidence will probably be your own testimony, but other documents and records will be used as well. These will include:

- ◆ pictures and telephone records that can prove frequency of contact with the children (if that is an issue);
- ◆ pay stubs and tax returns that can prove income;
- ◆ email and letters that can prove statements by the other party; and,
- ◆ DNA test results that can prove paternity or nonpaternity.

Write out your opening statement, all your questions for witnesses, and your closing argument. Determine which witnesses or documents will prove or corroborate which facts.

Pretrial Preparation Tips
The following are a few tips to help you prepare for trial.

- ◆ Review your discovery responses and a transcript of your deposition. Review any documents you will refer to during your testimony. Review any statement you made.
- ◆ Make sure you know the names of your children's teachers, coaches, doctor, dentist, and best friends. It does not hurt

to know your children's shoe sizes, clothing sizes, favorite pajamas, and bedtime story, because opposing counsel may ask you.

♦ This is a good time to subscribe to publications such as *Parents* magazine. Buy some books about children, parenting, and getting children through divorce. Attend seminars and keep the brochures and literature. Volunteer to coach your child's soccer team. The point is to do these things for your child and yourself, not just to impress the judge.

♦ Everyone is afraid of things they do not understand. Visiting the court before your case may make you more comfortable about your court appearance. After you watch a few cases, you will see that no one dies or is seriously injured when testifying. You will feel better when it is your turn.

♦ Try not to discuss your case much before trial if you can help it. One of the best ways for the opposition to trip you up is to get a statement you made before trial, especially to so-called mutual friends, that does not coincide exactly with your testimony at trial.

♦ It is a good idea to call the court clerk a couple of days before court to make sure your case will be heard. Often, cases are continued by the court for one reason or another, and you do not want to waste a trip if it is avoidable.

♦ Attorneys who do not prepare for trial rely on *thinking on their feet* and are said to be *gunslingers* who *shoot from the hip*. They are able to go to trial without a lot of preparation because they have tried hundreds of cases. You have not and must be prepared.

♦ Additionally, you now have the responses to your discovery, as well as the results of any evaluations ordered by the court or conducted by agreement. This is a good time to consider the likely outcome of a trial and whether or not a settlement is possible.

–12–

TRIAL

You prove the essential facts of your case at trial. The facts must be proven by evidence, including testimony of witnesses and documents. The trial is the dramatic end and phase three of the litigation process. This chapter tells you what you can expect at trial.

BEFORE THE TRIAL

Before the trial, review your trial notebook and read your discovery responses and a transcript of your deposition. Review any documents you will refer to during your testimony. Review any statement you made.

All testimony given and all papers filed in your case are matters of public record, and the public has a right to hear or see them—theoretically. However, the only people you are likely to see at court are other people who are getting divorced or involved in some other case that day, and they are probably far more concerned with their own problems than with your case.

BEHAVIOR AT TRIAL

Court is a formal place, and the judge will appreciate courtesy and good manners. The following are a few suggestions for appearing in court.

- Dress neatly, conservatively, and nicely for all court appearances. It is unfortunate that people judge others by the clothes they wear, but they do. If you want the judge to think you are one of the good guys, then dress like a good guy. Wear a suit and tie.

- Do not chew gum or smoke. Walk and stand erect. Do not slouch in the witness stand or slur your words. Be serious and forceful. Do not cover your mouth or avert your eyes.

- Do not use first names when you are talking about other people. It is always *Mrs. Smith* and never *Sally*. Look at the judge when you talk. Remember, you are trying to convince the judge, so talk to him or her, and not to your opposition or her lawyer. They will never believe you anyway.

- Only one person speaks at a time in court. You will have an opportunity to talk, so do not interrupt, especially if the judge is speaking. Be polite—it makes a good impression on the court. Answer *Yes sir* or *Yes madam*, and address the judge as *Your Honor*. The judge controls the courtroom, so defer to him or her. Listen when the judge asks questions. Sometimes the judge will help you, so follow his or her lead.

THE RULES

The court will conduct the trial in accordance with the *rules of procedure*. The rules of procedure are designed to give each side a chance to present their case fully and fairly.

The court uses the *rules of evidence* at trial. These rules govern the way your evidence is presented. Like the rules of chess, they are rather formal and complicated, and have been developed over the years by the legal system. The judge will know that you are not a lawyer, and may give you a little help. However, if there is a lawyer on the other side objecting, the judge has to follow the rules of evidence. You will generally be able to maneuver the rules of evidence in court if you remember the following general principles.

- Evidence must be *relevant,* which means it must somehow relate to the facts in the lawsuit. Judges appreciate it when you go straight to the heart of the matter and do not take them on long detours that are not relevant to the issues in dispute.

- Only testimony based on *personal knowledge* is permitted. You cannot testify about what someone else told you, because that is a statement made out of court, which is *hearsay* and not admissible in court. An important exception to this rule is that you can testify about what your spouse said.

THE TRIAL

When the trial begins, the clerk calls the name of the case. The judge asks if everyone is ready for trial, and the parties introduce themselves. Any preliminary matters are handled, then the parties present witnesses, testimony, and documents (called *exhibits*).

If there are any *preliminary matters* to resolve, such as any unresolved motions and the handling of witnesses, they are first addressed by the court. The *rule on witnesses*, which you usually must ask for to get, requires all witnesses except the parties to leave the courtroom until they are called. That is so they cannot listen to the testimony and be tempted to change what they are going to say.

The judge will then ask for *opening statements*. The plaintiff goes first and the defendant follows. Use the opening statement to give the judge a summary of your case. Tell him or her the important issues and what evidence you will present. The following is an example of what you might say in your opening statement.

> *Good morning, Your Honor. May it please the court, the evidence will show that I have been married to the defendant for five years and we have been separated for one year. We have one child together, Jake, and right now he lives with his mother primarily. I have four witnesses, including myself and the defendant, to prove that I should have joint legal and physical custody.*

The plaintiff presents his or her case first, questions witnesses, and presents documents (*direct examination*). The defendant can ask questions of the plaintiff's witnesses (*cross-examination*). Next, the defendant presents his or her case and the plaintiff cross-examines. Both parties make *closing arguments* to summarize the testimony and argue the result they want the judge to give them. At the conclusion of the trial, the judge will usually give a decision as to custody, visitation, child support, and legal fees, together with any other issues in dispute before the court.

PLAINTIFF'S CASE

After both sides give their opening statements, the plaintiff calls the first witness, usually him- or herself. If you are the plaintiff, you will take the stand and be sworn in by the court clerk. If you do not have an attorney, the judge may ask you questions or allow you to speak in a narrative to tell your story. Tell it in a direct, simple, and forceful fashion. Your objective is to tell the judge why you are the best parent to have custody of the child. If you know from discovery or from your history together that the defendant will bring up negative issues about you, then you can steal some of her thunder by anticipating and explaining those circumstances in your direct testimony. Your testimony will generally include:

- facts about you—your name, age, address, how long you have lived at that address, and occupation;
- if married, facts about the marriage—the date and place of your marriage and a present copy of your marriage certificate;
- facts about your children—their names and birth dates, and which parent the children are residing with;
- the reasons for your lawsuit;
- the facts about your finances—your financial statement, your opinions, and evidence of values of property; and,

◆ what you want—in the way of custody, visitation, child support, legal fees, and any other relief you are asking the court to grant.

The defendant or his or her attorney will then cross-examine you. He or she can ask you questions about your testimony and try to undermine it. Listen to the question and keep your answers short.

You can then ask the master or judge for permission to explain any answer you gave on cross-examination. This is called *redirect examination*.

Witnesses

When you must prove something in court, you need witnesses. Your witnesses are to support and corroborate your testimony. In the trial, you will present and conduct direct examination of your witnesses, including expert witnesses. The other side will cross-examine your witnesses. Then you may conduct redirect examination.

If you do not have an attorney, you will need to question the witness to get his or her testimony before the court. Ask the witness to identify him- or herself. Then, ask questions about what the witness knows and how he or she knows it.

In selecting a witness, choose an adult who can testify to all the essential facts from his or her own personal knowledge. Pick a person who will take the matter seriously, listen carefully to you before the hearing and at the hearing, appear on time, and testify truthfully.

Be sure to discuss the questions and answers with the witnesses before the trial so there are no surprises at trial. If a witness does not know the answer to one of your questions, or remembers events differently than you, then it is better to find out before the trial and find another witness.

Expert witnesses, unlike *fact witnesses*, can give their opinions on matters for which they are qualified. They have to be approved by the court as an expert witness first. You get this approval by asking questions at trial about such matters as the expert's education, experience, other training, associations, and publications.

Next, you move to have the witness qualified as an expert in the area in question. The other side may challenge your expert, and the judge will make a decision on whether to qualify the expert.

Once the expert is qualified by the judge, you ask the following questions to lay the *foundation* for his or her opinion.

- What steps do you normally take to form an opinion on this subject?
- Were those steps taken in this case?
- What documents did you review?
- What tests or interviews were given?
- What literature did you rely on?

After you have laid the foundation, you can ask the expert the big questions.

- Have you formed an opinion about who should have custody of the children in this case?
- What is that opinion?

If there are financial disputes, you need to prove income. You can prove this by calling the other side as a witness. Have her pay stub, financial statement, and tax return marked as exhibits. Ask her to identify them. Move them into evidence.

Documents

Documents, like letters, reports, and appraisals, require special treatment at trial. They may be objected to by the other side if there is not a live witness at court to authenticate them. You will want to have certain documents with you at the trial, depending on which type of case you are trying. In a custody trial, for example, you might introduce the following documents:

- stipulations, if any have been agreed upon;
- any prior orders for custody, visitation, and child support;
- a copy of your *Separation Agreement* or *Parenting Plan*, if applicable;
- a financial statement;
- child support guidelines;
- a map showing distance from the two homes of schools, work, child care, relatives, and extracurricular activities; and,
- a calendar showing time spent and proposed to be spent with each child.

If you are handy with a computer, many courts are now equipped with projectors and will permit PowerPoint presentations when you make arrangements in advance with the clerk.

It is a good idea to *lay a foundation* for documents. Then documents must be *identified* and *authenticated* by a witness, and moved into evidence. This is the proper way to handle a document that illustrates these points.

Q: Your salary is $40,000 a year, isn't it?

Defendant: Yes.

Q: And you brought a copy of your pay stub to trial under my subpoena, didn't you?

Defendant: Yes.

Hand pay stub to the clerk to mark it as an exhibit (e.g., Plaintiff's Exhibit Number 1). Then, show pay stub to the other side.

Q: I show you Plaintiff's Exhibit Number 1. Can you identify it?

Defendant: Yes.

Q: What is it?

Defendant: My pay stub.

Q: Is this your current pay stub?

Defendant: Yes.

Q: Your Honor, I move the admission of Plaintiff's Exhibit Number 1 into evidence.

Judge: Any objections?

Defendant: No.

Judge: It will be admitted.

It is easy to forget a step, especially asking the judge to move it into evidence, but the judge cannot base his or her decision on an exhibit you fail to move into evidence.

Children

In custody litigation, you must be able to show the judge that the child is better off with you. Photographs of you and your child having a good time doing things together is useful evidence.

Judges do not like to have children in the courtroom. It is also a terrible burden to place on children. They think that they must choose between mom and dad. The children will usually blame themselves for the outcome, whatever it may be. A recent study found that most children would prefer joint custody, if given the choice.

Usually, the children's wishes are expressed to the judge through the guardian ad litem, the evaluator, or the parties themselves. If you absolutely must have a child testify at trial, the judge will usually do it privately, *in camera*, which means in chambers or the judge's office. This is done without the parties present. You should request that a transcript be made of the judge's interview in case you need it for appeal purposes.

When you have finished presenting all of your testimony, witnesses, and documents, you should end your case formally like this: *Your Honor, that submits the plaintiff's case.*

DEFENDANT'S CASE

Next, the defendant will present her case, and you will have the opportunity to cross-examine the defendant and the defendant's witnesses. One of the best ways to do this is to use the witness's deposition. (This is one of the reasons it is so important to prepare for trial ahead of time.)

Take the witness through those (premarked and indexed) parts of the deposition that support your side of the case. In that way, cross-examination is not really examination at all. Done well, it is another chance for you to tell the judge your side of the story. You want to highlight any testimony that portrays you in a good light or helps your case. Remember, though—the witness is usually hostile to you and will take any chance you give him or her to hurt your case. There are times when it is better not to ask a question on cross-examination and not cross-examine certain witnesses at all.

Catching the other side in an inconsistency is called *impeachment of credibility*. It undermines the testimony of that witness and minimizes the effect of any testimony that is adverse to you. In your closing argument, you can remind the judge that if this witness would speak out of both sides of his or her mouth about one thing, he or she cannot be trusted to tell the truth about anything. Of course, it works both ways, so be sure to explain any inconsistencies in your own testimony.

If, for example, the mother of your children said at deposition that she never went to the children's soccer games, but testifies differently at trial, you cross-examine like the following example.

Q: *Mrs. Jones, do you remember the deposition you gave on January 10, 2007?*

A: *Yes.*

Q: *And you swore to tell the truth at that deposition, didn't you?*

A: *Yes.*

> *Q: This is the transcript of that deposition. At page 10, line 12, it says, "Question: Did you ever go to the children's soccer games? Answer: No." Did I read that correctly?*

By asking the question in this fashion, you are in control of the testimony and the witness. She does not have much chance to alter or explain her answer.

Experts

If the other side has an expert, you will want to obtain any written reports the expert prepared through document requests before trial. Show these to your own expert, who can tell you the weak points of the other expert's report. You will also want to depose your opponent's expert before trial. Your expert can help you prepare for this deposition, as well as cross-examination questions for trial.

In some cases, you may wish to hire an expert as a consultant and not as a witness. For example, you might hire an expert in custody evaluations to give you advice on how best to deal with the court evaluator and guardian ad litem, and to obtain custody in your case.

Rebuttal

At the close of the defendant's case, the judge will usually give you an opportunity for *rebuttal*. This is an opportunity for you to present new witnesses to rebut anything the defendant's witnesses said. You can also recall witnesses, including your expert witness, for rebuttal.

CLOSING

After both sides finish presenting their cases, they make a *closing argument* to the judge summarizing the evidence in their favor. The plaintiff goes first, the defendant follows, and then the plaintiff can respond to the defendant's argument. If all goes as planned, your closing argument will track what you have prepared from your trial notebook.

The judge will usually announce a *decision* right away. This is called *ruling from the bench*. A written order will follow. In more complex cases, the judge may take the case *under advisement* and give a decision later. The court's decision is sometimes called an order, judgment, or decree. You may be required to prepare a proposed order before or after the trial.

You may not like the judge's decision. The judge may not always believe everything you said, may not understand part of your case, or may just plain disagree with you. Judges are not always right, but we pay them to be the decision makers. If you disagree with the court's decision, you can ask the judge to reconsider by filing a *Motion to Alter or Amend Judgment* or a *Motion for Reconsideration*. If you are still not satisfied and believe the judge made a mistake, you can appeal his or her decision. These motions and processes are very technical with very strict and limited deadlines (only a matter of days). If you are not working with an attorney, now is the time to hire one, because once these deadlines pass, you may have no rights to change the decision.

–13–

TESTIMONY

This chapter gives you some tips for your testimony. It also contains questions that have actually been used in successful trials. Direct examination of the plaintiff is first, then cross-examination of the defendant, and finally direct examination of an expert witness. You can use these examples to be ready for the types of questions you will be asked or to prepare your own questions for depositions or trial.

YOUR TESTIMONY

The following are a few tips that will help you prepare for your own testimony.

- ◆ Stay calm and make all your remarks to the master or judge, not your spouse or your spouse's attorney, no matter how provoked you may be by the other side.

- ◆ Do not be a smart aleck or appear nervous, scared, argumentative, or angry. If your adversary baits you into becoming angry, she is probably trying to set you up for a trap, so keep your cool. Lose your temper and you may lose your case.

- ◆ Tell the truth. It is going to come out eventually anyway, and it is better coming from you than from the other side. If the other side catches you in a lie, you may lose your case.

- ◆ Listen carefully to all questions. Pause, make sure you understand the question, then take your time and answer that question. You cannot give a truthful and accurate answer if

you do not understand the question. If you ask, the attorney
will repeat the question.

♦ Do not tell the court "I think" or "it must have been." The
court does not normally care what you think or what could
have happened. It wants to know what actually happened.
However, if you estimate a time or a cost, make sure the
court knows it is an estimate. If you make a mistake during
your testimony, correct it as soon as possible. Politely say
something such as, "May I correct something I said earlier?"

♦ When the other side asks you a question that you do not
know the answer to, say, "I do not know." Witnesses are often
trapped by being led into areas about which their knowledge
is inadequate. They try to save face and end up making
statements that are incorrect. This gives the other side what
it needs to shoot them down. You can usually avoid the
problem by saying "I do not know." In cross-examinations,
most questions can be answered with yes, no, "I do not
know," or a simple sentence.

♦ Do not try to play with words. When you say, "To the best
of my recollection," people think you are getting ready to lie
to them. Do not volunteer information. Do not let the other
attorney pull you into testifying more than you need to by
standing there looking at you, waiting for you to add material.
When you are finished with your answer, stop talking.

♦ If the other side asks you if you have discussed the case with
anyone else, tell the truth—you have. The other side is not
asking you if you have fabricated the story, but it is asking
you if you have talked about it. Only a fool would go to
court without having discussed the case with his or her
witnesses. If they ask you if anyone has told you what to say,
say you were told to tell the truth.

- If the other side asks you if you are willing to swear to what you are saying, say you already did when you took the oath as a witness.

YOUR DIRECT EXAMINATION

Organize your questions under different headings. It helps the witness and the judge to mention the headings like this: *Now I'm going to ask you a little bit about the history of your marriage.* On direct examination, a lawyer cannot ask *leading* questions—questions that suggest an answer. The following are sample questions that a lawyer might ask you in a lawsuit. If you represent yourself, the judge may ask you these questions, but be prepared to give the answers in a narrative if the judge does not ask questions.

Background

- What is your name?
- What is your current address?
- How long have you lived there?
- Did you live there with the children and their mother?
- What is your age?
- Tell me a little bit about your educational background.
- What work experience have you had?
- What is the current state of your health?

Separation

- Drawing your attention to [date of separation], what happened on that date?
- How did you separate?
- Did she take the children?
- Did she tell you where they were?
- How far is her house from yours?
- Is it in the same school district?
- What has been the time-sharing arrangement since the separation?

History of the Relationship

- When did you and the defendant meet?
- Were there some good times in your relationship?
- Did you have disagreements?
- Did the disagreements ever result in you physically harming the defendant?
- Discuss each of the incidents that she claims you harmed her.
- Were you ever arrested for domestic violence?
- Was she ever arrested for domestic violence?
- Did she apply to the court for a domestic protection order?
- What happened?

The Children

- How old are your children?
- How would you describe them?
- Since their birth, what role have you played in caring for them?
- Who has been responsible for their care, for example, feeding, bathing, or taking them to school and doctor's appointments?

School

- Where do the children attend school?
- Have you been involved in dealing with the schools?
- Have you had an opportunity to meet with the teachers?
- How are the children doing in school?

Homework

- Do the children have much homework?
- How long does it take the children to do their homework?
- What is your role in seeing that the homework gets done?
- What time is allotted out of your day to helping the children with their homework on the weekdays? Weekends?

Medical

- Do the children have any health problems?
- What medical services have been required for the children?
- What role have you played in securing these services?
- Who interacts with the medical providers?
- What medications have been prescribed?
- Have you played a role in giving the medications?

Discipline

- How do you discipline the children?
- How does the defendant discipline the children?
- What methods do you think are most appropriate in disciplining the children?
- Do you think you do a better job of disciplining the children than she does?
- Why do you believe your methods are more effective than hers?

Activities

- What activities do you share with the children?
- Do you and the children get along well together?
- Do you give the children encouragement?
- Do you try to be a good role model for them?

Friends

- Do the children have friends?
- Do their friends seem important to them?
- How much time do they spend with their friends?
- Where do they live?
- Who are they?
- Do the children enjoy their friends?
- Do the children participate in extracurricular activities?

- Do you support these efforts? How?
- Does the defendant?
- What do you do to encourage friendships between the children and their peers?

Custody

- Has the defendant tried to alienate the children from you in any way?
- Has the defendant ever said anything disparaging to the children about you?
- Do you support her as a parent? How?
- What things do you think the defendant should do differently when it comes to the children?
- Are the children comfortable with you?
- Do the children enjoy spending time with you?
- Have the children expressed an interest in how much time they spend with either parent?
- Is their mother an important person in the children's lives?
- What do you think would be an appropriate amount of time for the children to spend with each parent?

Child Support

(*Getting Child Support Guidelines into evidence.*)

- I show you what has been marked as Plaintiff's Exhibit Number __, and ask you to identify it.
- Move to admit the exhibit into evidence.
- Are the gross incomes stated correctly for you and the defendant?
- What is the monthly child support indicated?

Summary
(*Asking for what you want.*)

◆ Are you asking the court to award joint legal custody?

◆ Are you asking the court to award shared physical custody on a week on/week off basis?

◆ Are you asking the court to award no child support based on the guidelines so that each party will pay the expenses of the children when they are in that party's care?

◆ Are you asking the court to deny the defendant's request for use and possession of the family home based on the fact that she now has her own home?

CROSS-EXAMINATION OF THE CHILDREN'S MOTHER

In cross-examination, all of your questions are leading. It is another chance for you to tell your story to the judge. It is almost as though you are testifying, while the witness merely punctuates your testimony with yeses and nos.

NOTE: *The father is referred to by the warm and personal term **father** or **dad**, while the mother is referred to by the cold and impersonal term **defendant**.*

The chief rule of cross-examination is *never ask a question you do not know the answer to*, because the answer may hurt your case. For some witnesses, especially those with nothing positive to add to your case, the best cross-examination is no cross-examination at all. The following are some sample questions for cross-examination of the defendant.

History of the Relationship

- You and the children's father both work full-time, do you not?
- Since you both work full-time, you have divided care of the children between you since they were born, have you not?
- Both of you have played a role in caring for the children—taking them to the doctor, feeding, bathing, baby-sitting, right?
- Even though you both were working, you both spent a lot of your spare time with the children, did you not?

Domestic Violence

- You called the police, correct?
- But they arrested you, did they not?
- And not the father, right?
- They took you to jail?
- Later, you filed for a protective order, correct?
- It was not granted, was it?

Separation

- You took the children and left on [date of separation], did you not?
- You bought a house in [month of separation] of this year?
- You did not tell the children's father that you bought a house, did you?
- You did not tell him you were leaving, did you?
- You did not tell him where the children were, did you?

The Children

- Is it not true the children have told you they want to spend equal time with their mother and father?
- Your son's friends are in his father's neighborhood, are they not?
- Is it not true that the father helps the children with their homework when they are together?

- ◆ The father has met with their teachers, correct?
- ◆ Their father has taken them to their doctors, right?
- ◆ Their father has taken them to extracurricular activities, correct?

Discipline

- ◆ You use corporal punishment to discipline the children?
- ◆ You spank your daughter?
- ◆ You spank your son?
- ◆ Does their father object to your hitting the children?

The Children and Their Father

- ◆ The children love their father, correct?
- ◆ And he loves them?
- ◆ They look forward to seeing him?
- ◆ They look up to him?
- ◆ As your son grows up, would you not agree that it is important for him to spend more time with his dad so that he can experience a male role model?

DIRECT EXAMINATION OF YOUR EXPERT WITNESS

Nonexpert witnesses are called *lay witnesses* or *fact witnesses*. They can only testify about facts and cannot give their opinions. Witnesses who qualify as experts, however, can give their opinions in the area of their expertise. What follows are sample questions to show you how to *qualify* a witness (a psychologist in this example) as an expert in custody evaluations and how to *present* expert opinion and testimony to the court.

An opposing lawyer might stipulate that your expert is qualified. You do not have to accept the stipulation. You want to ask all these questions to introduce the expert to the judge and give weight to the expert's opinion. On the other hand, you might want to stipulate to the defendant's expert to keep the expert from impressing the judge with his or her qualifications.

Terms of Engagement

- What is your name?
- What is your occupation?
- What were you hired to do in this case?
- How did you first learn of your assignment?
- What is your understanding of your assignment in this matter?
- Who paid you?

Qualifications

- Where did you obtain your undergraduate degree?
- When did you graduate?
- What is your degree?
- What other degrees do you have (Masters/PhD)?
- Are you licensed to practice psychology?
- When did you receive your license?
- Have you ever had your license suspended?
- Have you ever had your license restricted in any way?
- Have you ever been disciplined by any authorities in your field?
- What are the prerequisites to obtaining your license?
- Have you met those prerequisites?
- What, if anything, do you do to keep your professional license current and in good standing?
- What, if any, clinical training do you have in your field? Please explain what that involved.
- What experience do you have in the area of child psychology and development?
- Did you receive any special experience regarding the effects of divorce on children?

- What training do you have in the area of child custody evaluations?
- Do you read, on a regular basis, any professional journals or trade publications?
- What do you read?
- How often do you read them?
- Why do you read them?
- Have you ever authored or coauthored articles in any professional journals? Books?
- If yes, what were the names of the articles or books and when were they written?
- What professional organizations do you belong to?
- What are the entrance requirements?
- How often do these organizations meet?
- What happens at those meetings?
- Do you attend any continuing education programs in your field?
- What types of programs do you attend?
- Have you ever been a lecturer or presenter at any such continuing education programs?
- Please identify the names and dates of those presentations.
- Following your graduation, what was your first job?
- Explain what you did, for how long, and why you left. (Repeat for each job.)
- How many times in your career have you been consulted for a custody evaluation?
- How many times was your testimony required in court?

After you have asked your qualifying questions, you want to state, *Your Honor, I move to have this witness qualified as an expert in child custody evaluations.*

The Evaluation Process

- What procedure do you follow in performing a child custody evaluation?
- Did you follow that procedure in this case?
- With whom did you speak during the evaluation process?
- Explain why you met with the father and what information you learned from the interviews.
- Did you meet with the children?
- When?
- What did you do with the children?
- Did you perform any psychological tests?
- Why not?
- Did you review any documents in the course of your evaluation?
- What did you review?
- Where did those documents come from?
- How important were those documents to your ultimate conclusion?

The Opinion

- Based on the evaluation you conducted in this case, and in light of your professional experience, do you have an opinion as to which parent should have custody of the children?
- What is your opinion?
- Why did you reach that opinion?
- What weight did you give to the mother's allegations of domestic abuse?
- What role, if any, did the father's historical involvement in caring for the children—homework, medical services, school, extracurricular activities—play in your evaluation?
- What, if any, role does the gender of the child play in determining which parent should have custody?

- ◆ Do you believe that the children's best interests would be served if their father and the defendant had joint legal and physical custody as requested by their father?
- ◆ What would be the result to the children if the court grants the defendant's wishes and gives sole legal and physical custody to her?

–14–

POSTTRIAL LIFE

After the trial, life will be different. You and your children's mother will no longer be a couple. You have to adjust your view of yourself and the world as you restructure these relationships. It is not an easy transition. This chapter discusses some things to keep in mind as you set up your new life as a single father.

APPEALS

Your work does not end with the trial. First, if you are not happy with the outcome of your trial, you may appeal the result. However, this will mean more time and legal fees, and there is no guarantee that you will win. An appellate court does not retry the case or hear evidence. It looks at the record of the trial, and decides whether or not the judge made any mistakes. The appellate court may affirm the outcome of the trial, change it, or send it back to the trial judge to do all over again.

If you do want to appeal, you have to decide quickly because there is only a short time in which judgments may be appealed. There are detailed rules regarding filing appeals. You will have to file a notice with the court, pay a fee, and file a portion of the transcript and legal briefs. There will also be a hearing date set for legal argument before the appellate judges.

RECORDS

Next, make sure that you keep good records. If you pay child support directly to the mother of your children, pay by check and keep your canceled checks, so that you have evidence of payment if there is ever a question.

If you maintain a calendar, it will help the children know when they are going to be at dad's house and when they will be at mom's house. It is also a good record if there is ever a dispute about custody or visitation arrangements.

FINANCES

Complete all the financial transactions that result from the trial. Close any joint bank accounts and cancel any joint credit cards you had with the mother of your child. Transfer any household items you need to transfer. Follow up on any automobiles, stock, real estate, or retirement funds that need to be transferred. You may wish to change the beneficiaries on your life insurance, pension plans, and will at this time. If you were on your wife's health insurance plan, you will need to obtain your own health insurance now.

If your address has changed, you will want to notify the post office, the IRS, your state tax authority, and the children's schools. You will also need to have the address changed on your driver's license.

POSTTRIAL DISPUTES

While many clients think the trial resolves everything, most lawyers know that is not the case. If the mother of your children was difficult before the trial, the trial is not going to make her into a different person. She will still be difficult, you will have disputes regarding the children and you will need to resolve them somehow.

The court has the power to enforce its orders or the agreement of the parties. So the court can order a mother to allow visitation or can order a father to pay child support. However, the court will only do this if one of the parties asks it to do so by filing a petition.

The other party will then have an opportunity to respond and a hearing to present their side to the judge.

It is always better to resolve disputes yourselves if possible. If you have a settlement agreement, you can include a provision that disputes will be submitted to mediation before taking the other party back to court.

You can also include a Parenting Coordinator in an agreement. This would be someone that the parties can take their disputes to and let them make a decision. This is less costly and time consuming than litigation.

If you cannot resolve your dispute through one of these methods, then you must go back to court and ask the judge to decide. In some cases, it may be like trying your case all over again. In addition to resolving posttrial disputes, the court has the power to modify legal custody, physical custody, timesharing and child support after the trial, if circumstances change and the modification would be in the best interests of the child.

Changing Legal Custody

You can ask the court to change legal custody if you are not able to reach agreement with the mother of your children on long term parenting issues such as education, medical care or religious training.

For example, if you believe the children should be seeing a mental health therapist and their mother opposes this, you can ask the court to give you legal custody. Similarly, if the mother wants to enroll the children in private school and you believe they should be in public school, then you can seek a change in custody that will allow you to enroll them in public school.

In order to win, you must persuade the court that the children will be better off if you have sole legal custody. The court may appoint a custody evaluator or assessor to help it decide this issue, or you may hire your own expert witness to give an opinion to the court on the best custody arrangement for the child.

Changing Physical Custody

The court can change physical custody if there is a change in circumstances and it is in the best interests of the child.

An example of a change in circumstances is where the child's grades are going down dramatically in school or they are having emotional problems because of their home environment. Other examples are where the mother has withheld timesharing, or started a new relationship that exposes the child to domestic abuse, or neglected the child because of substance abuse or mental health issues.

In many jurisdictions, a noncustodial party can ask the court to change physical custody if the custodial parent intends to move away with the child. In some courts, relocation is automatically a change in circumstances, in some it is not and some let the judge decide.

You can deal with the issue of relocation ahead of time in an agreement. There are several different options. You can say that no party may relocate. You can say that relocation will require consent or a court order. You can say that either party may relocate and that will not result in a change in physical custody, or you can say that a relocating party will give the other notice and an opportunity to go to court to try to stop the move.

Relocation cases are basically custody cases. The court will focus on what is best for the child so you should too. And it will usually help the court to have the testimony of an expert on custody like a mental health professional.

Changing Time-sharing

Like custody, the court can change the time-sharing schedule when there is a change in circumstances and there is a reason to do so.

Relocation can be a reason to change the time-sharing schedule. A schedule of every other weekend may work when the parents are in the same town but not if they are hundreds of miles apart. Another reason might be a change in work schedule, or different schedules may be age appropriate.

If the parties cannot agree on a change in the time-sharing schedule, then they may petition the court to decide whether a change in the schedule will be good for the child.

Changing Child Support

Child support can always be modified by the court if circumstances change. If you need to change something because of a change in jobs, or other unforeseen events, you can agree to the change with the mother of your children. If you reach an agreement, be sure to put it in writing and have it signed by her. Do not just rely on the mother saying, "You don't have to pay child support for a year if you take the kids to Disneyland this summer." If you are amending a prior order of the court, you will want to ask the court to issue a new order.

MOVING ON

If you cannot get an agreement, then you can petition the court for a change. The change of circumstances that most impress the court are those changes that are unexpected, such as losing your job because the company went bankrupt. The courts are less sympathetic to people who just do not want to work as hard as they used to.

Another posttrial change may be decorating your new living environment. Getting the children involved in this is a good way to make sure they will enjoy their time with you. Make sure they have their own private spaces, and let them pick out colors and posters for their rooms. Pay attention to safety hazards, like stairways and windows. Put away the cleaning supplies if you have young children. Be sure to have lots of pictures of the children in your new place. Have plenty of clothes for them, and duplicate their favorite toys at your home, if possible.

Sooner or later, you will begin a new social life and you will be meeting people of the opposite sex. Remember that children need time to heal from the separation or divorce of their parents. New people should be introduced to them gradually and only after they have some time to get used to their new situation.

Now that you have won the hard-fought right to participate in raising your children, you have to participate. That means be a good parent. Talk to your children and listen to them. Spend time with them. Go to the parent-teacher conferences at school. Coach your children's soccer team.

It is hard to work to support a family, advance your career, and spend quality time with your children. There will be times when the children's time-sharing schedule has to yield to your work schedule, but try to be punctual in all your access time with the children. That will keep things running more smoothly with their mother, but more importantly, the children are depending on you to be there when you say you will be there.

Your objective is to become a business partner with the mother of your children. You will, after all, be in the business of raising your children for many years to come. Business partners usually do not love or hate each other. They are respectful and polite to one another. They protect and nurture the business. They keep their eye on the bottom line—in this case, the best interests of the children.

GLOSSARY

A

affidavit of paternity. A written sworn statement by a father admitting that he is the biological father of a certain child.

age of emancipation. The exact age at which a child becomes an adult; a matter of law in each state.

alternative dispute resolution. Any process by which legal adversaries reach a decision other than bringing the matter to trial for a judge's decision; in divorce cases, it usually refers to mediation.

appeal. Procedure by which a trial court decision is brought before a higher court for review.

arrearage. Unpaid child support payments for past periods owed by a parent who is obligated to pay.

B

biological father. The natural male parent of a child.

C

child support. The payment the noncustodial parent pays to the custodial parent for support of the parties' children.

child support guidelines. The charts or formula used to determine the amount of child support to be paid. The guidelines take into account objective economic factors that generally include the custodial parent's income, the noncustodial parent's income, alimony payable between the parties, the cost of health insurance, the cost of day care, and support obligations with respect to other children who are not children of both parties.

collaborative family law. A settlement process in which the lawyers contract to withdraw if one of the parties decides to litigate divorce.

custodial parent. The parent who has custody of the children. Child support is paid to the custodial parent.

custody. The legal right to act as parent to the children, have the children live with you, and make decisions about their welfare and upbringing, such as in the authority and responsibility to make major decisions in a child's best interests in the areas of residence, medical and dental treatment, education, child care, religion, and recreation. In a custody case, unless the parties reach an agreement, the court decides which parent will have custody of the children.

D

deposition. A discovery procedure. In a lawsuit, one party can compel the other party, or other witnesses, to answer questions under oath before a court reporter.

direct examination. A party's (or his or her attorney's) questioning of a witness whom the party has called as part of his or her case in a trial or hearing.

discovery. A variety of pretrial procedures that can be used to discover facts from the other party. The most common methods are depositions, interrogatories, requests for production of documents, and requests for admission.

domestic violence. Violence against a spouse or a person in another family or romantic relationship.

E

emancipate. Legal independence of children from their parents due to age or circumstance.

Employee Retirement Income Security Act (ERISA). Federal statute regulating employee benefit plans and private pension plans.

evidence. The proof presented at trial. A witness's answer under oath, or documents or other tangible things presented by a party and accepted by the court.

G

garnishment. A legal proceeding whereby a person's property, money, or credit in the possession of or under the control of a third person (garnishee) is withheld from the defendant and applied to the payment of the defendant's debt to the plaintiff. The most common example would be an employer having to withhold wages and pay them to the court or possibly directly to the plaintiff on account of the defendant's owed debt.

genetic testing. Testing of DNA that is used to conclusively prove the paternity of a child. This may be a Buccal Swab Test involving the alleged father, the mother, and child.

guardian ad litem. An attorney appointed to act as the children's advocate or an advocate for the best interests of the children in a custody case.

guidelines. A standard method of setting child support obligations based upon the income of the parent(s) and other factors as determined by state law.

I

income withholding. An order or other legal process directed to an obligor's employer or other income payer to withhold court-ordered sums from the obligor's wage or other income.

interrogatories. A discovery procedure. A party's written questions to the other party that have to be answered in writing under oath.

J

joint custody. An order of the court awarding custody of a child to both parents. Joint custody does not imply an equal division of the child's time between the parents or an equal division of financial responsibility for the child.

jurisdiction. The power of the court to hear and decide the matter that is before it, and bind the parties by its decision.

L

legal custody. The right to make long-term parenting decisions about the child's upbringing, health care, education, religion, and so on.

M

mediation. A process by which the parties meet to discuss the disputed issues with a skilled, neutral person who guides the process and helps the parties reach agreements on the issues in the case.

modification of support. Change of prior support orders based upon a substantial change in circumstances (such as a change in amount of income). A modification can be either a decrease or an increase in the amount of support.

N

noncustodial parent. The parent who does not have custody of the children, or if custody is shared, the parent who has less custody.

P

parent. A natural parent, adoptive parent, or person who is found by the court to be a parent.

Parental Kidnapping Prevention Act (PKPA). A federal statute designed to combat child snatching and forum shopping for a more favorable court to hear your case.

parenting classes. Classes on the negative impact of divorce on children and how to minimize it, as well as related subjects, that the court may order parties to attend in contested custody cases.

parenting plan. An agreement between parents setting forth the responsibilities of each parent individually and the parents jointly in a custody arrangement. It may include child support and visitation schedules.

paternity. The legal determination of fatherhood by court order, administrative order, acknowledgment, or other method provided for under state law.

pendente lite. Latin for *during the litigation*. Many courts still use this term when classifying motion hearings leading up to trial.

physical custody. Refers to the home in which the children primarily reside. The parent who lives in that home has physical custody of the children.

pleadings. Papers filed with the court, such as a Complaint, Answer, and Counterclaim, asking the court for relief or providing information.

presumed father. When a man is considered to be the father of a child by reasonable assumption. A man can be presumed to be the father of a child when: 1) he signs the child's birth certificate or 2) he is married to a woman and a child is born during the legal marriage.

pretrial conference. Final conference with the court before trial. At or before the conference, the parties have to file a joint statement of marital property and a pretrial statement regarding such things as identification of witnesses, documents, and pending motions.

putative father. Males alleged or reputed to be biological fathers of children born out of wedlock.

R

request for production of documents. A discovery procedure. A party's written request to the other party to produce the documents for inspection and copying.

S

scheduling conference. First court appearance at which the court schedules various hearings depending on the issues in the case, and may schedule mediation or order the parties to attend parenting classes.

shared custody. The noncustodial parent has custody a significant amount of the time. Child support will be calculated under the shared custody child support guidelines.

sole custody. An order of the court awarding custody of a child to one parent.

split custody. Each parent has physical custody of one or more of the party's children.

statute of limitations. A state statute that determines a specific time within which a legal action must be filed in a court, or the matter be forever barred or prohibited from litigation.

subpoena. A document issued by a court of administrative agency to compel a person to attend a hearing or to produce documents for inspection at a specified time and location.

support order. An order issued by a court of law or other tribunal that directs the noncustodial parent to pay an amount of money to the custodial parent for the benefit and support of a child.

T

time-sharing. The noncustodial parent's time with the children. Also often referred to in agreements and orders as *visitation*.

trial. A hearing at which the parties to litigation present witnesses, documents, and other evidence about the facts bearing on the contested issues in the case.

U

Uniform Child Custody Jurisdiction and Enforcement Act (UCCJEA). Designed to avoid jurisdictional competition and conflict among state courts that can arise when parents shift children from state to state in search of a favorable custody decision.

Uniform Interstate Family Support Act (UIFSA). A model law used by all fifty states to process interstate cases, providing a mechanism for establishing and enforcing support obligations when the noncustodial parent lives in one state and the custodial parent lives in another.

use and possession. In some states, a spouse with custody of minor children of the parties can obtain exclusive use and possession of the family home, furniture, and automobile.

V

visitation. The noncustodial parent's time with the children. Sometimes referred to in an agreement and orders as *time-sharing*.

W

waiver. Voluntary and knowing release of personal obligations, such as the right to contest parentage actions, the right to paternity testing, and the right to separate counsel.

STATE-BY-STATE CUSTODY PRESUMPTIONS AND FACTORS

Each state has its own presumptions that it follows in deciding custody matters. These presumptions guide and direct the judge as he or she is making a custody decision. If a presumption is in your favor, it should be easier for you to get the court to rule how you want. If the presumption is not in your favor, you must overcome it, and prove to the court why you should receive what you are asking. Presumptions can be powerful tools in custody battles. All of the states determine which parent gets custody based on *best interests of the children*. Most of the states have established factors the court must consider in making that determination. Here are the custody factors that you will need to establish in each state.

ALABAMA

Presumptions:

It is the policy of this state to assure that minor children have frequent and continuing contact with parents who have shown the ability to act in the best interest of their children and to encourage parents to share in the rights and responsibilities of rearing their children after the parents have separated or dissolved their marriage. Joint custody does not necessarily mean equal physical custody. *Alabama Code Sec. 30-3-150.*

In every proceeding where there is at issue a dispute as to the custody of a child, a determination by the court that domestic or family violence has occurred raises a rebuttable presumption by the court that it is detrimental to the child and not in the best interest of the child to be placed in sole custody, joint legal custody, or joint physical custody with the perpetrator of domestic or family violence. *Alabama Code Sec. 30-3-131.*

If both parents request joint custody, the presumption is that joint custody is in the best interest of the child. *Alabama Code Sec. 30-3-152(c).*

There shall be a rebuttable presumption in favor of visitation by any grandparent. *Alabama Code Sec. 30-3-4.1(e).*

Factors:

1. Agreement or lack of agreement of the parents on joint custody.

2. Past and present ability of the parents to cooperate with each other and make decisions jointly.
3. Ability of the parents to encourage the sharing of love, affection, and contact between the child and the other parent.
4. History of, or potential for, child abuse, spouse abuse, or kidnapping.
5. Geographic proximity of the parents to each other as this relates to the practical considerations of joint physical custody.
Alabama Code Sec. 30-3-152.

ALASKA

Presumptions:

The court may award shared custody to both parents if shared custody is determined by the court to be in the best interests of the child. An award of shared custody shall assure that the child has frequent and continuing contact with each parent to the maximum extent possible. *Alaska Statutes Sec. 25.20.060(b).*

Neither parent, regardless of the question of the child's legitimacy, is entitled to preference in the awarding of custody. *Alaska Statutes Sec. 25.20.060(a).*

Factors:

1. Physical, emotional, mental, religious, and social needs of the child.
2. Capability and desire of each parent to meet these needs.
3. Child's preference if the child is of sufficient age and capacity to form a preference.
4. Love and affection existing between the child and each parent.
5. Length of time the child has lived in a stable, satisfactory environment and the desirability of maintaining continuity.
6. Desire and ability of each parent to allow an open and loving frequent relationship between the child and the other parent.
7. Domestic violence, child abuse, or child neglect in the proposed custodial household or a history of violence between the parents.
8. Substance abuse by either parent or other members of the household directly affects the emotional or physical well-being of the child.
9. Other factors that the court considers pertinent.
10. The court may consider only those facts that directly affect the well-being of the child.
Alaska Statutes Sec. 25.24.150(c).

ARIZONA

Presumptions:

In awarding child custody, the court may order sole custody or joint custody. This section does not create a presumption in favor of one custody arrangement over another. The court in determining custody shall not prefer a parent as custodian because of that parent's sex. *Arizona Revised Statutes Sec. 25-403B.*

The court may issue an order for joint custody of a child if both parents agree and submit a written parenting plan and the court finds such an order is in the best interests of the child. The court may order joint legal custody without ordering joint physical custody. *Arizona Revised Statutes Sec. 25-403C.*

Joint custody shall not be awarded in cases of significant domestic violence. *Arizona Revised Statutes Sec. 25-403E.*

If the court determines that a parent has been convicted of certain drug offenses within twelve months before the petition or the request for custody is filed, there is a rebuttable presumption that sole or joint custody by that parent is not in the child's best interests. *Arizona Revised Statutes Sec. 25-403K.*

If the court determines that a parent who is seeking custody has committed an act of domestic violence against the other parent, there is a rebuttable presumption that an award of custody to the parent who committed the act of domestic violence is contrary to the child's best interests. This presumption does not apply if both parents have committed an act of domestic violence. *Arizona Revised Statutes Sec. 25-403N.*

If a person other than a child's legal parent is seeking custody there is a rebuttable presumption that it is in the child's best interest to award custody to a legal parent because of the physical, psychological and emotional needs of the child to be reared by the child's legal parent. *Arizona Revised Statutes Sec. 25-415B.*

Factors:

1. Wishes of the child's parent or parents as to custody.
2. Wishes of the child as to the custodian.
3. Interaction and interrelationship of the child with parent or parents, siblings, and any other person who may significantly affect the child's best interest.
4. Child's adjustment to home, school, and community.
5. Mental and physical health of all individuals involved.
6. Which parent is more likely to allow the child frequent and meaningful continuing contact with the other parent.
7. Whether one parent, both parents or neither parent has provided primary care of the child.
8. Nature and extent of coercion or duress used by a parent in obtaining an agreement regarding custody.
9. Whether a parent has complied with chapter 3, article 5 of this title.
10. Whether either parent was convicted of an act of false reporting of child abuse or neglect.

Arizona Revised Statutes Sec. 25-403.

ARKANSAS

Presumptions:

In an action for divorce, the award of custody of a child of the marriage shall be made without regard to the sex of a parent, but solely in accordance with the welfare and best interest of the child. *Arkansas Code Sec. 9-13-101(a)(1)(A).*

There shall be a rebuttable presumption that it is not in the best interest of the child to be placed in the custody of an abusive parent where there is a pattern of domestic abuse. *Arkansas Code Sec. 9-13-101(c)(2).*

Factors:
1. The court shall determine custody in accordance with the best interests of the child. *Arkansas Code Sec. 9-13-101.*

CALIFORNIA

Presumptions:
There is a presumption, affecting the burden of proof, that joint custody is in the best interest of a minor child, where the parents have agreed to joint custody or so agree in open court at a hearing for the purpose of determining the custody of the minor child. *California Family Code Sec. 3080.*

On application of either parent, joint custody may be ordered in the discretion of the court. *California Family Code Sec. 3081.*

The mother and the father are equally entitled to the custody of a minor child. *California Family Code Sec. 3082.*

There is a rebuttable presumption that an award of sole or joint physical or legal custody of a child to a person, who has perpetrated domestic violence against the other party, the child or the child's siblings within five years, is detrimental to the best interest of the child. *California Family Code Sec. 3044(a).*

Factors:
1. Health, safety, and welfare of the child.
2. History of abuse by one parent or any other person seeking custody against (a) a child, (b) the other parent, or (c) a parent, current spouse, cohabitant, fiancee of, or one who is in a dating relationship with, the parent or person seeking custody.
3. Nature and amount of contact with both parent.
4. Drug or alcohol abuse.
California Family Code Sec. 3011.

COLORADO

Presumptions:
In a divorce action, the legislative intent of Colorado declares that "it is in the best interest of all parties to encourage frequent and continuing contact between each parent and the minor children of the marriage after the parents have separated or dissolved their marriage. In order to effectuate this goal, the general assembly urges parents to share the rights and responsibilities of child-rearing and to encourage the love, affection, and contact between the children and the parents." *Colorado Revised Statutes Sec. 14-10-124(1).*

The court shall determine the allocation of parental responsibilities, including parenting time and decision-making responsibilities, in accordance with the best interests of the child giving paramount consideration to the physical, mental, and emotional conditions and needs of the child. *Colorado Revised Statutes Sec. 14-10-124(1.5).*

If the court makes a finding of fact that one of the parties has been a perpetrator of child abuse or neglect, then it shall not be in the best interests of the child to allocate mutual decision-making with respect to any issue over the objection of the other party or the representative of the child. *Colorado Revised Statutes Sec. 14-10-124(1)(V).*

In determining parenting time or decision-making responsibilities, the court shall not presume that any person is better able to serve the best interests of the child because of that person's sex. *Colorado Revised Statutes Sec. 14-10-124(3).*

The court may order mediation to assist the parties in formulating or modifying a parenting plan or in implementing a parenting plan and may allocate the cost of said mediation between the parties. *Colorado Revised Statutes Sec. 14-10-124(8).*

In determining a custodial dispute between a parent and a non-parent, Colorado courts recognize that the best interests standard is subject to a presumption that the biological parent has a first and prior right to custody. This presumption may be rebutted by evidence establishing that the welfare of the child, *i.e.*, the best interests of the child, is better served by granting custody to a nonparent. *Abrams v. Connolly*, 781 P.2d 651 (Colo. 1989); *In re Custody of C.C.R.S.*, 892 P.2d 246 (Colo. 1995).

Factors:

Legal Custody (Decision Making):
1. Ability of the parties to cooperate and to make decisions jointly.
2. Past pattern of involvement of the parties with the child that reflects a system of values, time commitment, and mutual support that would indicate an ability as mutual decision makers to provide a positive and nourishing relationship with the child.
3. Promotion of more frequent or continuing contact between the child and each of the parties.
4. Child abuse or neglect.
5. Spouse abuse.
6. The court shall not consider conduct of a party that does not affect that party's relationship to the child.
7. The court shall not presume that any person is better able to serve the best interests of the child because of that person's sex.
8. A parenting plan submitted by either party.

Physical Custody (Parenting Time):
1. Wishes of the child's parents as to parenting time.
2. Wishes of the child if he or she is sufficiently mature to express reasoned and independent preferences as to the parenting time schedule.
3. Interaction and interrelationship of the child with his or her parents, his or her siblings, and any other person who may significantly affect the child's best interests.
4. Child's adjustment to his or her home, school, and community.
5. Mental and physical health of all individuals involved, except that a disability alone shall not be a basis to deny or restrict parenting time.
6. Ability of the parties to encourage the sharing of love, affection, and contact between the child and the other party.
7. Whether the past pattern of involvement of the parties with the child reflects a system of values, time commitment, and mutual support.
8. Physical proximity of the parties to each other as this relates to the practical considerations of parenting time.
9. Child abuse or neglect.
10. Spouse abuse.
11. Ability of each party to place the needs of the child ahead of his or her own needs.
Colorado Revised Statutes Sec. 14-10-124.

CONNECTICUT

Presumptions:

In any dispute as to the custody of a minor child involving a parent and a nonparent, there shall be a presumption that it is in the best interest of the child to be in the custody of the parent, which presumption may be rebutted by showing that it would be detrimental to the child to permit the parent to have custody. *Connecticut General Statutes Sec. 46b-56b.*

Factors:

1. Best interests of the child.

Connecticut General Statutes Sec. 46b-56.

DELAWARE

Presumptions:

The Court shall determine the legal custody and residential arrangements for a child in accordance with the best interests of the child. *Delaware Code tit. 13 Sec. 722.*

The Court shall not presume that a parent, because of his or her sex, is better qualified than the other parent to act as a joint or sole legal custodian for a child or as the child's primary residential parent, nor shall it consider conduct of a proposed sole or joint custodian or primary residential parent that does not affect his or her relationship with the child. *Delaware Code tit. 13 Sec. 722(7)(b).*

There shall be a rebuttable presumption that no perpetrator of domestic violence shall be awarded sole or joint custody of any child. *Delaware Code tit. 13 Sec. 705(A)(a).* There shall be a rebuttable presumption that no child shall primarily reside with a perpetrator of domestic violence. *Delaware Code tit. 13 Sec. 705(A)(b).*

Factors:

1. Wishes of the child's parent or parents as to his or her custody and residential arrangements.
2. Wishes of the child as to his or her custodian(s) and residential arrangements.
3. Interaction and interrelationship of the child with his or her parents, grandparents, siblings, persons cohabiting in the relationship of husband and wife with a parent of the child, any other residents of the household or persons who may significantly affect the child's best interests.
4. Child's adjustment to his or her home, school and community.
5. Mental and physical health of all individuals involved.
6. Past and present compliance by both parents with their rights and responsibilities to their child.
7. Evidence of domestic violence.
8. The Court shall not presume that a parent, because of his or her sex, is better qualified than the other parent to act as a joint or sole legal custodian for a child or as the child's primary residential parent, nor shall it consider conduct of a proposed sole or joint custodian or primary residential parent that does not affect his or her relationship with the child.

Delaware Code tit. 13 Sec. 722.

DISTRICT OF COLUMBIA

Presumptions:

In any proceeding between parents in which the custody of a child is raised as an issue, the best interest of the child shall be the primary consideration. The race, color, national origin, political affiliation, sex, or sexual orientation of a party, in and of itself, shall not be a conclusive consideration. The Court shall make a determination as to the legal custody and the physical custody of a child. *D.C. Code Sec. 16-914(a)(1).*

There shall be a rebuttable presumption that joint custody is in the best interest of the child or children, except in instances of an intrafamily offense, child abuse, child neglect or parental kidnaping. *D.C. Code Sec. 16-914(2).*

Factors:

 1. Wishes of the child as to his or her custodian.
 2. Wishes of the child's parent or parents as to the child's custody.
 3. Interaction and interrelationship of the child with his or her parent or parents, his or her siblings, and any other person who may emotionally or psychologically affect the child's best interest.
 4. Child's adjustment to his or her home, school, and community.
 5. Mental and physical health of all individuals involved.
 6. Evidence of an intrafamily offense.
 7. Capacity of the parents to communicate and reach shared decisions affecting the child's welfare.
 8. Willingness of the parents to share custody.
 9. Prior involvement of each parent in the child's life.
10. Potential disruption of the child's social and school life.
11. Geographic proximity of the parental homes as this relates to the practical considerations of the child's residential schedule.
12. Demands of parental employment.
13. Age and number of children.
14. Sincerity of each parent's request.
15. Parent's ability to financially support a joint custody arrangement.
16. Impact on social welfare programs.
17. Benefit to the parents.
    D.C. Code Sec. 16-914(3).

FLORIDA

Presumptions:

The court shall order that the parental responsibility for a minor child be shared by both parents unless the court finds that shared parental responsibility would be detrimental to the child.

Evidence that a parent has been convicted of a felony of the third degree or higher involving domestic violence creates a rebuttable presumption of detriment to the child. If the presumption is not rebutted, shared parental responsibility, including visitation, residence of the child, and decisions made regarding the child, may not be granted to the convicted parent. If the court determines that shared parental responsibility would be detrimental to the child, it may order sole parental responsibility and make such arrangements for visitation as will best protect the child or abused spouse from further harm.

Whether or not there is a conviction of any offense of domestic violence or child abuse or the existence of an injunction for protection against domestic violence, the court shall consider evidence of domestic violence or child abuse as evidence of detriment to the child. *Florida Statutes Sec. 61-13(2)(b)(2).*

Factors:

For purposes of shared parental responsibility and primary residence, the best interests of the child shall include an evaluation of all factors affecting the welfare and interests of the child, including, but not limited to:

1. The parent who is more likely to allow the child frequent and continuing contact with the nonresidential parent.
2. The love, affection, and other emotional ties existing between the parents and the child.
3. The capacity and disposition of the parents to provide the child with food, clothing, medical care or other remedial care recognized and permitted under the laws of this state in lieu of medical care, and other material needs.
4. The length of time the child has lived in a stable, satisfactory environment and the desirability of maintaining continuity.
5. The permanence, as a family unit, of the existing or proposed custodial home.
6. The moral fitness of the parents.
7. The mental and physical health of the parents.
8. The home, school, and community record of the child.
9. The reasonable preference of the child, if the court deems the child to be of sufficient intelligence, understanding, and experience to express a preference.
10. The willingness and ability of each parent to facilitate and encourage a close and continuing parent-child relationship between the child and the other parent.
11. Evidence that any party has knowingly provided false information to the court regarding a domestic violence proceeding.
12. Evidence of domestic violence or child abuse.
13. Any other fact considered by the court to be relevant.
    Florida Statutes Sec. 61-13(3).

GEORGIA

Presumptions:

In all cases in which the custody of any minor child or children is at issue between the parents, there shall be no prima-facie right to the custody of the child or children in the father or mother. *Georgia Code Sec. 19-9-3(a)(1).*

The duty of the court in all such cases shall be to exercise its discretion to look to and determine solely what is for the best interest of the child or children and what will best promote their welfare and happiness and to make its award accordingly. *Georgia Code Sec. 19-9-3(2).*

Joint custody may be considered as an alternative form of custody by the court. This provision allows a court at any temporary or permanent hearing to grant sole custody, joint custody, joint legal custody, or joint physical custody where appropriate. *Georgia Code Sec. 19-9-3(5)*.

Before custody of [a] child may be awarded to third party, presumption that it will be in best interest of child to be with his parent must be rebutted by clear and convincing showing that parent is unfit to be awarded custody. *Larson v. Gambrell*, 157 Ga. App. 193, 276 S.E.2d 686 (1981).

Factors:

1. All the circumstances of the case, including the improvement of the health of the party seeking a change in custody provision.
2. What is for the best interest of the child or children and what will best promote their welfare and happiness.
3. Safety and well-being of the child and of the parent who is the victim of family violence.
4. If the child has reached the age of 14 years, the child shall have the right to select the parent with whom he or she desires to live. The child's selection shall be controlling unless the parent so selected is determined not to be a fit and proper parent.
5. In all custody cases in which the child has reached the age of at least 11 but not 14 years, the court shall consider the desires and educational needs of the child, but the child's selection shall not be controlling.
6. The court may order a psychological custody evaluation of the family or an independent medical evaluation.

Georgia Code Sec. 19-9-3.

HAWAII

Presumptions:

In Hawaii, Custody should be awarded to either parent or to both parents according to the best interests of the child. *Hawaii Revised Statutes Sec. 571-46(1)*.

In every proceeding where there is at issue a dispute as to the custody of a child, a determination by the court that family violence has been committed by a parent raises a rebuttable presumption that it is detrimental to the child and not in the best interest of the child to be placed in sole custody, joint legal custody, or joint physical custody with the perpetrator of family violence. *Hawaii Revised Statutes Sec. 571-46(9)*.

Factors:

1. Child's wishes as to custody, if of sufficient age and capacity to reason, so as to form an intelligent preference.
2. Court may require an investigation and report concerning the care, welfare, and custody of any minor child of the parties.
3. The court may hear the testimony of any person or expert, produced by any party or upon the court's own motion, whose skill, insight, knowledge, or experience is such that the person's or expert's testimony is relevant to a just and reasonable determination of what is for the best physical, mental, moral, and spiritual well-being of the child.
4. Safety and well-being of the child and of the parent who is the victim of family violence.

Hawaii Revised Statues Sec. 571-46.

IDAHO

Presumptions:

In Idaho, there shall be a presumption that joint custody is in the best interests of a minor child or children. *Idaho Code Sec. 32-717B(4).*

There shall be a presumption that joint custody is not in the best interests of a minor child if one (1) of the parents is found by the court to be a habitual perpetrator of domestic violence. *Idaho Code Sec. 32-717B(5).*

Factors:

1. The court may award either joint physical custody or joint legal custody or both as between the parents or parties as the court determines is for the best interests of the minor child or children.

Idaho Code Sec. 32-717B.

ILLINOIS

Presumptions:

Unless the court finds the occurrence of ongoing abuse, the court shall presume that the maximum involvement and cooperation of both parents regarding the physical, mental, moral, and emotional well-being of their child is in the best interest of the child. There shall be no presumption in favor of or against joint custody. *750 ILCS 5/602(c).*

In the case of a custody proceeding in which a stepparent has standing, it is presumed to be in the best interest of the minor child that the natural parent have the custody of the minor child unless the presumption is rebutted by the stepparent. *750 ILCS 5/602(8).*

Factors:

1. Ability of the parents to cooperate effectively and consistently in matters that directly affect the joint parenting of the child.
2. Residential circumstances of each parent.
3. All other factors which may be relevant to the best interest of the child.

750 ILCS 5/602.1(c).

INDIANA

Presumptions:

The court shall determine custody and enter a custody order in accordance with the best interests of the child. In determining the best interests of the child, there is no presumption favoring either parent. *Indiana Code Sec. 31-17-2-8.*

If a court finds that a noncustodial parent has been convicted of a crime involving domestic or family violence that was witnessed or heard by the noncustodial parent's child, the court may order supervised visits. The supervised visits could last (1) for at least one year and not more than two years immediately following the crime involving domestic or family violence; or (2) until the child becomes emancipated, whichever occurs first. There is created a rebuttable presumption that the court shall order that the noncustodial parent's visitation with the child must be supervised. *Indiana Code Sec. 31-17-2-8.3.*

Factors:
1. Age and sex of the child.
2. Wishes of the child's parent or parents.
3. Wishes of the child, with more consideration given to the child's wishes if the child is at least fourteen years of age.
4. Interaction and interrelationship of the child with (a) parent or parents, (b) siblings and (c) any other person who may significantly affect the child's best interests.
5. Child's adjustment to (a) home, (b) school and (c) community.
6. Mental and physical health of all individuals involved.
7. Pattern of domestic or family violence by either parent.
8. Evidence that the child has been cared for by a de facto custodian.
Indiana Code Sec. 31-17-2-8.

IOWA

Presumptions:
The court, insofar as is reasonable and in the best interest of the child, shall order the custody award, including liberal visitation rights where appropriate, which will assure the child the opportunity for the maximum continuing physical and emotional contact with both parents after the parents have separated or dissolved the marriage, and which will encourage parents to share the rights and responsibilities of raising the child unless direct physical harm or significant emotional harm to the child, other children, or a parent is likely to result from such contact with one parent. *Iowa Code Sec. 598.41(1)(a).*

If the court finds that a history of domestic abuse exists, a rebuttable presumption against the awarding of joint custody exists. *Iowa Code Sec. 598.41(1)(b).*

On the application of either parent, the court shall consider granting joint custody in cases where the parents do not agree to joint custody. *Iowa Code Sec. 598.41(2)(a).*

If the court does not grant joint custody, the court shall cite clear and convincing evidence that joint custody is unreasonable and not in the best interest of the child to the extent that the legal custodial relationship between the child and a parent should be severed. *Iowa Code Sec. 598.41(2)(b).*

Factors:
1. Whether each parent would be a suitable custodian for the child.
2. Whether the psychological and emotional needs and development of the child will suffer due to lack of active contact with and attention from both parents.
3. Whether the parents can communicate with each other regarding the child's needs.
4. Whether both parents have actively cared for the child before and since the separation.
5. Whether each parent can support the other parent's relationship with the child.
6. Whether the custody arrangement is in accord with the child's wishes or whether the child has strong opposition, taking into consideration the child's age and maturity.
7. Whether one or both the parents agree or are opposed to joint custody.
8. Geographic proximity of the parents.
9. Whether the safety of the child, other children, or the other parent will be jeopardized by the awarding of joint custody or by unsupervised or unrestricted visitation.
10. Whether a history of domestic abuse exists.
Iowa Code Sec. 598.41.3.

KANSAS

Presumptions:

The court shall determine custody or residency of a child in accordance with the best interests of the child. *Kansas Statutes Sec. 60-1610(a)(3).*

A finding by the court that a history of domestic abuse exists...which is not rebutted, shall outweigh consideration of any other factor...in the determination of the awarding of custody *Kansas Statutes Sec. 60-1610(2)(c).*

Factors:

1. Length of time that the child has been under the actual care and control of any person other than a parent and the circumstances.
2. Desires of the parents as to custody or residency.
3. Desires of the child as to custody or residency.
4. Interaction and interrelationship of the child with parents, siblings and any other person who may significantly affect the child's best interests.
5. Child's adjustment to the child's home, school and community.
6. Willingness and ability of each parent to respect and appreciate the bond between the child and the other parent and to allow for a continuing relationship between the child and the other parent.
7. Spousal abuse.

Kansas Statutes Sec. 60-1610(3)(B).

KENTUCKY

Presumptions:

The court shall determine custody in accordance with the best interests of the child and equal consideration shall be given to each parent and to any de facto custodian. *Kentucky Revised Statutes Sec. 403.270(2).*

KRS Section 403.270 directs the trial court to continue the status quo in a custody arrangement unless certain proven facts indicate a need for change. *Dexter v. Spainhoward,* 563 S.W.2d 474 (Ky. Ct. App. 1978).

The purpose of KRS section [403.340] is to maximize the finality of a custody decree without jeopardizing the health and welfare of the child; moreover, this section creates a presumption that the present custodian is entitled to continue as the child's custodian. *West v. West,* 664 S.W.2d 948 (Ky. Ct. App. 1984).

Factors:

1. Wishes of the parent or parents, or any other custodian.
2. Wishes of the child as to his custodian.
3. Interaction and interrelationship of the child with his parent or parents, his siblings, and any other person who may significantly affect the child's best interests.
4. The child's adjustment to his home, school, and community.
5. Mental and physical health of all individuals involved.
6. Information, records, and evidence of domestic violence.
7. Extent to which the child has been cared for, nurtured, and supported by any *de facto* custodian.

8. Intent of the parent or parents in placing the child with a *de facto* custodian.

9. Circumstances under which the child was placed or allowed to remain in the custody of a *de facto* custodian.

Kentucky Revised Statutes Sec. 403.270.

LOUISIANA

Presumptions:

In a proceeding for divorce or thereafter, the court shall award custody of a child in accordance with the best interest of the child. *Louisiana Civil Code art. 131.*

Rebuttable presumptions noted in case law:

"Although joint custody was not legally available when a father agreed to the mother's sole custody of their children, he was entitled to the rebuttable joint custody presumption when awarded increased visitation, because the joint custody presumption could not be waived before joint custody became legally possible, and because the record showed no concerns relative to the father indicating that joint custody was not in the children's best interests." *Smith v. Smith,* 459 So. 2d 646 (La.App. 4 Cir. 1984).

"In a father's rule for joint custody, an order of sole custody was changed to joint custody because there was a rebuttable presumption in favor of joint custody; the joint custody plan was reasonable, feasible, and in the child's best interest." *Plemer v. Plemer,* 436 So. 2d 1348 (La.App. 4 Cir. 1983).

Factors:

1. In a proceeding for divorce or thereafter, the court shall award custody of a child in accordance with the best interest of the child.

2. If the parents agree who is to have custody, the court shall award custody in accordance with their agreement unless the best interest of the child requires a different award.

3. In the absence of agreement, or if the agreement is not in the best interest of the child, the court shall award custody to the parents jointly; however, if custody in one parent is shown by clear and convincing evidence to serve the best interest of the child, the court shall award custody to that parent.

Louisiana Civil Code Sec. 3, arts. 131, 132.

MAINE

Presumptions:

No rebuttable presumptions regarding custody in the statutes or caselaw.

Factors:

1. The father and mother are the joint natural guardians of their minor children and are jointly entitled to the care, custody, control, services and earnings of their children.

2. Neither parent has any rights paramount to the rights of the other with reference to any matter affecting their children.

Maine Revised Statutes Sec. 19-A-1651.

MARYLAND

Presumptions:

The parents are the joint natural guardians of their minor child. *Maryland Family Law Code Sec. 5-203(a)(1)*.

"The child's best interest is subserved by custody in the parent, but that presumption is overcome and such custody will be denied if: (a) The parent is unfit to have custody; or (b) if there are such exceptional circumstances as make such custody detrimental to the best interest of the child." *Ross v. Hoffman*, 280 Md. 172, 372 A.2d 582 (1977).

Factors:

1. Capacity of the parents to communicate and to reach shared decisions affecting the child's welfare.
2. Willingness of the parents to share custody.
3. Fitness of the parents.
4. Relationship established between the child and each parent.
5. Preference of the child.
6. Potential disruption of the child's social and school life.
7. Geographic proximity of parental homes.
8. Demands of parental employment.
9. Age and number of children.
10. Sincerity of parent's request.
11. Financial status of the parents.
12. Impact on state and federal assistance.
13. Benefit to parents.
14. Any other factor or circumstance related to the issue.
Taylor v. Taylor, 306 Md. 290, 508 A.2d 964 (1986).

MASSACHUSETTS

Presumptions:

There shall be no presumption either in favor of or against shared legal or physical custody at the time of the trial on the merits. *Massachusetts General Laws ch.208 Sec. 31*.

Nothing herein shall be construed to create any presumption of temporary shared physical custody. *Massachusetts General Laws ch.208 Sec. 31*.

A probate and family court's finding by a preponderance of the evidence, that a pattern or serious incident of abuse has occurred shall create a rebuttable presumption that it is not in the best interests of the child to be placed in sole custody, shared legal custody, or shared physical custody with the abusive parent. Such presumption may be rebutted by a preponderance of the evidence that such custody award is in the best interests of the child. For the purposes of this section, an "abusive parent" shall mean a parent who has committed a pattern of abuse or a serious incident of abuse. *Massachusetts General Laws, ch.209C, Sec. 10*.

"There is no presumption that custody should be awarded to primary caretaking parent." *Custody of Zia*, 50 Mass. App. 237; 736 N.E.2d 449 (2000).

Factors:

1. The rights of the parents shall, in the absence of misconduct, be held to be equal.

2. The happiness and welfare of the children shall determine their custody.

3. When considering the happiness and welfare of the child, the court shall consider whether or not the child's present or past living conditions adversely affect his physical, mental, moral or emotional health.

4. At the trial on the merits, if the issue of custody is contested and either party seeks shared legal or physical custody, the parties, jointly or individually, shall submit to the court at the trial a shared custody implementation plan setting forth the details of shared custody including, but not limited to, the child's education; the child's health care; procedures for resolving disputes between the parties with respect to child-raising decisions and duties; and the periods of time during which each party will have the child reside or visit with him, including holidays and vacations, or the procedure by which such periods of time shall be determined.

Massachusetts General Laws 208-31.

MICHIGAN

Presumptions:

If a child custody dispute is between the parents, between agencies, or between third persons, the best interests of the child control. If the child custody dispute is between the parent or parents and an agency or a third person, the court shall presume that the best interests of the child are served by awarding custody to the parent or parents, unless the contrary is established by clear and convincing evidence. *(Michigan Compiled Laws Sec. 722.25.*

In the case of a child born out of wedlock:

After a mother and father sign an acknowledgment of parentage, the mother is presumed to have custody of the minor child unless otherwise determined by the court or otherwise agreed upon by the parties in writing. *(Michigan Compiled Laws Sec. 722.1006).*

The Child Custody Act "is properly applicable to disputes as between natural parents and third parties pursuant to presumption that best interests of child shall be served by placement of custody with natural parents unless third parties prove opposite." *In re Weldon*, 397 Mich. 225, 244 N.W.2d 827 (1976).

The Child Custody Act "does not create substantive rights of entitlement to custody of child; rather, it creates presumptions and standards by which competing claims to right of custody are to be judged, sets forth procedures to be followed in litigation regarding custody claims, and authorizes the forms of relief available in circuit court." *Ruppel v Lesner,* 421 Mich. 559, 364 N.W.2d 665 (1984).

"It is presumed that the best interests of the child are served by awarding custody to the parent or parents, unless the contrary is established by clear and convincing evidence, where a custody dispute is between the parent or parents and an agency or a third person; a trial court's failure to consider the statutory prescription to that effect is reversible error." *Williamson v. Williamson*, 122 Mich. App. 667, 333 N.W.2d 6 (1982).

Factors:

1. Love, affection, and other emotional ties existing between the parties involved and the child.

2. Capacity and disposition of the parties involved to give the child love, affection, and guidance and to continue the education and raising of the child in his or her religion or creed, if any.
3. Capacity and disposition of the parties involved to provide the child with food, clothing, medical care or other remedial care recognized and permitted under the laws of this state in place of medical care, and other material needs.
4. Length of time the child has lived in a stable, satisfactory environment, and the desirability of maintaining continuity.
5. Permanence, as a family unit, of the existing or proposed custodial home or homes.
6. Moral fitness of the parties involved.
7. Mental and physical health of the parties involved.
8. Home, school, and community record of the child.
9. Reasonable preference of the child, if the court considers the child to be of sufficient age to express preference.
10. Willingness and ability of each of the parties to facilitate and encourage a close and continuing parent-child relationship between the child and the other parent or the child and the parents.
11. Domestic violence, regardless of whether the violence was directed against or witnessed by the child.
12. Any other factor considered by the court to be relevant to a particular child custody dispute.
Michigan Compiled Laws Sec. 722.23(3).

MINNESOTA

Presumptions:
The court shall use a rebuttable presumption that upon request of either or both parties, joint legal custody is in the best interests of the child. However, the court shall use a rebuttable presumption that joint legal or physical custody is not in the best interests of the child if domestic abuse...has occurred between the parents. *Minnesota Statutes Sec. 518.17.*

Factors:
1. Wishes of the child's parent or parents as to custody.
2. Reasonable preference of the child, if the court deems the child to be of sufficient age to express preference.
3. Child's primary caretaker.
4. Intimacy of the relationship between each parent and the child.
5. Interaction and interrelationship of the child with a parent or parents, siblings, and any other person who may significantly affect the child's best interests.
6. Child's adjustment to home, school, and community.
7. Length of time the child has lived in a stable, satisfactory environment and the desirability of maintaining continuity.
8. Permanence, as a family unit, of the existing or proposed custodial home.
9. Mental and physical health of all individuals involved; except that a disability, of a proposed custodian or the child shall not be determinative of the custody of the child, unless the proposed custodial arrangement is not in the best interest of the child.

10. Capacity and disposition of the parties to give the child love, affection, and guidance, and to continue educating and raising the child in the child's culture and religion or creed, if any.
11. Child's cultural background.
12. Effect on the child of the actions of an abuser, if related to domestic abuse that has occurred between the parents or between a parent and another individual, whether or not the individual alleged to have committed domestic abuse is or ever was a family or household member of the parent.
13. Disposition of each parent to encourage and permit frequent and continuing contact by the other parent with the child (except in cases of domestic abuse).
14. The court may not use one factor to the exclusion of all others. The primary caretaker factor may not be used as a presumption in determining the best interests of the child. The court must make detailed findings on each of the factors and explain how the factors led to its conclusions and to the determination of the best interests of the child.
15. The court shall not consider conduct of a proposed custodian that does not affect the custodian's relationship to the child.
16. Evidence of false allegations of child abuse.
Additional factors for joint custody:
1. Ability of parents to cooperate in the rearing of their children.
2. Methods for resolving disputes regarding any major decision concerning the life of the child, and the parents' willingness to use those methods.
3. Whether it would be detrimental to the child if one parent were to have sole authority over the child's upbringing.
4. Whether domestic abuse has occurred between the parents.
Minnesota Statutes Sec. 518.17.

MISSISSIPPI

Presumptions:

There shall be a presumption that joint custody is in the best interest of a minor child where both parents have agreed to an award of joint custody. *Mississippi Code Sec. 93-5-24(4).*

There shall be no presumption that it is in the best interest of a child that a mother be awarded either legal or physical custody. *Mississippi Code Sec. 93-5-24(7).*

In every proceeding where the custody of a child is in dispute, there shall be a rebuttable presumption that it is detrimental to the child and not in the best interest of the child to be placed in sole custody, joint legal custody or joint physical custody of a parent who has a history of perpetrating family violence. The court may find a history of perpetrating family violence if the court finds, by a preponderance of the evidence, one (1) incident of family violence that has resulted in serious bodily injury to, or a pattern of family violence against, the party making the allegation or a family household member of either party. The court shall make written findings to document how and why the presumption was or was not triggered. *Mississippi Code Sec. 93-5-24(9)(a)(i).*

This presumption may only be rebutted by a preponderance of the evidence. *Mississippi Code Sec. 93-5-24(9)(a)(ii).*

Factors:

Custody shall be awarded as follows according to the best interests of the child:

1. Upon a finding by the court that both of the parents of the child have abandoned or deserted such child or that both such parents are mentally, morally or otherwise unfit to rear and train the child the court may award physical and legal custody to.
2. The person in whose home the child has been living in a wholesome and stable environment.
3. Physical and legal custody to any other person deemed by the court to be suitable and able to provide adequate and proper care and guidance for the child.
4. In making an order for custody to either parent or to both parents jointly, the court, in its discretion, may require the parents to submit to the court a plan for the implementation of the custody order.
5. Joint custody may be awarded where irreconcilable differences is the ground for divorce, in the discretion of the court, upon application of both parents.
6. In other cases, joint custody may be awarded, in the discretion of the court, upon application of one or both parents.
7. There shall be a presumption that joint custody is in the best interest of a minor child where both parents have agreed to an award of joint custody.

Mississippi Code Sec. 93-5-24.

MISSOURI

Presumptions:

The court shall determine custody in accordance with the best interests of the child. *Missouri Revised Statutes Sec. 452.375.2.*

"Mo. Rev. Statutes Sec. 452.375 carries a rebuttable presumption that custody of a child should be with the child's parent." *Young v. Young,* 59 S.W.3d 23, (Mo. Ct. App. 2001).

"Mo. Rev. Statutes Sec. 452.375.5 creates a rebuttable presumption that parents are fit, suitable, and able custodians of their children and that their welfare is best served by awarding their custody to their parents." *Flathers v. Flathers,* 948 S.W.2d 463, (Mo. Ct. App. 1997).

Factors:

1. Wishes of the child's parents as to custody and the proposed parenting plan submitted by both parties.
2. Needs of the child for a frequent, continuing and meaningful relationship with both parents and the ability and willingness of parents to actively perform their functions as mother and father for the needs of the child.
3. Interaction and interrelationship of the child with parents, siblings, and any other person who may significantly affect the child's best interests.
4. Which parent is more likely to allow the child frequent, continuing and meaningful contact with the other parent.
5. Child's adjustment to the child's home, school, and community.
6. The mental and physical health of all individuals involved, including any history of abuse of any individuals involved. If the court finds that a pattern of domestic violence has occurred, and, if the court also finds that awarding custody to the abusive parent

is in the best interest of the child, then the court shall enter written findings of fact and conclusions of law. Custody and visitation rights shall be ordered in a manner that best protects the child and the parent or other family or household member who is the victim of domestic violence from any further harm.

7. Intention of either parent to relocate the principal residence of the child.
8. Wishes of a child as to the child's custodian.
9. The fact that a parent sends his or her child or children to a home school shall not be the sole factor that a court considers in determining custody of such child or children.
10. The court shall not award custody of a child to a parent if such parent has been found guilty of, or pled guilty to, a felony sex crime when the child was the victim.
11. As between the parents of a child, no preference may be given to either parent in the awarding of custody because of that parent's age, sex, or financial status, nor because of the age or sex of the child.

Missouri Revised Statutes Sec. 452.375.1.

MONTANA

Presumptions:

The court shall determine the parenting plan in accordance with the best interest of the child. *Montana Code Sec. 40-4-212(1).*

The following are rebuttable presumptions and apply unless contrary to the best interest of the child:

(a) A parenting plan action brought by a parent within 6 months after a child support action against that parent is vexatious.

(b) A motion to amend a final parenting plan is vexatious if a parent seeks to amend a final parenting plan without making a good faith effort to comply with the provisions of the parenting plan or with dispute resolution provisions of the final parenting plan. *Montana Code Sec. 40-4-212(3).*

Factors:

1. Wishes of the child's parent or parents.
2. Wishes of the child.
3. Interaction and interrelationship of the child with the child's parent or parents and siblings and with any other person who significantly affects the child's best interest.
4. Child's adjustment to home, school, and community.
5. Mental and physical health of all individuals involved.
6. Physical abuse or threat of physical abuse by one parent against the other parent or the child.
7. Chemical dependency or abuse on the part of either parent.
8. Continuity and stability of care.
9. Developmental needs of the child.
10. Whether a parent has knowingly failed to pay birth-related costs that the parent is able to pay, which is considered to be not in the child's best interests.
11. Whether a parent has knowingly failed to financially support a child that the parent is able to support, which is considered to be not in the child's best interests.
12. Whether the child has frequent and continuing contact with both parents, which is considered to be in the child's best interests unless the court determines, after a

hearing, that contact with a parent would be detrimental to the child's best interests. In making that determination, the court shall consider evidence of physical
abuse or threat of physical abuse by one parent against the other parent or the
child, including but not limited to whether a parent or other person residing in that
parent's household has been convicted of certain crimes.
13. Adverse effects on the child resulting from continuous and vexatious parenting plan
    amendment actions.
    Montana Code Sec. 40-4-212.

NEBRASKA

Presumptions:
No presumptions.
Factors:
1. Relationship of the child to each parent prior to the commencement of the action or
   any subsequent hearing.
2. Desires and wishes of the child if of an age of comprehension when such desires and
   wishes are based on sound reasoning.
3. General health, welfare, and social behavior of the minor child.
4. Credible evidence of abuse inflicted on any family or household member.
5. In determining custody arrangements and the time to be spent with each parent, the
   court shall not give preference to either parent based on the sex of the parent and no
   presumption shall exist that either parent is more fit or suitable than the other.
   Nebraska Statutes Sec. 42-364(2).

NEVADA

Presumptions:
Except as otherwise provided a determination by the court after an evidentiary hearing and
finding by clear and convincing evidence that either parent or any other person seeking custody has engaged in one or more acts of domestic violence against the child, a parent of the
child or any other person residing with the child creates a rebuttable presumption that sole
or joint custody of the child by the perpetrator of the domestic violence is not in the best
interest of the child. *Nevada Revised Statutes Sec. 125.480(5).*
　　There is a presumption, affecting the burden of proof, that joint custody would be in
the best interest of a minor child if the parents have agreed to an award of joint custody or
so agree in open court at a hearing for the purpose of determining the custody of the minor
child or children of the marriage. *Nevada Revised Statutes Sec. 125.490(1).*
Factors:
1. Wishes of the child if the child is of sufficient age and capacity to form an intelligent
   preference as to his custody.
2. Any nomination by a parent or a guardian for the child.
3. Whether either parent or any other person seeking custody has engaged in an act of
   domestic violence against the child, a parent of the child or any other person residing
   with the child.

4. Preference must not be given to either parent for the sole reason that the parent is the mother or the father of the child.
Nevada Revised Statutes Sec. 125.480(4).

NEW HAMPSHIRE

Presumptions:
Except as provided, in the making of any order relative to such custody there shall be a presumption, affecting the burden of proof, that joint legal custody is in the best interest of minor children. *New Hampshire Revised Statutes Sec. 458:17(II).*

Factors:
In all cases where there shall be a decree of divorce or nullity, the court shall make such further decree in relation to the custody of the children as shall be most conducive to their benefit.

1. Where the parents have agreed to an award of joint legal custody or so agree in open court joint legal custody is presumed to be in the best interest of the children.
2. Upon the application of either parent for joint legal custody, in which case it may be awarded in the discretion of the court.
3. Where the court finds that abuse has occurred, the court shall consider such abuse as harmful to children and as evidence in determining whether joint legal custody is appropriate. In such cases, the court shall make custody and visitation orders that best protect the children or the abused spouse or both.
4. The paramount and controlling consideration in deciding child custody is the overall welfare of the child, and there is no one formula for all cases, each case being determined by its particular facts.
5. Considerable weight may be given to the stated preference of a mature minor, provided that preference was not unduly influenced.

New Hampshire Revised Statutes Sec. 458:17.

NEW JERSEY

Presumptions:
In a custody dispute between a parent and a third party, a presumption exists in favor of the parent; a third party can overcome that presumption by satisfying the standard required for termination of the rights of the non-consenting parent. *Watkins v. Nelson,* 163 N.J. 235, 748 A.2d 558 (2000).

Factors:
1. Parents' ability to agree, communicate and cooperate in matters relating to the child.
2. Parents' willingness to accept custody and any history of unwillingness to allow parenting time not based on substantiated abuse.
3. Interaction and relationship of the child with its parents and siblings.
4. History of domestic violence, if any.
5. Safety of the child and the safety of either parent from physical abuse by the other parent.

6. Preference of the child when of sufficient age and capacity to reason so as to form an intelligent decision.
7. Needs of the child.
8. Stability of the home environment offered.
9. Quality and continuity of the child's education.
10. Fitness of the parents.
11. Geographical proximity of the parents' homes.
12. Extent and quality of the time spent with the child prior to or subsequent to the separation.
13. Parents' employment responsibilities.
14. Age and number of the children.
New Jersey Statutes 9:2-4.

NEW MEXICO

Presumptions:
No presumptions.
Factors:
1. Wishes of the child's parent or parents as to his custody.
2. Wishes of the child as to his custodian.
3. Interaction and interrelationship of the child with his parents, his siblings and any other person who may significantly affect the child's best interest.
4. Child's adjustment to his home, school and community.
5. Mental and physical health of all individuals involved.
6. If the child is fourteen years of age or older, the court shall consider the desires of the minor as to with whom he wishes to live before awarding custody of such minor.
In addition, for joint custody:
1. Whether the child has established a close relationship with each parent.
2. Whether each parent is capable of providing adequate care for the child throughout each period of responsibility, including arranging for the child's care by others as needed.
3. Whether each parent is willing to accept all responsibilities of parenting, including a willingness to accept care of the child at specified times and to relinquish care to the other parent at specified times.
4. Whether the child can best maintain and strengthen a relationship with both parents through predictable, frequent contact and whether the child's development will profit from such involvement and influence from both parents.
5. Whether each parent is able to allow the other to provide care without intrusion, that is, to respect the other's parental rights and responsibilities and right to privacy.
6. Suitability of a parenting plan for the implementation of joint custody, preferably, although not necessarily, one arrived at through parental agreement.
7. Geographic distance between the parents' residences.
8. Willingness or ability of the parents to communicate, cooperate or agree on issues regarding the child's needs.

9. Whether a judicial adjudication has been made in a prior or the present proceeding that either parent or other person seeking custody has engaged in one or more acts of domestic abuse against the child, a parent of the child or other household member.
10. The court shall not prefer one parent as a custodian solely because of gender.
New Mexico Statutes Sec. 40-4-9.1.

NEW YORK

Presumptions:
There is presumption that, absent extraordinary circumstances, child should be in custody of natural parent, but presumption should be rebuttable where child has developed secure, stable and continuing parent-child relationship with third party who has become psychological parent. *Doe v. Doe* 92 Misc. 2d 184, 399 N.Y.S.2d 977 (1977).
Factors:
There are no custody factors in New York.

NORTH CAROLINA

Presumptions:
"The presumption in favor of the natural parents is rebuttable" *Best v. Best,* 81 N.C. App. 337, 344 S.E.2d 363 (1986); *Petersen v. Rowe,* 337 N.C. 397, 445 S.E.2d 901 (1994).
    "Although there is a rebuttable presumption in favor of a natural parent, it is not necessary to prove unfitness in order to overcome the presumption." *Black v. Glawson,* 114 N.C. App. 442, 442 S.E.2d 79 (1994).
Factors:
   1. Acts of domestic violence between the parties.
   2. Safety of the child.
   3. Safety of either party from domestic violence by the other party.
   4. Between the mother and father, whether natural or adoptive, no presumption shall apply as to who will better promote the interest and welfare of the child.
North Carolina General Statutes Sec. 50-13.2(a).

NORTH DAKOTA

Presumptions:
In awarding custody or granting rights of visitation, the court shall consider evidence of domestic violence. If the court finds credible evidence that domestic violence has occurred, and there exists one incident of domestic violence which resulted in serious bodily injury or involved the use of a dangerous weapon or there exists a pattern of domestic violence within a reasonable time proximate to the proceeding, this combination creates a rebuttable presumption that a parent who has perpetrated domestic violence may not be awarded sole or joint custody of a child. This presumption may be overcome only by clear and convincing evidence that the best interests of the child require that parent's participation as a custodial parent. *North Dakota Century Code Sec. 14-09-06.2(1)(j).*

Factors:

1. Love, affection, and other emotional ties existing between the parents and child.
2. Capacity and disposition of the parents to give the child love, affection, and guidance and to continue the education of the child.
3. Disposition of the parents to provide the child with food, clothing, medical care, or other remedial care in lieu of medical care, and other material needs.
4. Length of time the child has lived in a stable satisfactory environment and the desirability of maintaining continuity.
5. Permanence, as a family unit, of the existing or proposed custodial home.
6. Moral fitness of the parents.
7. Mental and physical health of the parents.
8. Home, school, and community record of the child.
9. Reasonable preference of the child, if the court deems the child to be of sufficient intelligence, understanding, and experience to express a preference.
10. Evidence of domestic violence.
11. Interaction and interrelationship, or the potential for interaction and interrelationship, of the child with any person who resides in, is present, or frequents the household of a parent and who may significantly affect the child's best interests. The court shall consider that person's history of inflicting, or tendency to inflict, physical harm, bodily injury, assault, or the fear of physical harm, bodily injury, or assault, on other persons.
12. False allegations, not made in good faith, by one parent against the other, of harm to a child.
13. Any other factors considered by the court to be relevant to a particular child custody dispute.

North Dakota Century Code Sec. 14-09-06.2.

OHIO

Presumptions:
No presumptions.

Factors:

For custody determination:
1. Wishes of the child's parents regarding the child's care.
2. Wishes and concerns of the child, as expressed to the court in chambers.
3. Child's interaction and interrelationship with the child's parents, siblings, and any other person who may significantly affect the child's best interest.
4. Child's adjustment to the child's home, school, and community.
5. Mental and physical health of all persons involved in the situation.
6. Parent more likely to honor and facilitate court-approved parenting time rights or visitation and companionship rights.
7. Whether either parent has failed to make all child support payments, including all arrearages, that are required of that parent pursuant to a child support order under which that parent is an obligor.
8. Child abuse or neglect.

9. Whether the residential parent or one of the parents subject to a shared parenting decree has continuously and willfully denied the other parent's right to parenting time in accordance with an order of the court.
10. Whether either parent has established a residence, or is planning to establish a residence, outside this state.

Additional factors for shared parenting:
1. Ability of the parents to cooperate and make decisions jointly, with respect to the children.
2. Ability of each parent to encourage the sharing of love, affection, and contact between the child and the other parent.
3. Any history of, or potential for, child abuse, spouse abuse, other domestic violence, or parental kidnapping by either parent.
4. Geographic proximity of the parents to each other, as the proximity relates to the practical considerations of shared parenting.
5. The recommendation of the guardian ad litem of the child, if the child has a guardian ad litem.
6. The court shall not give preference to a parent because of that parent's financial status or condition.

Ohio Revised Code Sec. 3109.04(F)(1).

OKLAHOMA

Presumptions:
No presumptions.

Factors:
1. Which parent is more likely to allow the child or children frequent and continuing contact with the noncustodial parent.
2. The court shall not prefer a parent as a custodian of the child because of the gender of that parent.

Oklahoma Statutes tit. 43 Sec. 112.

OREGON

Presumptions:
The best interests and welfare of the child in a custody matter shall not be determined by isolating any one of the relevant factors, or any other relevant factor, and relying on it to the exclusion of other factors. However, if a parent has committed abuse, there is a rebuttable presumption that it is not in the best interests and welfare of the child to award sole or joint custody of the child to the parent who committed the abuse. *Oregon Revised Statutes Sec. 107.137(2).*

Factors:
1. Emotional ties between the child and other family members.
2. Interest of the parties in and attitude toward the child.
3. Desirability of continuing an existing relationship.

4. Abuse of one parent by the other.
5. Preference for the primary caregiver of the child, if the caregiver is deemed fit by the court.
6. Willingness and ability of each parent to facilitate and encourage a close and continuing relationship between the other parent and the child. However, the court may not consider such willingness and ability if one parent shows that the other parent has sexually assaulted or engaged in a pattern of behavior of abuse against the parent or a child and that a continuing relationship with the other parent will endanger the health or safety of either parent or the child.

Oregon Revised Statutes Sec. 107.137.

PENNSYLVANIA

Presumptions:

No presumptions.

Factors:

1. Preference of the child.
2. Any other factor which legitimately impacts the child's physical, intellectual and emotional well-being.
3. Which parent is more likely to encourage, permit and allow frequent and continuing contact and physical access between the noncustodial parent and the child.
4. Each parent and adult household member's present and past violent or abusive conduct.
5. Criminal conviction or conduct of a parent.

Pennsylvania Consolidated Statutes Sec. 5303.

RHODE ISLAND

Presumptions:

No presumptions.

Factors:

1. The fact that a parent is receiving public assistance shall not be a factor in awarding custody.
2. Evidence of past or present domestic violence. The court shall consider as primary the safety and well-being of the child and of the parent who is the victim of domestic or family violence. The court shall also consider the perpetrator's history of causing physical harm, bodily injury or assault to another person.

Rhode Island Code Sec. 15-5-16(d).

SOUTH CAROLINA

Presumptions:

No presumptions.

Factors:

1. Court may issue orders touching the care, custody and maintenance of the children of the marriage and what, if any, security shall be given for the same as from the circumstances of the parties and the nature of the case and the best spiritual as well as other interests of the children may be fit, equitable and just.
2. In placing the child in the custody of an individual or a private agency or institution, the court shall, whenever practicable, select a person or an agency or institution governed by persons of the same religious faith as that of the parents of such child, or, in case of a difference in the religious faith of the parents, then of the religious faith of the child, or, if the religious faith of the child is not ascertainable, then of the faith of either of the parents.

South Carolina Code Secs. 20-3-160 and 20-7-1520.

SOUTH DAKOTA

Presumptions:

No presumptions.

Factors:

1. The court shall be guided by consideration of what appears to be for the best interests of the child in respect to the child's temporal and mental and moral welfare.
2. If the child is of a sufficient age to form an intelligent preference, the court may consider that preference in determining the question.
3. As between parents adversely claiming the custody, neither parent may be given preference over the other in determining custody.
3. Fault shall not be taken into account with regard to child custody, except as it may be relevant to the fitness of either parent.
4. The expressed desires of the parents for joint legal custody.

South Dakota Statutes Secs. 25-4-45, 25-4-45.1, and 25-5-7.1.

TENNESSEE

Presumptions:

Notwithstanding any common law presumption to the contrary, a finding that child abuse, or child sexual abuse has occurred within the family shall give rise to a rebuttable presumption that it is detrimental to the child and not in the best interests of the child to award sole custody, joint legal or joint physical custody to the perpetrator of such abuse. *Tennessee Code Sec. 36-6-101(4).*

Factors:

1. Child abuse or child sexual abuse within the family (rebuttable presumption that it is detrimental to the child and not in the best interests of the child to award sole custody, joint legal or joint physical custody to the perpetrator of such abuse).
2. Gender of the party seeking custody shall not give rise to a presumption of parental fitness or cause a presumption or constitute a factor in favor or against the award of custody to such party.

Tennessee Code Sec. 36-6-101.

TEXAS

Presumptions:

The court may not appoint joint managing conservators if credible evidence is presented of a history or pattern of past or present child neglect, or physical or sexual abuse by one parent directed against the other parent, a spouse, or a child, including a sexual assault that results in the other parent becoming pregnant with the child. A history of sexual abuse includes a sexual assault that results in the other parent becoming pregnant with the child, regardless of the prior relationship of the parents. It is a rebuttable presumption that the appointment of a parent as the sole managing conservator of a child or as the conservator who has the exclusive right to determine the primary residence of a child is not in the best interest of the child if credible evidence is presented of a history or pattern of past or present child neglect, or physical or sexual abuse by that parent directed against the other parent, a spouse, or a child. *Texas Family Code Sec. 153.004(b).*

It is a rebuttable presumption that it is not in the best interest of a child for a parent to have unsupervised visitation with the child if credible evidence is presented of a history or pattern of past or present child neglect or physical or sexual abuse by that parent directed against the other parent, a spouse, or a child. *Texas Family Code Sec. 153.004(e).*

Factors:

1. Qualifications of the parties without regard to their marital status or to the sex of the party or the child.
2. Evidence of the intentional use of abusive physical force by a party against the party's spouse, a parent of the child, or any person younger than 18 years of age committed within a two-year period preceding the filing of the suit or during the pendency of the suit.
3. The court may not appoint joint managing conservators if credible evidence is presented of a history or pattern of past or present child neglect, or physical or sexual abuse by one parent directed against the other parent, a spouse, or a child, including a sexual assault that results in the other parent becoming pregnant with the child.
4. Family violence.
5. Age, developmental status, circumstances, needs, and best interest of the child.
6. Circumstances of the managing conservator and of the parent named as a possessory conservator.
7. Any other relevant factor.

Texas Family Code Secs. 153.002, 153.003, 153.004, and 153.256.

UTAH

Presumptions:

If the parties are unable to agree on a parent-time schedule, the court may establish a parent-time schedule consistent with the best interests of the child. *Utah Code Sec. 30-3-34(1).*

The advisory guidelines and the parent-time schedule shall be presumed to be in the best interests of the child. The parent-time schedule shall be considered the minimum parent-time to which the noncustodial parent and the child shall be entitled unless a parent can establish otherwise by a preponderance of the evidence that more or less parent-time should be awarded. *Utah Code Sec. 30-3-34(1)(2).*

Factors:

1. Whether the physical, psychological, and emotional needs and development of the child will benefit from joint legal or physical custody.
2. Ability of the parents to give first priority to the welfare of the child and reach shared decisions in the child's best interest.
3. Whether each parent is capable of encouraging and accepting a positive relationship between the child and the other parent, including the sharing of love, affection, and contact between the child and the other parent.
4. Whether both parents participated in raising the child before the divorce.
5. Geographical proximity of the homes of the parents.
6. Preference of the child if the child is of sufficient age and capacity to reason so as to form an intelligent preference as to joint legal or physical custody.
7. Maturity of the parents and their willingness and ability to protect the child from conflict that may arise between the parents.
8. Past and present ability of the parents to cooperate with each other and make decisions jointly.
9. Any history of, or potential for, child abuse, spouse abuse, or kidnaping.
10. Any other factors the court finds relevant.

Utah Code Sec. 30-3-10.2.

VERMONT

Presumptions:

No presumptions.

Factors:

1. Relationship of the child with each parent and the ability and disposition of each parent to provide the child with love, affection and guidance.
2. Ability and disposition of each parent to assure that the child receives adequate food, clothing, medical care, other material needs and a safe environment.
3. Ability and disposition of each parent to meet the child's present and future developmental needs.
4. Quality of the child's adjustment to the child's present housing, school and community and the potential effect of any change.
5. Ability and disposition of each parent to foster a positive relationship and frequent and continuing contact with the other parent, including physical contact, except where contact will result in harm to the child or to a parent.
6. Quality of the child's relationship with the primary care provider, if appropriate given the child's age and development.
7. Relationship of the child with any other person who may significantly affect the child.
8. Ability and disposition of the parents to communicate, cooperate with each other and make joint decisions concerning the children where parental rights and responsibilities are to be shared or divided.

9. Evidence of abuse, and the impact of the abuse on the child and on the relationship between the child and the abusing parent.
10. The court shall not apply a preference for one parent over the other because of the sex of the child, the sex of a parent or the financial resources of a parent. The court may order a parent who is awarded responsibility for a certain matter involving a child's welfare to inform the other parent when a major change in that matter occurs.
Vermont Statutes tit. 15 Sec. 665.

VIRGINIA

Presumptions:
"The law presumes that the best interest will be served when the child is in the custody of the natural parents" *Judd v. Van Horn,* 195 Va. 988, 81 S.E.2d 432 (1954); *Tanner v. Price,* 48 Va. Cir. 314 (1999).

"This presumption is rebuttable, however, if the non-parent adduces clear and convincing evidence that (1) the parents are unfit; (2) a court previously has granted an order of divestiture; (3) the parents voluntarily relinquished custody; (4) the parents abandoned the child; or (5) special facts and circumstances constitute an extraordinary reason to take the child from the parents. *Bailes v. Sours,* 231 Va. 96, 340 S.E.2d 824, (1986).

"Once the presumption favoring parental custody is rebutted, the natural parents who are seeking to regain custody must bear the burden of proving that custody with them is in the child's best interests." *Shortridge v. Deel,* 224 Va. 589, 299 S.E.2d 500 (1983).

Factors:
1. Age and physical and mental condition of the child, giving due consideration to the child's changing developmental needs.
2. Age and physical and mental condition of each parent.
3. Relationship existing between each parent and each child, giving due consideration to the positive involvement with the child's life, the ability to accurately assess and meet the emotional, intellectual and physical needs of the child.
4. Needs of the child, giving due consideration to other important relationships of the child, including but not limited to siblings, peers and extended family members.
5. Role which each parent has played and will play in the future, in the upbringing and care of the child.
6. Propensity of each parent to actively support the child's contact and relationship with the other parent, including whether a parent has unreasonably denied the other parent access to or visitation with the child.
7. Relative willingness and demonstrated ability of each parent to maintain a close and continuing relationship with the child, and the ability of each parent to cooperate in and resolve disputes regarding matters affecting the child.
8. Reasonable preference of the child, if the court deems the child to be of reasonable intelligence, understanding, age and experience to express such a preference.
9. Any history of family abuse.
10. Such other factors as the court deems necessary and proper to the determination.
Virginia Code Sec. 20-124.3.

WASHINGTON

Presumptions:

There *is* a rebuttable presumption that custody orders will not be disturbed, absent some showing that it would be in the best interests of the child. "Litigation on the custody issue is inconsistent with the welfare of the children. It should be avoided unless first there is a showing that a custody change is in their best interest." *Re: Marriage of Roorda*, 25 Wash. App. 849, 611 P.2d 794 (1980); *Potts v. Potts*, 40 Wash. App. 582; 699 P.2d 799 (1985).

Factors:

For Joint Legal Custody:
1. Agreements between the parties.
2. The existence of a limitation under RCW 26.09.191.
3. History of participation of each parent in decision making.
4. Whether the parents have a demonstrated ability and desire to cooperate with one another in decision making.
5. Parents' geographic proximity to one another, to the extent that it affects their ability to make timely mutual decisions.

For Physical Custody:
1. Relative strength, nature, and stability of the child's relationship with each parent, including whether a parent has taken greater responsibility for performing parenting functions relating to the daily needs of the child.
2. Agreements of the parties, provided they were entered into knowingly and voluntarily.
3. Each parent's past and potential for future performance of parenting functions.
4. Emotional needs and developmental level of the child.
5. Child's relationship with siblings and with other significant adults, as well as the child's involvement with his or her physical surroundings, school, or other significant activities.
6. Wishes of the parents and the wishes of a child who is sufficiently mature to express reasoned and independent preferences as to his or her residential schedule.
7. Each parent's employment schedule, and shall make accommodations consistent with those schedules.

Washington Revised Code Sec. 26.09.187.

WEST VIRGINIA

Presumptions:

"The primary caretaker presumption is rebuttable and may be overcome if the primary caretaker parent is shown by a clear preponderance of the evidence to be an unfit person to have custody of a child of tender years."
J.B. v. A.B., 161 W. Va. 332.

Factors:

"The primary caretaker presumption is rebuttable and may be overcome if the primary caretaker parent is shown by a clear preponderance of the evidence to be an unfit person to have custody of a child of tender years."
J.B. v. A.B., 161 W. Va. 332.

WISCONSIN

Presumptions:

Joint legal custody will not be awarded when the court finds that the parties will not be able to cooperate in the future decision making required under an award of joint legal custody. In making this finding the court shall consider, along with any other pertinent items, any reasons offered by a party objecting to joint legal custody. Evidence that either party engaged in abuse of the child or evidence of interspousal battery, or domestic abuse, creates a rebuttable presumption that the parties will not be able to cooperate in the future decision making required. *Wisconsin Statutes Sec. 767.24(2)(c).*

Factors:

1. Wishes of the child's parent or parents, as shown by any stipulation between the parties, any proposed parenting plan or any legal custody or physical placement proposal submitted to the court at trial.
2. Wishes of the child, which may be communicated by the child or through the child's guardian ad litem or other appropriate professional.
3. Interaction and interrelationship of the child with his or her parent or parents, siblings, and any other person who may significantly affect the child's best interest.
4. Amount and quality of time that each parent has spent with the child in the past, any necessary changes to the parents custodial roles and any reasonable life-style changes that a parent proposes to make to be able to spend time with the child in the future.
5. Child's adjustment to the home, school, religion and community.
6. Age of the child and the child's developmental and educational needs at different ages.
7. Mental and physical health of the parties, the minor children and other persons living in a proposed custodial household.
8. Need for regularly occurring and meaningful periods of physical placement to provide predictability and stability for the child.
9. Availability of public or private child care services.
10. Cooperation and communication between the parties and whether either party unreasonably refuses to cooperate or communicate with the other party.
11. Whether each party can support the other party's relationship with the child, including encouraging and facilitating frequent and continuing contact with the child, or whether one party is likely to unreasonably interfere with the child's continuing relationship with the other party.
12. Whether there is evidence that a party engaged in abuse of the child.
13. Whether there is evidence of interspousal battery or domestic abuse.
14. Whether either party has or had a significant problem with alcohol or drug abuse.
15. The reports of appropriate professionals if admitted into evidence.
16. Such other factors as the court may in each individual case determine to be relevant.
17. The court may not prefer one parent or potential custodian over the other on the basis of the sex or race of the parent or potential custodian.

Wisconsin Statutes Sec. 767.24(5).

WYOMING

Presumptions:

No presumptions.

Factors:

1. Quality of the relationship each child has with each parent.
2. Ability of each parent to provide adequate care for each child throughout each period of responsibility, including arranging for each child's care by others as needed.
3. Relative competency and fitness of each parent.
4. Each parent's willingness to accept all responsibilities of parenting, including a willingness to accept care for each child at specified times and to relinquish care to the other parent at specified times.
5. How the parents and each child can best maintain and strengthen a relationship with each other.
6. How the parents and each child interact and communicate with each other and how such interaction and communication may be improved.
7. Ability and willingness of each parent to allow the other to provide care without intrusion, respect the other parent's rights and responsibilities, including the right to privacy.
8. Geographic distance between the parents' residences.
9. Current physical and mental ability of each parent to care for each child.
10. Evidence of spousal abuse or child abuse.
11. Any other factors the court deems necessary and relevant.
12. The court shall not prefer one parent as a custodian solely because of gender.

Wyoming Code Sec. 20-2-201.

CHILD SUPPORT AGE OF TERMINATION AND COLLEGE EXPENSES

The following is a state-by-state breakdown of the age at which child support terminates and a father's obligation to pay for college expenses under state law. If you have an agreement with the mother of your children that identifies a different termination age or obligation for college expenses, it will override the state law.

Alabama
Age: 19, or graduation from high school.
Alabama Code Sec. 26-1-1.
College: Court may order parents to pay for college.
Ex Parte Bayliss, 550 So. 2d 1038 (1989); *Alabama Code Sec. 30-3-1.*

Alaska
Age: 18, or 19 if child is in high school or equivalent and lives with custodial parent.
Alaska Statutes Title 20.
College: No requirement to pay for college.
H.P.A. v. S.C.A., 704 P.2d 205 (Alaska 1985).

Arizona
Age: 18, or graduation from high school.
Arizona Revised Statutes Sec. 8-101.
College: No requirement to pay for college, but courts will enforce agreements to pay.
Solomon v. Findley, 167 Ariz. 409, 808 P.2d 294 (1991).

Arkansas
Age: 18, or graduation from high school.
Arkansas Code Sec. 9-2501.
College: No requirement to pay for college.
Towery v. Towery, 285 Ark. 113, 685 S.W.2d 155 (1985).

California
Age: 18, or if child is in high school, then 19 or graduation, whichever is first.
California Family Code Sec. 6502.
College: No requirement to pay for college.

Colorado
Age: 19, or court order.
Colorado Revised Statutes Sec. 19-1-103.
College: Court may order parents to pay for college.
Colorado Revised Statutes Sec. 14-10-115(1.5)(b); In re marriage of Robb, 934 P.2d 927 (Col. Ct. App. 1997).

Connecticut
Age: 18.
Connecticut General Statutes Sec. 1-1d.
College: No requirement to pay for college.
Cariseo v. Cariseo, 190 Conn. 141, 459 A.2d 523 (1983).

Delaware
Age: 18, or if child is in high school, then 19 or graduation, whichever is first.
Delaware Code tit. 1 Sec. 701.
College: No requirement to pay for college.

District of Columbia
Age: 21, or emancipation.
D.C. Code Sec. 46-101.
College: No requirement to pay for college.

Florida
Age: 18, or 19 if child will graduate from high school by that age.
Florida Statutes Sec. 743.07.
College: Courts may order parents to pay for college of actual dependents, but attending college does not necessarily make a child a dependent.
Slaton v. Slaton, 428 So. 2d 347 (Fla. DCA 1983).

Georgia
Age: 18.
Georgia Code Annotated Sec. 39-1-1.
College: The court may order parents to pay college until age 20.
Georgia Code Annotated Sec. 19-6-15(e).

Hawaii
Age: 18.
Hawaii Revised Statutes Sec. 577-1.
College: The court may order parents to pay for college to age 23.
Hawaii Revised Statutes Sec. 580-47.

Idaho
Age: 18, or 19 by court order if child is in school.
Idaho Statutes Sec. 32-101.
College: No requirement to pay for college.

Illinois
Age: 18.
755 ILCS 5/11-1.
College: The court may order parents to pay for college.
750 ILCS 5/51.

Indiana
Age:	21.
	Indiana Code Sec. 31-16-6-6.
College:	Order may include amounts for college expenses.
	Indiana Code Sec. 31-16-6-2.

Iowa
Age:	18, or if child is between 18 and 19, then high school graduation by court order.
	Iowa Code Sec. 599.1.
College:	No requirement to pay for college.

Kansas
Age:	18, extended to end of school year in which child turns 18, and may be extended to 19 on agreement of parents.
	Kansas Statutes Sec. 38-101.
College:	No requirement to pay for college.

Kentucky
Age:	18, or 19 if child is still attending high school.
	Kentucky Revised Statutes Sec. 2.015.
College:	No requirement to pay for college.

Louisiana
Age:	18, or emancipation; if child is still in secondary school or an equivalent, until 19 or graduation, whichever is first; or 22 if child is disabled.
	Louisiana Civil Code art. 29
College:	No requirement to pay for college.

Maine
Age:	18, or if child is still in high school, then 19.
	Maine Revised Statutes tit. 1 Sec. 72(2-a).
College:	No requirement to pay for college.

Maryland
Age:	18, or if child is in high school, then 19 or graduation, whichever is first.
	Maryland Family Law Code Sec. 24.
College:	No requirement to pay for college.

Massachusetts
Age:	18, or to 21 if child lives with and is dependent upon a parent, or age 23 if in school.
	Massachusetts General Laws ch.4 Sec. 7(51).
College:	College expenses are part of support.

Michigan
Age:	18, but may be ordered until 19½ for completion of high school.
	Michigan Compiled Laws Sec. 722.52.
College:	No requirement to pay for college.

Minnesota
Age:	18, or 20 if child is in school.
	Minnesota Statutes Sec. 645.451.
College:	No requirement to pay for college.

Mississippi
Age: 21.
          Mississippi Code Sec. 93-11-65(8a).
College: The court may order parents to pay college expenses to age 21.
          Stokes v. Martin, 596 So. 2d 879 (Miss. 1992).

Missouri
Age: 18, or upon graduation from high school or age 21, whichever is first.
          Missouri Revised Statutes Sec. 452.240.
College: If child is in institution of higher learning, then child support will be
          extended to 22 or graduation, whichever is first.

Montana
Age: 18, or 19 if in high school.
          Montana Code Sec. 41-1-101.
College: No requirement to pay for college.

Nebraska
Age: 19.
          Nebraska Statutes Sec. 43-2101.
College: No requirement to pay for college costs, but parents agreements
          will be enforced.
          Zetterman v. Zetterman, 245 Neb. 255, 512 N.W.2d 622 (1994).

Nevada
Age: 18, or 19 if in high school.
          Nevada Revised Statutes Sec. 129-010.
College: No requirement to pay for college.

New Hampshire
Age: 18, or graduation from high school, whichever is later.
          New Hampshire Revised Statutes Sec. 21:24.
College: Court may order parents of adult children to pay for college in appropriate
          circumstances.
          Gnirk v. Gnirk, 134 N.H. 199, 589 A.2d 1008 (1991).

New Jersey
Age: 18, or as determined by the court.
          New Jersey Statutes Sec. 9-17B-3.
College: Court may order parents to pay for college even though the child
          has reached the age of majority.
          Newburgh v. Newburgh, 88 N.J. 529, 443 A.2d 1031 (1982).

New Mexico
Age: 18.
          New Mexico Statute Sec. 28-6-1 (2004).
College: No requirement to pay for college.

New York
Age: 21.
New York Domestic Relations Law Sec. 2.
College: Court may order parents to pay for college, private school or special enriched education. Court may not, however, order a parent to pay for college after 21.
Setford v. Cavanaugh, 175 A.D.2d 665, 572 N.Y.S.2d 591 (1991).

North Carolina
Age: 18, or through secondary school or age 20, whichever comes first.
North Carolina General Statutes Sec. 48A-2.
College: No requirement to pay for college.

North Dakota
Age: 18, but if in high school, then 19 or graduation.
North Dakota Century Code Sec. 14-10-02.
College: Court may order parents to pay for college.
North Dakota Century Code Sec. 14-09-08; Johnson v. Johnson, 527 N.W.2d 663 (N.D. 1995).

Ohio
Age: 18, or graduation from high school, whichever occurs later.
Ohio Code Sec. 3109.01.
College: Court can order parents to pay for college beyond the age of majority.
Ohio Code Sec. 3103.03.

Oklahoma
Age: 18, or until completion of high school.
Oklahoma Statutes tit. 10 Sec. 91-4.
College: No requirement to pay for college.

Oregon
Age: 18, or 21 if in school half-time or more.
Oregon Revised Statutes Sec. 109.510.
College: Court can order parents to pay for college to 21.
Oregon Revised Statutes Sec. 107.108; Crocker and Crocker, 332 Or. 42, 22 P.3d 759 (2001).

Pennsylvania
Age: 18, or completion of high school, whichever is later.
Pennsylvania Consolidated Statutes Sec. 5101.
College: No requirement to pay for college, but court will enforce agreement of the parties.
Curtis v. Kline, 542 Pa. 249, 666 A.2d 265 (1995).

Rhode Island
Age: 18, or if child is in high school, then 19 or 90 days past graduation, whichever is first.
Rhode Island General Laws Sec. 15-12-1.
College: No requirement to pay for college.

South Carolina
Age: 18, or until graduation from high school.
             South Carolina Code of Laws Sec. 20-7-30.
College: Court may order parents to pay for college.
             Risinger v. Risinger, 273 S.C. 36, 253 S.E.2d 652 (1979); *West v. West,*
             309 S.C. 28, 419 S.E.2d 804 (Ct. App. 1992).

South Dakota
Age: 18, or 19 if attending secondary school.
             South Dakota Codified Laws Sec. 26-1-1.
College: No requirement to pay for college.

Tennessee
Age: 18, or if in high school, then graduation.
             Tennessee Code Sec. 1-3-113.
College: No requirement to pay for college.

Texas
Age: 18, or graduation from high school, whichever is later.
             Texas Family Code Sec. 101.003.
College: No requirement to pay for college.

Utah
Age: 18, or graduation from high school.
             Utah Code Sec. 15-2-1.
College: The court may order parents to pay for college to age 21.
             Utah Code Sec. 15-2-1.

Vermont
Age: 18, or graduation from secondary school.
             Vermont Statutes Sec. 1-173.
College: No requirement to pay for college.

Virginia
Age: 18, unless child is in high school, then 19 or graduation, whichever comes first.
             Virginia Code Sec. 1-13.42.
College: No requirement to pay for college.

Washington
Age: 18.
             Washington Revised Code Sec. 26.28.010.
College: The court may, in its discretion, order parents to pay for college
             according to certain factors.
             Washington Revised Code Sec. 26.19.090.

West Virginia
Age: 21.
             West Virginia Code Sec. 36-7-1.
College: No requirement to pay for college.

Wisconsin

Age: 18, or if still in school, 19 or graduation from high school, whichever is first. *Wisconsin Statutes Sec. 990.01(3).*

College: No requirement to pay for college.

Wyoming

Age: 18, or to 20 or graduation for secondary education. *Wyoming Statutes Sec. 14-1-101.*

College: No requirement to pay for college.

–Appendix C–

LAWS TO PREVENT CHILD SNATCHING

This appendix contains two federal laws and one treaty that you will want to know about if you fear that your children may be taken to another state or country by your spouse, or if that has already happened. The first section is selected sections of the *Parental Kidnapping Prevention Act*. This law determines which state makes custody decisions when the parents are in different states (similar to the uniform statutes adopted by the states, the UCJA and the UCJEA discussed in Chapter 8).

PARENTAL KIDNAPPING PREVENTION ACT

The Hague Convention is a treaty adopted by the United States and several other countries to return children who are removed from their country of residence. The International Child Abduction Remedies Act is the law passes by Congress which sets forth the legal procedures for enforcing the Hague Convention in the United States.

Sec. 1738A. - Full faith and credit given to child custody determinations
(a) The appropriate authorities of every State shall enforce according to its terms, and shall not modify except as provided in subsections (f), (g), and (h) of this section, any custody determination or visitation determination made consistently with the provisions of this section by a court of another State.
(b) As used in this section, the term -
(1) "child" means a person under the age of eighteen;
(2) "contestant" means a person, including a parent or grandparent, who claims a right to custody or visitation of a child;

(3) "custody determination" means a judgment, decree, or other order of a court providing for the custody of a child, and includes permanent and temporary orders, and initial orders and modifications;
(4) "home State" means the State in which, immediately preceding the time involved, the child lived with his parents, a parent, or a person acting as parent, for at least six consecutive months, and in the case of a child less than six months old, the State in which the child lived from birth with any of such persons. Periods of temporary absence of any of such persons are counted as part of the six-month or other period;

(5) "modification" and "modify" refer to a custody or visitation determination which modifies, replaces, supersedes, or otherwise is made subsequent to, a prior custody or visitation determination concerning the same child, whether made by the same court or not;

(6) "person acting as a parent" means a person, other than a parent, who has physical custody of a child and who has either been awarded custody by a court or claims a right to custody;

(7) "physical custody" means actual possession and control of a child;

(8) "State" means a State of the United States, the District of Columbia, the Commonwealth of Puerto Rico, or a territory or possession of the United States; and

(9) "visitation determination" means a judgment, decree, or other order of a court providing for the visitation of a child and includes permanent and temporary orders and initial orders and modifications.

(c) A child custody or visitation determination made by a court of a State is consistent with the provisions of this section only if -

(1) such court has jurisdiction under the law of such State; and

(2) one of the following conditions is met:

(A) such State

(i) is the home State of the child on the date of the commencement of the proceeding, or

(ii) had been the child's home State within six months before the date of the commencement of the proceeding and the child is absent from such State because of his removal or retention by a contestant or for other reasons, and a contestant continues to live in such State;

(B) (i) it appears that no other State would have jurisdiction under subparagraph (A), and (ii) it is in the best interest of the child that a court of such State assume jurisdiction because

(I) the child and his parents, or the child and at least one contestant, have a significant connection with such State other than mere physical presence in such State, and

(II) there is available in such State substantial evidence concerning the child's present or future care, protection, training, and personal relationships;

(C) the child is physically present in such State and

(i) the child has been abandoned, or

(ii) it is necessary in an emergency to protect the child because the child, a sibling, or parent of the child has been subjected to or threatened with mistreatment or abuse;

(D)(i) it appears that no other State would have jurisdiction under subparagraph (A), (B), (C), or (E), or another State has declined to exercise jurisdiction on the ground that the State whose jurisdiction is in issue is the more appropriate forum to determine the custody or visitation of the child, and

(ii) it is in the best interest of the child that such court assume jurisdiction; or

(E) the court has continuing jurisdiction pursuant to subsection (d) of this section.

(d) The jurisdiction of a court of a State which has made a child custody or visitation determination consistently with the provisions of this section continues as long as the requirement of subsection (c)(1) of this section continues to be met and such State remains the residence of the child or of any contestant.

(e) Before a child custody or visitation determination is made, reasonable notice and opportunity to be heard shall be given to the contestants, any parent whose parental rights have not been previously terminated and any person who has physical custody of a child.

(f) A court of a State may modify a determination of the custody of the same child made by a court of another State, if -

(1) it has jurisdiction to make such a child custody determination; and

(2) the court of the other State no longer has jurisdiction, or it has declined to exercise such jurisdiction to modify such determination.

(g) A court of a State shall not exercise jurisdiction in any proceeding for a custody or visitation determination commenced during the pendency of a proceeding in a court of another State where such court of that other State is exercising jurisdiction consistently with the provisions of this section to make a custody or visitation determination.

(h) A court of a State may not modify a visitation determination made by a court of another State unless the court of the other State no longer has jurisdiction to modify such determination or has declined to exercise jurisdiction to modify such determination.

Sec. 1738B. - Full faith and credit for child support orders

(a) General Rule. - The appropriate authorities of each State -

(1) shall enforce according to its terms a child support order made consistently with this section by a court of another State; and

(2) shall not seek or make a modification of such an order except in accordance with subsections (e), (f), and (i).

(b) Definitions. - In this section:

"child" means -

(A) a person under 18 years of age; and

(B) a person 18 or more years of age with respect to whom a child support order has been issued pursuant to the laws of a State. "child's State" means the State in which a child resides. "child's home State" means the State in which a child lived with a parent or a person acting as parent for at least 6 consecutive months immediately preceding the time of filing of a petition or comparable pleading for support and, if a child is less than 6 months old, the State in which the child lived from birth with any of them. A period of temporary absence of any of them is counted as part of the 6-month period. "child support" means a payment of money, continuing support, or arrearages or the provision of a benefit (including payment of health insurance, child care, and educational expenses) for the support of a child. "child support order" -

(A) means a judgment, decree, or order of a court requiring the payment of child support in periodic amounts or in a lump sum; and

(B) includes -

(i) a permanent or temporary order; and

(ii) an initial order or a modification of an order.

"contestant" means -

(A) a person (including a parent) who -

(i) claims a right to receive child support;

(ii) is a party to a proceeding that may result in the issuance of a child support order; or

(iii) is under a child support order; and

(B) a State or political subdivision of a State to which the right to obtain child support has been assigned. "court" means a court or administrative agency of a State that is authorized by State law to establish the amount of child support payable by a contestant or make a modification of a child support order. "modification" means a change in a child support order that affects the amount, scope, or duration of the order and modifies, replaces, supersedes, or otherwise is made subsequent to the child support order. "State" means a State of the United States, the District of Columbia, the Commonwealth of Puerto Rico, the territories and possessions of the United States, and Indian country (as defined in section 1151 of title 18).

(c) Requirements of Child Support Orders. - A child support order made by a court of a State is made consistently with this section if -

(1) a court that makes the order, pursuant to the laws of the State in which the court is located and subsections (e), (f), and (g) -

(A) has subject matter jurisdiction to hear the matter and enter such an order; and

(B) has personal jurisdiction over the contestants; and

(2) reasonable notice and opportunity to be heard is given to the contestants.

(d) Continuing Jurisdiction. - A court of a State that has made a child support order consistently with this section has continuing, exclusive jurisdiction over the order if the State is the child's State or the residence of any individual contestant unless the court of another State, acting in accordance with subsections (e) and (f), has made a modification of the order.

(e) Authority To Modify Orders. - A court of a State may modify a child support order issued by a court of another State if -

(1) the court has jurisdiction to make such a child support order pursuant to subsection (i); and

(2)(A) the court of the other State no longer has continuing, exclusive jurisdiction of the child support order because that State no longer is the child's State or the residence of any individual contestant; or

(B) each individual contestant has filed written consent with the State of continuing, exclusive jurisdiction for a court of another State to modify the order and assume continuing, exclusive jurisdiction over the order.

(f) Recognition of Child Support Orders. - If 1 or more child support orders have been issued with regard to an obligor and a child, a court shall apply the following rules in determining which order to recognize for purposes of continuing, exclusive jurisdiction and enforcement:

(1) If only 1 court has issued a child support order, the order of that court must be recognized.

(2) If 2 or more courts have issued child support orders for the same obligor and child, and only 1 of the courts would have continuing, exclusive jurisdiction under this section, the order of that court must be recognized.

(3) If 2 or more courts have issued child support orders for the same obligor and child, and more than 1 of the courts would have continuing, exclusive jurisdiction under this section, an order issued by a court in the current home State of the child must be recognized, but if an order has not been issued in the current home State of the child, the order most recently issued must be recognized.

(4) If 2 or more courts have issued child support orders for the same obligor and child, and none of the courts would have continuing, exclusive jurisdiction under this section, a court having jurisdiction over the parties shall issue a child support order, which must be recognized.

(5) The court that has issued an order recognized under this subsection is the court having continuing, exclusive jurisdiction under subsection (d).

(g) Enforcement of Modified Orders. - A court of a State that no longer has continuing, exclusive jurisdiction of a child support order may enforce the order with respect to nonmodifiable obligations and unsatisfied obligations that accrued before the date on which a modification of the order is made under subsections (e) and (f).

(h) Choice of Law. -

(1) In general. - In a proceeding to establish, modify, or enforce a child support order, the forum State's law shall apply except as provided in paragraphs (2) and (3).

(2) Law of state of issuance of order. - In interpreting a child support order including the duration of current payments and other obligations of support, a court shall apply the law of the State of the court that issued the order.

(3) Period of limitation. - In an action to enforce arrears under a child support order, a court shall apply the statute of limitation of the forum State or the State of the court that issued the order, whichever statute provides the longer period of limitation.

(i) Registration for Modification. - If there is no individual contestant or child residing in the issuing State, the party or support enforcement agency seeking to modify, or to modify and enforce, a child support order issued in another State shall register that order in a State with jurisdiction over the nonmovant for the purpose of modification.

Sec. 1738C. - Certain acts, records, and proceedings and the effect thereof

No State, territory, or possession of the United States, or Indian tribe, shall be required to give effect to any public act, record, or judicial proceeding of any other State, territory, possession, or tribe respecting a relationship between persons of the same sex that is treated as a marriage under the laws of such other State, territory, possession, or tribe, or a right or claim arising from such relationship.

INTERNATIONAL CHILD ABDUCTION REMEDIES ACT

Sec. 11601. Findings and declarations

(a) Findings

The Congress makes the following findings:

(1) The international abduction or wrongful retention of children is harmful to their well-being.

(2) Persons should not be permitted to obtain custody of children by virtue of their wrongful removal or retention.

(3) International abductions and retentions of children are increasing, and only concerted cooperation pursuant to an international agreement can effectively combat this problem.

(4) The Convention on the Civil Aspects of International Child Abduction, done at The Hague on October 25, 1980, establishes legal rights and procedures for the prompt return of children who have been wrongfully

removed or retained, as well as for securing the exercise of visitation rights. Children who are wrongfully removed or retained within the meaning of the Convention are to be promptly returned unless one of the narrow exceptions set forth in the Convention applies. The Convention provides a sound treaty framework to help resolve the problem of international abduction and retention of children and will deter such wrongful removals and retentions.

(b) Declarations

The Congress makes the following declarations:

(1) It is the purpose of this chapter to establish procedures for the implementation of the Convention in the United States.

(2) The provisions of this chapter are in addition to and not in lieu of the provisions of the Convention.

(3) In enacting this chapter the Congress recognizes -

(A) the international character of the Convention; and

(B) the need for uniform international interpretation of the Convention.

(4) The Convention and this chapter empower courts in the United States to determine only rights under the Convention and not the merits of any underlying child custody claims.

Sec. 11602. Definitions

For the purposes of this chapter -

(1) the term "applicant" means any person who, pursuant to the Convention, files an application with the United States Central Authority or a Central Authority of any other party to the Convention for the return of a child alleged to have been wrongfully removed or retained or for arrangements for organizing or securing the effective exercise of rights of access pursuant to the Convention;

(2) the term "Convention" means the Convention on the Civil Aspects of International Child Abduction, done at The Hague on October 25, 1980;

(3) the term "Parent Locator Service" means the service established by the Secretary of Health and Human Services under section 653 of this title;

(4) the term "petitioner" means any person who, in accordance with this chapter, files a petition in court seeking relief under the Convention;

(5) the term "person" includes any individual, institution, or other legal entity or body;

(6) the term "respondent" means any person against whose interests a petition is filed in court, in accordance with this chapter, which seeks relief under the Convention;

(7) the term "rights of access" means visitation rights;

(8) the term "State" means any of the several States, the District of Columbia, and any commonwealth, territory, or possession of the United States; and

(9) the term "United States Central Authority" means the agency of the Federal Government designated by the President under section 11606(a) of this title.

Sec. 11603. Judicial remedies

(a) Jurisdiction of courts

The courts of the States and the United States district courts shall have concurrent original jurisdiction of actions arising under the Convention.

(b) Petitions

Any person seeking to initiate judicial proceedings under the Convention for the return of a child or for arrangements for organizing or securing the effective exercise of rights of access to a child may do so by commencing a civil action by filing a petition for the relief sought in any court which has jurisdiction of such action and which is authorized to exercise its jurisdiction in the place where the child is located at the time the petition is filed.

(c) Notice

Notice of an action brought under subsection (b) of this section shall be given in accordance with the applicable law governing notice in interstate child custody proceedings.

(d) Determination of case

The court in which an action is brought under subsection (b) of this section shall decide the case in accordance with the Convention.

(e) Burdens of proof

(1) A petitioner in an action brought under subsection (b) of this section shall establish by a preponderance of the evidence -

(A) in the case of an action for the return of a child, that the child has been wrongfully removed or retained within the meaning of the Convention; and

(B) in the case of an action for arrangements for organizing or securing the effective exercise of rights of access, that the petitioner has such rights.

(2) In the case of an action for the return of a child, a respondent who opposes the return of the child has the burden of establishing -

(A) by clear and convincing evidence that one of the exceptions set forth in article 13b or 20 of the Convention applies; and

(B) by a preponderance of the evidence that any other exception set forth in article 12 or 13 of the Convention applies.

(f) Application of Convention

For purposes of any action brought under this chapter -

(1) the term "authorities", as used in article 15 of the Convention to refer to the authorities of the state of the habitual residence of a child, includes courts and appropriate government agencies;

(2) the terms "wrongful removal or retention" and "wrongfully removed or retained", as used in the Convention, include a removal or retention of a child before the entry of a custody order regarding that child; and

(3) the term "commencement of proceedings", as used in article 12 of the Convention, means, with respect to the return of a child located in the United States, the filing of a petition in accordance with subsection (b) of this section.

(g) Full faith and credit

Full faith and credit shall be accorded by the courts of the States and the courts of the United States to the judgment of any other such court ordering or denying the return of a child, pursuant to the Convention, in an action brought under this chapter.

(h) Remedies under Convention not exclusive

The remedies established by the Convention and this chapter shall be in addition to remedies available under other laws or international agreements.

Sec. 11604. Provisional remedies

(a) Authority of courts

In furtherance of the objectives of article 7(b) and other provisions of the Convention, and subject to the provisions of subsection (b) of this section, any court exercising jurisdiction of an action brought under section 11603(b) of this title may take or cause to be taken measures under Federal or State law, as appropriate, to protect the well-being of the child involved or to prevent the child's further removal or concealment before the final disposition of the petition.

(b) Limitation on authority

No court exercising jurisdiction of an action brought under section 11603(b) of this title may, under subsection (a) of this section, order a child removed from a person having physical control of the child unless the applicable requirements of State law are satisfied.

Sec. 11605. Admissibility of documents

With respect to any application to the United States Central Authority, or any petition to a court under section 11603 of this title, which seeks relief under the Convention, or any other documents or information included with such application or petition or provided after such submission which relates to the application or petition, as the case may be, no authentication of such application, petition, document, or information shall be required in order for the application, petition, document, or information to be admissible in court.

Sec. 11606. United States Central Authority

(a) Designation

The President shall designate a Federal agency to serve as the Central Authority for the United States under the Convention.

(b) Functions

The functions of the United States Central Authority are those ascribed to the Central Authority by the Convention and this chapter.

(c) Regulatory authority

The United States Central Authority is authorized to issue such regulations as may be necessary to carry out its functions under the Convention and this chapter.

(d) Obtaining information from Parent Locator Service

The United States Central Authority may, to the extent authorized by the Social Security Act (42 U.S.C. 301 et seq.), obtain information from the Parent Locator Service.

Sec. 11607. Costs and fees

(a) Administrative costs

No department, agency, or instrumentality of the Federal Government or of any State or local government may impose on an applicant any fee in relation to the administrative processing of applications submitted under the Convention.

(b) Costs incurred in civil actions

(1) Petitioners may be required to bear the costs of legal counsel or advisors, court costs incurred in connection with their petitions, and travel costs for the return of the child involved and any accompanying persons, except as provided in paragraphs (2) and (3).

(2) Subject to paragraph (3), legal fees or court costs incurred in connection with an action brought under section 11603 of this title shall be borne by the petitioner unless they are covered by payments from Federal, State, or local legal assistance or other programs.

(3) Any court ordering the return of a child pursuant to an action brought under section 11603 of this title shall order the respondent to pay necessary expenses incurred by or on behalf of the petitioner, including court costs, legal fees, foster home or other care during the course of proceedings in the action, and transportation costs related to the return of the child, unless the respondent establishes that such order would be clearly inappropriate.

Sec. 11608. Collection, maintenance, and dissemination of information

(a) In general

In performing its functions under the Convention, the United States Central Authority may, under such conditions as the Central Authority prescribes by regulation, but subject to subsection (c) of this section, receive from or transmit to any department, agency, or instrumentality of the Federal Government or of any State or foreign government, and receive from or transmit to any applicant, petitioner, or respondent, information necessary to locate a child or for the purpose of otherwise implementing the Convention with respect to a child, except that the United States Central Authority -

(1) may receive such information from a Federal or State department, agency, or instrumentality only pursuant to applicable Federal and State statutes; and

(2) may transmit any information received under this subsection notwithstanding any provision of law other than this chapter.

(b) Requests for information

Requests for information under this section shall be submitted in such manner and form as the United States Central Authority may prescribe by regulation and shall be accompanied or supported by such documents as the United States Central Authority may require.

(c) Responsibility of government entities

Whenever any department, agency, or instrumentality of the United States or of any State receives a request from the United States Central Authority for information authorized to be provided to such Central Authority under subsection (a) of this section, the head of such department, agency, or instrumentality shall promptly cause a search to be made of the files and records maintained by such department, agency, or instrumentality in order to determine whether the information requested is contained in any such files or records. If such search discloses the information requested, the head of such department, agency, or instrumentality shall immediately transmit such information to the United States Central Authority, except that any such information the disclosure of which -

(1) would adversely affect the national security interests of the United States or the law enforcement interests of the United States or of any State; or

(2) would be prohibited by section 9 of title 13; shall not be transmitted to the Central Authority. The head of such department, agency, or instrumentality shall, immediately upon completion of the requested search, notify the Central Authority of the results of the search, and whether an exception set forth in paragraph (1) or (2) applies. In the event that the United States Central Authority receives information and the appropriate Federal or State department, agency, or instrumentality thereafter notifies the Central Authority that an exception set forth in paragraph (1) or (2) applies to that information, the Central Authority may not disclose that information under subsection (a) of this section.

(d) Information available from Parent Locator Service
To the extent that information which the United States Central Authority is authorized to obtain under the provisions of subsection (c) of this section can be obtained through the Parent Locator Service, the United States Central Authority shall first seek to obtain such information from the Parent Locator Service, before requesting such information directly under the provisions of subsection (c) of this section.
(e) Recordkeeping
The United States Central Authority shall maintain appropriate records concerning its activities and the disposition of cases brought to its attention.

Sec. 11609. Interagency coordinating group
The Secretary of State, the Secretary of Health and Human Services, and the Attorney General shall designate Federal employees and may, from time to time, designate private citizens to serve on an interagency coordinating group to monitor the operation of the Convention and to provide advice on its implementation to the United States Central Authority and other Federal agencies. This group shall meet from time to time at the request of the United States Central Authority. The agency in which the United States Central Authority is located is authorized to reimburse such private citizens for travel and other expenses incurred in participating at meetings of the interagency coordinating group at rates not to exceed those authorized under subchapter I of chapter 57 of title 5 for employees of agencies.

Sec. 11610. Authorization of appropriations
There are authorized to be appropriated for each fiscal year such sums as may be necessary to carry out the purposes of the Convention and this chapter.

HAGUE CONVENTION

The States signatory to the present Convention,

Firmly convinced that the interests of children are of paramount importance in matters relating to their custody, Desiring to protect children internationally from the harmful effects of their wrongful removal or retention and to establish procedures to ensure their prompt return to the State of their habitual residence, as well as to secure protection for rights of access,

Have resolved to conclude a Convention to this effect, and have agreed upon the following provisions -

CHAPTER I - SCOPE OF THE CONVENTION
Article 1
The objects of the present Convention are-
a) to secure the prompt return of children wrongfully removed to or retained in any Contracting State; and
b) to ensure that rights of custody and of access under the law of one Contracting State are effectively respected in other Contracting States.
Article 2
Contracting States shall take all appropriate measures to secure within their territories the implementation of the objects of the Convention. For this purpose they shall use the most expeditious procedures available.

Article 3
The removal or the retention of a child is to be considered wrongful where -
a) it is in breach of rights of custody attributed to a person, an institution or any other body, either jointly or alone, under the law of the State in which the child was habitually resident immediately before the removal or retention; and
b) at the time of removal or retention those rights were actually exercised, either jointly or alone, or would have been so exercised but for the removal or retention.
The rights of custody mentioned in subparagraph a above, may arise in particular by operation of law or by reason of a judicial or administrative decision, or by reason of an

agreement having legal effect under the law of that State.

Article 4

The Convention shall apply to any child who was habitually resident in a Contracting State immediately before any breach of custody or access rights. The Convention shall cease to apply when the child attaint the age of 16 years.

Article 5

For the purposes of this Convention -

a) 'rights of custody' shall include rights relating to the care of the person of the child and, in particular, the right to determine the child's place of residence;

b) 'rights of access' shall include the right to take a child for a limited period of time to a place other than the child's habitual residence.

CHAPTER II - CENTRAL AUTHORITIES

Article 6

A Contracting State shall designate a Central Authority to discharge the duties which are imposed by the Convention upon such authorities.

Federal States, States with more than one system of law or States having autonomous territorial organizations shall be free to appoint more than one Central Authority and to specify the territorial extent of their powers. Where a State has appointed more than one Central Authority, it shall designate the Central Authority to which applications may be addressed for transmission to the appropriate Central Authority within that State.

Article 7

Central Authorities shall co-operate with each other and promote co-operation amongst the competent authorities in their respective States to secure the prompt return of children and to achieve the other objects of this Convention.

In particular, either directly or through any intermediary, they shall take all appropriate measures -

a) to discover the whereabouts of a child who has been wrongfully removed or retained;

b) to prevent further harm to the child or prejudice to interested parties by taking or causing to be taken provisional measures;

c) to secure the voluntary return of the child or to bring about an amicable resolution of the issues;

d) to exchange, where desirable, information relating to the social background of the child;

e) to provide information of a general character as to the law of their State in connection with the application of the Convention;

f) to initiate or facilitate the institution of judicial or administrative proceedings with a view to obtaining the return of the child and, in a proper case, to make arrangements for organizing or securing the effective exercise of rights of access;

g) where the circumstances so require, to provide or facilitate the provision of legal aid and advice, including the participation of legal counsel and advisers;

h) to provide such administrative arrangements as may be necessary and appropriate to secure the safe return of the child;

i) to keep other each other informed with respect to the operation of this Convention and, as far as possible, to eliminate any obstacles to its application.

CHAPTER III - RETURN OF CHILDREN

Article 8

Any person, institution or other body claiming that a child has been removed or retained in breach of custody rights may apply either to the Central Authority of the child's habitual residence or to the Central Authority of any other Contracting State for assistance in securing the return of the child.

The application shall contain -

a) information concerning the identity of the applicant, of the child and of the person alleged to have removed or retained the child;

b) where available, the date of birth of the child;

c) the grounds on which the applicant's claim for return of the child is based;

d) all available information relating to the whereabouts of the child and the identity of the person with whom the child is presumed to be.

The application may be accompanied or supplemented by -

e) an authenticated copy of any relevant decision or agreement;

f) a certificate or an affidavit emanating from a Central Authority, or other competent authority of the State of the child's habitual residence, or from a qualified person, concerning the relevant law of that State;

g) any other relevant document.

Article 9

If the Central Authority which receives an application referred to in Article 8 has reason to believe that the child is in another Contracting State, it shall directly and without delay transmit the application to the Central Authority of that Contracting State and inform the requesting Central Authority, or the applicant, as the case may be.

Article 10

The Central Authority of the State where the child is shall take or cause to be taken all appropriate measures in order to obtain the voluntary return of the child.

Article 11

The judicial or administrative authorities of Contracting States shall act expeditiously in proceedings for the return of children.

If the judicial or administrative authority concerned has not reached a decision within six weeks from the date of commencement of the proceedings, the applicant or the Central Authority of the requested State, on its own initiative or if asked by the Central Authority of the requesting State, shall have the right to request a statement of the reasons for the delay. If a reply is received by the Central Authority of the requested State, that Authority shall transmit the reply to the Central Authority of the requesting State, or to the applicant, as the case may be.

Article 12

Where a child has been wrongfully removed or retained in terms of Article 3 and, at the date of the commencement of the proceedings before the judicial or administrative authority of the Contracting State where the child is, a period of less than one year has elapsed from the date of the wrongful removal or retention, the authority concerned shall order the return of the child forthwith.

The judicial or administrative authority, even where the proceedings have been commenced after the expiration of the period of one year referred to in the preceding paragraph, shall also order the return of the child, unless it is demonstrated that the child is now settled in its new environment. Where the judicial or administrative authority in the requested State has reason to believe that the child has been taken to another State, it may stay the proceedings or dismiss the application for the return of the child.

Article 13

Notwithstanding the provisions of the preceding Article, the judicial or administrative authority of the requested State is not bound to order the return of the child if the person, institution or other body which opposes its return establishes that -

a) the person, institution or other body having the care of the person of the child was not actually exercising the custody rights at the time of removal or retention, or had consented to or subsequently acquiesced in the removal of retention; or

b) there is a grave risk that his or her return would expose the child to physical or psychological harm or otherwise place the child in an intolerable situation.

The judicial or administrative authority may also refuse to order the return of the child if it finds that the child objects to being returned and has attained an age and degree of maturity at which it is appropriate to take account of its views.

In considering the circumstances referred to in this Article, the judicial and administrative authorities shall take into account the information relating to the social background of the child provided by the Central Authority or other competent authority of the child's habitual residence.

Article 14

In ascertaining whether there has been a wrongful removal of retention within the meaning of Article 3, the judicial or administrative authorities of the requested State may take notice directly of the law of, and of judicial or administrative decisions, formally recognized or not in the State of the habitual residence of the child, without recourse to the specific procedures for the proof of that law or for the recognition of foreign decisions which would otherwise be applicable.

Article 15

The judicial or administrative authorities of a Contracting State may, prior to the making of an order for the return of the child, request that the applicant obtain from the authorities of the State of the habitual residence of the child a decision or other determination that the removal or retention was wrongful within the meaning of Article 3 of the Convention, where such a decision or determination may be obtained in that State. The Central Authorities of the Contracting States shall so far as practicable assist applicants to obtain such a decision or determination.

Article 16

After receiving notice of a wrongful removal or retention of a child in the sense of Article 3, the judicial or administrative authorities of the Contracting State to which the child has been removed or in which it has been retained shall not decide on the merits of rights of custody until it has been determined that the child is not to be returned under this Convention or unless an application under the Convention is not lodged within a reasonable time following receipt of the notice.

Article 17

The sole fact that a decision relating to custody has been given in or is entitled to recognition in the requested State shall not be a ground for refusing to return a child under this Convention, but the judicial or administrative authorities of the requested State may take account of the reasons for that decision in applying this Convention.

Article 18

The provisions of this Chapter do not limit the power of a judicial or administrative authority to order the return of the child at any time.

Article 19

A decision under this Convention concerning the return of the child shall not be taken to be determination on the merits of any custody issue.

Article 20

The return of the child under the provision of Article 12 may be refused if this would not be permitted by the fundamental principles of the requested State relating to the protection of human rights and fundamental freedoms.

CHAPTER IV - RIGHTS OF ACCESS

Article 21

An application to make arrangements for organizing or securing the effective exercise of rights of access may be presented to the Central Authorities of the Contracting States in the same way as an application for the return of a child.

The Central Authorities are bound by the obligations of co-operation which are set forth in Article 7 to promote the peaceful enjoyment of access rights and the fulfillment of any conditions to which the exercise of such rights may be subject. The central Authorities shall take steps to remove, as far as possible, all obstacles to the exercise of such rights. The Central Authorities, either directly or through intermediaries, may initiate or assist in the institution of proceedings with a view to organizing or protecting these rights and securing respect for the conditions to which the exercise of these rights may be subject.

CHAPTER V - GENERAL PROVISIONS

Article 22

No security, bond or deposit, however described, shall be required to guarantee the payment of costs and expenses in the judicial or administrative proceedings falling within the scope of this Convention.

Article 23

No legalization or similar formality may be required in the context of this Convention.

Article 24

Any application, communication or other document sent to the Central Authority of the requested State shall be in the original language, and shall be accompanied by a translation into the official language or one of the official languages of the requested State or, where that is not feasible, a translation into French or English.

However, a Contracting State may, by making a reservation in accordance with Article 42, object to the use of either French or English, but not both, in any application, communication or other document sent to its Central Authority.

Article 25

Nationals of the Contracting States and persons who are habitually resident within those States shall be entitled in matters concerned with the application of this Convention to legal aid and advice in any other Contracting State on the same conditions as if they themselves were nationals of and habitually resident in that State.

Article 26

Each Central Authority shall bear its own costs in applying this Convention.

Central Authorities and other public services of Contracting States shall not impose any charges in relation to applications submitted under this Convention. In particular, they may not require any payment from the applicant towards the costs and expenses of the proceedings or, where applicable, those arising from the participation of legal counsel or advisers. However, they may require the payment of the expenses incurred or to be incurred in implementing the return of the child.

However, a Contracting State may, by making a reservation in accordance with Article 42, declare that it shall not be bound to assume any costs referred to in the preceding paragraph resulting from the participation of legal counsel or advisers or from court proceedings, except insofar as those costs may be covered by its system of legal aid and advice. Upon ordering the return of a child or issuing an order concerning rights of access under this Convention, the judicial or administrative authorities may, where appropriate, direct the person who removed or retained the child, or who prevented the exercise of rights of access, to pay necessary expenses incurred by or on behalf of the applicant, including travel expenses, any costs incurred or payments made for locating the child, the costs of legal representation of the applicant, and those of returning the child.

Article 27

When it is manifest that the requirements of this Convention are not fulfilled or that the application is otherwise not well founded, a Central Authority is not bound to accept the application. In that case, the Central Authority shall forthwith inform the applicant or the Central Authority through which the application was submitted, as the case may be, of its reasons.

Article 28

A Central Authority may require that the application be accompanied by a written authorization empowering it to act on behalf of the applicant, or to designate a representative so to act.

Article 29

This Convention shall not preclude any person, institution or body who claims that there has been a breach of custody or access rights within the meaning of Article 3 or 21 from applying directly to the judicial or administrative authorities of a Contracting State, whether or not under the provisions of this Convention.

Article 30

Any application submitted to the Central Authorities or directly to the judicial or administrative authorities of a Contracting State in accordance with the terms of this Convention, together with documents and any other information appended thereto or provided by a Central Authority, shall be admissible in the courts or administrative authorities of the Contracting States.

Article 31

In relation to a State which in matters of custody of children has two or more systems of law applicable in different territorial units —

a) any reference to habitual residence in that State shall be construed as referring to habitual residence in a territorial unit of that State;

b) any reference to the law of the State of habitual residence shall be construed as referring to the law of the territorial unit in that State where the child habitually resides.

Article 32

In relation to a State which in matters of custody of children has two or more systems of law applicable to different categories of persons, any reference to the law of that State shall be construed as referring to the legal system specified by the law of that State.

Article 33

A State within which different territorial units have their own rules of law in respect of custody of children shall not be bound to apply this Convention where a State with a unified system of law would not be bound to do so.

Article 34

This Convention shall take priority in matters within its scope over the Convention of 5 October 1961 concerning the powers of authorities and the law applicable in respect of the protection of minors, as between

Parties to both Conventions. Otherwise the present Convention shall not restrict the application of an international instrument in force between the State of origin and the State addressed or other law of the State addressed for the purposes of obtaining the return of a child who has been wrongfully removed or retained or of organizing access rights.

Article 35

This Convention shall apply as between Contracting States only to wrongful removals or retentions occurring after its entry into force in those States.

Where a declaration has been made under Article 39 or 40, the reference in the preceding paragraph to a Contracting State shall be taken to refer to the territorial unit or units in relation to which this Convention applies.

Article 36

Nothing in this Convention shall prevent two or more Contracting State, in order to limit the restrictions to which the return of the child may be subject, from agreeing among themselves to derogate from any provision of this Convention which may imply such a restriction.

CHAPTER VI - FINAL CLAUSES

Article 37

The Convention shall be open for signature by the States which were Members of the Hague Conference on Private International Law at the time of its Fourteenth Session.

It shall be ratified, accepted or approved and the instruments of ratification, acceptance or approval shall be deposited with the Ministry of Foreign Affairs of the Kingdom of the Netherlands.

Article 38

Any other State may accede to the Convention. The instrument of accession shall be deposited with the Ministry of Foreign Affairs of the Kingdom of the Netherlands.

The Convention shall enter into force for a State acceding to it on the first day of the third calendar month after the deposit of its instrument of accession.

The accession will have effect only as regards the relations between the acceding State and such Contracting States as will have declared their acceptance of the accession. Such a declaration will also have to be made by any

Member State ratifying, accepting or approving the Convention after an accession. Such declaration shall be deposited at the Ministry of Foreign Affairs of the Kingdom of the Netherlands; this Ministry shall forward, through diplomatic channels, a certified copy to each of the Contracting States.

The Convention will enter into force as between the acceding State and the State that has declared its acceptance of the accession on the first day of the third calendar month after the deposit of the declaration of acceptance.

Article 39

Any State may, at the time of signature, ratification, acceptance, approval or accession, declare that the Convention shall extend to all the territories for the international relations of which it is responsible, or to one or more of them. Such a declaration shall take effect at the time the Convention enters into force for that State.

Such declaration, as well as any subsequent extension, shall be notified to the Ministry of Foreign Affairs of the Kingdom of the Netherlands.

Article 40

If a Contracting State has two or more territorial units in which different systems of law are applicable in relation to matters dealt with in this Convention, it may at the time of signature, ratification, acceptance, approval or accession declare that this Convention shall extend to all its territorial units or only to one or more of them and may modify this declaration by submitting another declaration at any time.

Any such declaration shall be notified to the Ministry of Foreign Affairs of the Kingdom of the Netherlands and shall state expressly the territorial units to which the Convention applies.

Article 41

Where a Contracting State has a system of government under which executive, judicial and legislative powers are distributed between central and other authorities within that State, its signature or ratification, acceptance or approval of, or accession to this Convention, or its making of any declaration in terms of Article 40 shall carry no implication as to the internal distribution of powers within that State.

Article 42

Any State may, not later than the time of ratification, acceptance, approval or accession, or at the time of making a declaration in terms of Article 39 or 40, make one or both of the reservations provided for in Article 24 and Article 26, third paragraph. No other reservations shall be permitted.

Any State may at any time withdraw a reservation it has made. The withdraw shall be notified to the Ministry of Foreign Affairs of the Kingdom of the Netherlands. The reservation shall cease to have effect on the first day of the third calendar month after the notification referred to in the preceding paragraph.

Article 43

The Convention shall enter into force on the first day of the third calendar month after the deposit of the third instrument of ratification, acceptance, approval or accession referred to in Articles 37 and 38.

Thereafter the Convention shall enter into force -

1 for each State ratifying, accepting, approving or acceding to it subsequently, on the first day of the third calendar month after the deposit of its instrument of ratification, acceptance, approval or accession;

2 for any territory or territorial unit to which the Convention has been extended in conformity with Article 39 or 40, on the first day of the third calendar month after the notification referred to in that Article.

Article 44

The Convention shall remain in force for five years form the date of its entry into force in accordance with the first paragraph of Article 43 even for States which subsequently have ratified, accepted, approved it or acceded to it.

If there has been no denunciation, it shall be renewed tacitly every five years.

Any denunciation shall be notified to the Ministry of Foreign Affairs of the Kingdom of the netherlands at least six months before the expiry of the five year period. It may be limited to certain of the territories or territorial units to which the Convention applies.

The denunciation shall have effect only as regards the State which has notified it. The Convention shall remain in force for the other Contracting States.

Article 45

The Ministry of Foreign Affairs of the Kingdom of the Netherlands shall notify the States Members of the Conference, and the States which have acceded in accordance with Article 38, of the following -

1. the signatures and ratifications, acceptances and approvals referred to in Article 37;

2. the accession referred to in Article 38;

3. the date on which the Convention enters into force in accordance with Article 43;

4. the extensions referred to in Article 39;

5. the declarations referred to in Articles 38 and 40;

6. the reservations referred to in Article 24 and Article 26, third paragraph, and the withdrawls referred to in Article 42;

7. the denunciation referred to in Article 44.

In witness whereof the undersigned, being duly authorized thereto, have signed this Convention.

Done at The Hague, on the 25th day of October, 1980, in the English and French languages, both texts being equally authentic, in a single copy which shall be deposited in the archives of the Government of the Kingdom of the Netherlands, and of which a certified copy shall be sent, through diplomatic channels, to each of the States Members of the Hague Conference on Private International Law at the date of its Fourteenth Session.

–Appendix D–

CHILD ABDUCTION RESOURCES

If your child is snatched by his or her other parent or removed from the United States, the following resources may be able to assist you in the return of your son of daughter.

Child Quest International
> 1060 North 4th Street
> Suite 200
> San Jose, CA 95112
> 408-287-4673
> www.childquest.org
> Email: info@childquest.org

Child Watch of North America
> 7380 Sand Lake Road
> Suite 500
> Orlando, FL 32819
> 407-290-5100
> 800-928-2445
> www.childwatch.org
> Email: info@childwatch.org

International Center for the Search and Recovery of Missing Children
> 6146 Clark Centre Avenue
> Sarasota, FL 34238
> Email: csrmc@aol.com

Lost Children's Network
9794 Forest Lane
Box 170
Dallas, TX 75243
Founder: Randy Smith
www.lostchildren.org
Email: lostchildren@usa.net

Missing Children Investigation Center, Inc.
P.O. Box 4138
Burbank, CA 91503
818-382-1999
www.MCIC4help.org

National Center for Missing and Exploited Children
Charles B. Wang International Children's Building
699 Prince Street
Alexandria, VA 22314
703-235-3900
800-435-5678
www.ncmec.org

New York Police Department
Missing Children's Unit
1 Police Plaza
New York, NY 10038
212-374-0501

PARENT International
P.O. Box 134
Capron, VA 23829
434-658-3050
www.parentinternational.com
Email: prevent01@aol.com

Parental Abduction in Divorce
Article and links by Lee Borden
www.divorceinfo.com/parentalabduction.htm

Parental Kidnapping: Prevention and Remedies
Article by Patricia M. Hoff (ABA 2000)
www.abanet.org/child/pkprevrem.pdf

Prevent International Parental Child Abduction (PIPCA)
P.O. Box 270362
Houston, TX 77277
www.pipca.org
Email: all@pipca.org

The Polly Klaas Foundation
P.O. Box 800
Petaluma, CA 94953
800-587-4357
www.pollyklass.org
Email: info@pollyklaas.org

U.S. Department of State
Office of Children's Issues
2201 C Street, NW, SA-29
Washington, D.C. 20520
202-736-9130
888-407-4747
http://travel.state.gov/family/abduction/abduction_580.html

Vanished Children's Alliance-West Coast
991 West Hedding Street
Suite 101
San Jose, CA 95126
408-296-1113
www.vca.org
Email: vca001@aol.com

Voice of America
330 Independence SW
Room 3334
Washington, D.C. 20547
202-203-4959
When a federal arrest warrant is issued, VOA will make an international radio broadcast of an internationally abducted child and establish a website about the child and the abductor.

–Appendix E–

CHILD SUPPORT ENFORCEMENT AGENCIES

This appendix contains a listing of each state's child support enforcement agency. Contact your state's agency if you need assistance collecting child support owed to you.

Federal

Administration for Children and Families:
Office of Child Support Enforcement
370 L'Enfant Promenade, SW
Washington, D.C. 20447
www.acf.dhhs.gov/programs/cse

Alabama

Alabama Department of Human Resources
Child Support Enforcement Partnership
P.O. Box 304000
Montgomery, AL 36130
334-242-9300
www.dhr.state.al.us./page.asp?pageid=288

Alaska

Alaska Child Support Enforcement Division
550 West 7th Avenue
Anchorage, AK 99501
907-269-6901
www.csed.state.ak.us

Arizona

Arizona Division of Child Support Enforcement
Central Office North and South Maricopa
2222 West Encanto Boulevard
Phoenix, AZ 85009
602-252-4045
www.de.state.az.us/dcse

Arkansas

Office of Child Support Enforcement
400 East Capitol
P.O. Box 8133
Little Rock, AR 72203
501-371-5349
www.state.ar.us/dfa/childsupport

California

California Department of Child Support Services
3701 Power Inn Road
Sacramento, CA 95826
916-875–7400
www.childsup.cahwnet.gov

Colorado

Colorado Office of Child Support Enforcement
1575 Sherman Street
5th floor
Denver, CO 80203
303-866-4300
www.childsupport.state.co.us/home/indexIndex.jsp

Connecticut

Central Office of Child Support Enforcement
25 Sigourney Street
Hartford, CT 06106
800-842-1508
www.dss.state.ct.us

Delaware

Division of Child Support Enforcement
P.O. Box 904
84A Christiana Road
New Castle, DE 19720
302-326-6200
www.state.de.us/dhss

District of Columbia

Office of the Attorney General
Child Support Services Division
441 4th Street NW
Suite 550N
Washington, DC 20001
202-442-9900
www.csed.dc.gov

Florida

State Program Office
The Florida Department of Revenue
Child Support Enforcement
P.O. Box 8030
Tallahassee, FL 32314
800-622-5437
www.myflorida.com/dor/childsupport

Georgia

Atlanta Regional Office
Child Support Enforcement
1718 Peachtree Street, NW
Suite 385
Atlanta, GA 30309
404-206-5362
800-227-7993
www.ocse.dhr.georgia.gov

Hawaii

Hilo Child Support Enforcement Agency
Waiakea Kai Shopping Plaza
88 Kanoelehua Avenue
Suite 202
Hilo, HI 96720
808-933-0644
www.hawaii.gov/ag/csea

Idaho

Idaho Department of Health & Welfare
450 West State Street
Boise, ID 83702
208-334-5500
www2.state.id.us/dhw/childsupport/index.htm

Illinois

Cook County Office of Child Support Enforcement
32 W. Randolph
Chicago, IL 60601
800-447-4278
www.ilchildsupport.com

Indiana

Division of Family and Children
129 East Market Street
Suite 1200
Indianapolis, IN 46204
317-232-3645
www.in.gov/dcs/support

Iowa

The Iowa Department of Human Services
Hoover State Office Building
Des Moines, IA 50319
888-229-9223
http://childsupport.dhs.state.ia.us

Kansas

Kansas Department of Social and Rehabilitative Services
915 SW Harrison Street
Topeka, KS 66612
785-296-3959
www.srskansas.org

Kentucky

Child Support Enforcement Commission
1024 Capital Center Drive
Suite 200
Frankfort, KY 40601
502-564-2285
http://chfs.ky.gov/dcbs/dcs

Louisiana

Service Baton Rouge Regional Support Enforcements Office
333 Laurel Street
Second Floor
P.O. Box 829
Baton Rouge, LA 70821
225-342-5760
www.dss.state.la.us/departments/ofs/OFS_Regional_Offices.html

Maine

Division of Support Enforcement & Recovery
11 SHS Whitten Road
Augusta, ME 04333
207-287-3110
www.state.me.us/dhs/bfi/dser

Maryland

Office of Child Support Enforcement (OCSE)
44 Calvert Street
2nd Floor
Annapolis, MD 21401
800-332-6347
www.dhr.state.md.us/csea

Massachusetts

Department of Revenue
Customer Service Bureau
P.O. Box 7057
Boston, MA 02204
800-332-2733
www.cse.state.ma.us

Michigan

Michigan Family Independence Agency
P.O. Box 30037
Lansing, MI 48909
517-373-2035
www.michigan.gov/dhs

Minnesota

Minnesota Department of Human Services
444 Lafayette Road North
Saint Paul, MN 55155
651-215-5630
www.dhs.state.mn.us/ECS/ChildSupport

Mississippi

Mississippi Department of Human Services
Division of Child Support Enforcement
750 North State Street
Jackson, MS 39205
866-388-2836
www.mdhs.state.ms.us/cse.html

Missouri

Missouri Department of Social Services
Child Support Enforcement
615 Howerton Court
PO Box 2320
Jefferson City, MO 65102
573-751-4301
www.dss.mo.gov/cse

Montana

Montana Child Support Enforcement Division
3075 North Montana Avenue
Helena, MT 59601
406-444-9855
800-346-KIDS
www.dphhs.mt.gov/aboutus/divisions/childsupportenforcement

Nebraska

Nebraska Department of Health and Human Services
Child Support Enforcement
P.O. Box 94728
Lincoln, NE 68509
402-441-8715
877-631-9973
www.hhs.state.ne.us/cse/cseindex.htm

Nevada

Nevada Department of Human Resources
Welfare Division
1470 East College Parkway
Carson City, NV 89706
775-684-0500
www.welfare.state.nv.us/child.htm

New Hampshire

NH DHHS
Division of Child Support Services
129 Pleasant Street
Concord, NH 03301
603-271-4745
www.dhhs.state.nh.us/DHHS/DCSS/default.htm

New Jersey

Mercer County Family Court Building
175 South Broad Street
P.O. Box 8068
Trenton, NJ 08650
609-989-6741
www.njchildsupport.org

New Mexico

CSED Central Office
P.O. Box 25110
Santa Fe, NM 87504
800-288-7207 (In-State)
800-585-7631 (Out of State)
www.state.nm.us/hsd/csed.html

New York

Albany County Child Support Enforcement Unit
162 Washington Avenue
5th Floor
Albany, NY 12210
518-447-7390
https://newyorkchildsupport.com

North Carolina

Child Support Enforcement
NC DHHS-Division of Social Services
Albermarle Building
8th Floor
325 North Salisbury Street
Raleigh, NC 27601
919-255-3800
www.dhhs.state.nc.us/dss/cse

North Dakota

North Dakota DHS
600 East Boulevard Avenue
Department 325
Bismarck, ND 58505
701-328-2310
800-472-2622
www.state.nd.us/humanservices/services/childsupport

Ohio

Office of Child Support
30 East Broad Street
32nd Floor
Columbus, OH 43215
614-752-6561
800-686-1556
www.jfs.ohio.gov/OCS

Oklahoma

Oklahoma Department of Human Services
P.O. Box 53552
Oklahoma City, OK 73152
800-522-2922
www.okdhs.org/childsupport

Oregon

Oregon Department of Justice
Division of Child Support
1495 Edgewater Street, NW
Suite 170
Salem, OR 97304
503-986-6090
www.dcs.state.or.us

Pennsylvania

Domestic Relations Section
Child Support Enforcement Program
25 South Front Street
8th Floor
P.O. Box 1295
Harrisburg, PA 17108
717-255-2796
www.childsupport.state.pa.us

Rhode Island

Office of Child Support Enforcement
Rhode Island Department of Administration
Division of Taxation—Child Support Enforcement
77 Dorrance Street
Providence, RI 09203
401-222-2847
www.cse.ri.gov

South Carolina

Child Support Enforcement Division
Central Inquiry Unit
P.O. Box 1469
Columbia, SC 29202
803-898-9210
800-768-5858
www.state.sc.us/dss/csed

South Dakota

Department of Social Services
Office of Child Support Enforcement
700 Governors Drive
Pierre, SD 57501
605-773-3641
http://dss.sd.gov/childsupport

Tennessee

Child Support Enforcement
Department of Human Services
400 Deaderick Street
15th Floor
Nashville, TN 37248
615-253-4394
800-838-6911
www.state.tn.us/humanserv/child-support.htm

Texas

Office of the Attorney General
300 West 15th Street
Austin, TX 78701
512-463-2100
800-252-8011
www.oag.state.tx.us/child

Utah

Office of Recovery Services Administration
515 East 100 South
Salt Lake City, UT 84102
801-536-8500
800-662-8525
www.ors.state.ut.us

Vermont

Office of Child Support
Vermont Agency of Human Services
103 South Main Street
Waterbury, VT 05671
800-786-3214
www.ocs.state.vt.us

Virginia

Virginia Department of Social Services
7 North Eighth Street
Richmond, VA 23219
804-726-7000
www.dss.virginia.gov/family/dcse.html

Washington

DSHS Constituent Services
P.O. Box 45130
Olympia, WA 98504-5130
800-737-0617
www1.dshs.wa.gov/dcs

West Virginia

Bureau for Child Support Enforcement
231 Capitol Street
Village Place
Suite 111
Charleston, WV 25332
304-347-8688
www.wvdhhr.org/bcse

Wisconsin

Bureau of Child Support
City-County Building
Room 106
210 Martin Luther King, Jr. Boulevard
Madison, WI 53709
608-266-4031
www.dwd.state.wi.us/bcs

Wyoming

Wyoming Child Support Enforcement
2300 Capitol Avenue
3rd Floor
Cheyenne, WY 82002-0490
307-777-6948
http://dfsweb.state.wy.us/csehome/cs.htm

–Appendix F–

FATHERS' RIGHTS ORGANIZATIONS

The following are some of the national organizations advocating for fathers' rights. There are also many local father's rights organizations in each state. Menstuff maintains and updates a directory of resources on the Internet at **www.menstuff.org**.

American Coalition for Fathers and Children
1718 M Street NW #187
Washington, D.C. 20036
800-978-3237
www.acfc.org

BOND
P.O. Box 35090
Los Angeles, CA 90035-0090
323-782-1980
www.bondinfo.org

Center for Successful Fathering
13740 Research Boulevard
Suite L-2
Austin, TX 78750
800-537-0853
512-335-8106
www.fathering.org

Children of Divorce and Separation
P.O. Box 202
Glenside, PA 19038
215-576-0177
http://users.snip.net/%7Ecodas/

CPF-The Fatherhood Coalition
P.O. Box 700
Milford, MA 01757
617-723-DADS
www.fatherhoodcoalition.org

Dads and Daughters
2 West 1ˢᵗ Street
Suite 101
Duluth, MN 55802
218-722-3942
www.dadsanddaughters.org/

DivorceCare
P.O. Box 1739
Wake Forest, NC 27588
800-489-7778
www.divorcecare.org

Divorce Wizards
5015 Birch Street
Newport Beach, CA 92660
949-622-1750
www.divorcewizards.com

False Allegations
6 Appletree Lane
Andover, MA 01810
978-474-0833
www.falseallegations.com

Fathers and Families
20 Park Plaza
Suite 628
Boston, MA 02116
617-542-9300
www.fathersandfamilies.org

Men & Fathers Resource Center
807 Brazos Street
Suite 315
Austin, TX 78701
512-472-3237
www.fathers.org

Fathers Rights Foundation
10325 Winterhue
Baton Rouge, LA 70810
225-766-0707
www.fathers-rights.com

Separated Parenting Access & Resource Center
P.O. Box 82764
Kenmore WA 98028
www.deltabravo.net

Joint Custody Association
10606 Wilkins Avenue
Los Angeles, CA 90024
310-475-5352
www.jointcustody.org

MBRACE Fatherhood
5520 Groveland Avenue
Baltimore, Maryland 21215
443-527-5527
www.mbracefatherhood.com

National Association for Fathers
1075D North Railroad Avenue #111
Stanton Island, NY 10306
800-HELP-DAD

National Center for Fathering
P.O. Box 413888
Kansas City, MO 64141
913-384-4661
800-593-DADS
www.fathers.com

National Congress for Fathers & Children
9454 Wilshire Boulevard
Suite 907
Beverly Hills, CA 90212
760-758-0268
www.ncfc.net

National Fatherhood Initiative
101 Lake Forest Boulevard
Suite 360
Gaithersburg, MD 20877
301-948-0599
www.fatherhood.org

INDEX

I

income shares model, 84, 87
individual retirement account
  (IRA), 33
insurance, 6, 19, 32, 88, 89, 90, 95,
  98, 104, 105, 158, 196, 201
interest-based bargaining, 116, 117
Internal Revenue Service (IRS), 87,
  99, 100, 101, 158, 196
International Child Abduction
  Remedies Act (ICARA), 108
International Parental Kidnapping
  Crime Act (IPKCA), 108
Interrogatories, 144, 145, 149, 150,
  151, 154, 166, 202, 203
interventions, 14, 18

J

joint custody, 28, 53, 56, 57, 149,
  176, 203
judges, 2, 3, 6, 8, 10, 11, 16, 18,
  20, 21, 26, 29, 30, 31, 32, 35,
  36, 37, 40, 43, 45, 46, 47, 48,
  49, 50, 54, 55, 56, 60, 61, 62,
  65, 69, 74, 75, 77, 79, 87, 89,
  90, 93, 97, 99, 111, 113, 116,
  119, 127, 128, 129, 130, 134,
  136, 142, 143, 148, 162, 163,
  165, 166, 167, 168, 169, 170,
  171, 172, 173, 174, 176, 177,
  178, 179, 181, 183, 187, 189,
  190, 195, 197, 198, 201

L

lawyers. *See attorneys*
legal custody, 53, 56, 57, 58, 59,
  60, 61, 80, 119, 121, 187, 197,
  203
limited scope of engagement, 40
litigation, 1, 10, 26, 41, 42, 48, 49,
  75, 115, 127, 129, 149, 156,
  169, 176, 197, 204, 205, 206

M

Marital Settlement Agreement, 91
Martindale-Hubbel attorney rating,
  43
mediation, 21, 22, 51, 68, 72, 114,
  116, 117, 118, 125, 128, 142,
  143, 146, 197, 201, 204, 205
medical treatment, 4, 6, 7, 8, 32,
  57, 76, 78, 83, 88, 89, 90, 98,
  104, 119, 121, 122, 123, 124,
  150, 153, 165, 185, 192, 197,
  202
Melson model, 86, 87
military service, 111, 136
misconduct, 17, 25, 26, 52, 86
modification of child support, 78,
  93, 94, 107, 154, 197, 204
Motion for Judgment, 132
move out agreement, 26, 27, 28
moving out, 25, 26

N

ne exeat order, 29
negotiation, 117, 128

About the Author

James J. Gross is co-founder and managing partner of the law firm of Thyden Gross and Callahan in Chevy Chase, Maryland. He has practiced family law and business law for thirty years. He has represented hundreds of fathers in their efforts to secure their parental rights.

Mr. Gross received his Masters of Laws in Taxation from Georgetown University in 1982; a Juris Doctor from the University of Missouri in 1975, and a Bachelor of Science in Chemical Engineering from the University of Missouri in 1970.

Mr. Gross was named as one of the top divorce lawyers by Washingtonian Magazine. He appears frequently on television and radio in connection with fathers' rights. He is the coauthor of *File for Divorce in Maryland, Virginia and the District of Columbia* and *Money and Divorce*. Mr. Gross writes the columns *The Daily Answer Desk* for DivorceNet.Com and *In the Courts* for ShagMail.Com. He is the Maryland legal expert for DivorceInfo.Com, and writes three blogs—*Maryland Divorce Legal Crier, Not Just Every Other Weekend,* and *Married Guy/Single Guy.*

Mr. Gross teaches divorce classes at the Montgomery County Commission for Women and presents programs for other family lawyers through the Montgomery County Bar Association. He was recently a co-presenter on *Shame as a Tactic in Divorce Trials* at the Association of Family Courts and Conciliators.

He is on the Board of Directors of the D.C. Capitols Track and Field Club, and was formerly the President of the Metropolitan

Washington Mensa. He is a member of the Family Law Sections of the American, District of Columbia, Maryland, and Montgomery County Bar Associations. Mr. Gross is a trained mediator and collaborative lawyer. He is the co-founder and director of the Collaborative Family Law Society of Maryland, Virginia, and the District of Columbia.

Mr. Gross, formerly in-house counsel to Satellite Business Systems and an attorney with the Federal Communications Commission, is rated *AV* by his fellow attorneys—the highest rating in Martindale-Hubbel.

He lives with his wife, Holly; two sons, Jake and Nicholas; and two cats, Xena and Lola; in Chevy Chase, Maryland. He may be contacted at **tgclawyers@smart.net** or by calling 301-907-4580.